GOJU RYU LEGENDS

Jose M. Fraguas

EMPIRE BOOKS/AWP LLC
Los Angeles, California

Disclaimer
Please note that the author and publisher of this book are NOT RESPONSIBLE in any manner whatsoever for any injury that may result from practicing the techniques and/or following the instructions given within. Since the physical activities described herein may be too strenuous in nature for some readers to engage in safely, it is essential that a physician be consulted prior to training.

Published in 2020 by Empire Books/AWP LLC.
Copyright (c) 2020 by Jose M. Fraguas
All rights reserved. No part of this publication may be reproduced or utilized in any form or by any means, electronic or mechanical, including photocopying, recording, or by any information storage and retrieval system, without prior written permission from Empire Books/AWP LLC.

Library of Congress Cataloging-in-Publication Data

Name: Fraguas, Jose M., author.
Title: Goju Ryu Legends / by Jose M. Fraguas.
Description: Los Angeles, California: Empire Books, 2020. | Description based on print version record and CIP data provided by publisher; resource not viewed.
Identifiers: ISBN: 9781949753264 (pbk.: alk. paper)

1. karate-goju ryu-Interviews I. Fraguas, Jose M. II. Title GV1115.M340 2020
797.704 '2' 0899151-dc23

29041125450

Empire Books/AWP
Los Angeles, CA 90049
First Edition
20 19 18 17 16 15 14 13 12 11 10

Printed in the United States of America.

"We should open Karate to the public and receive criticism, opinions and studies from other prominent fighting artists."

- Chojun Miyagi

Dedication

I dedicate this book to the memory of Chojun Miyagi Sensei.

Acknowledgments

Many people were responsible for making this book possible, some more directly than others. I want to extend my gratitude to all those whom so generously contributed their time and experience to the preparation of this work. A very special thanks to my teacher, Masahiro Okada Sensei, whose flights of guidance throughout my Budo life and karate-do journey, have been always on the wings of excitement and self-discovery.

A word of appreciation is also due to my good friend Masahiro Ide, president of JK Fan and Champ videos, for his generosity and cooperation in this project. Without his support, kindness and commitment to preserve the art of karate-do, this book would not exist.

I also want to thank France's Thierry Plee, long-time friend and president of Sedirep and Budo Editions; Mr. Schlatt, kind friend and founder of Schlatt-Books in Germany; Harold E. Sharp, a true legend in the world of martial arts who kindly supplied great photos of his personal archives; Germany's Norbert Schiffer (director of Satori-Verlag and Budo magazine); Don Warrener (director of Rising Sun Productions); Isaac Florentine (film director and passionate karateka); and finally to Oleg Larinov, a great karateka, impeccable filmmaker and better human being; I truly admire your passion for the art of karate-do.

And last but not least, to all the instructors who shared their knowledge and experience with me, past and present, for giving me the understanding and knowledge to undertake all the karate-do projects I've done during my life. My understanding of the art has grown over the years thanks to the questions they made me ask myself. These questions — both perceptive and practical — have sent me further and deeper in search for answers. This book would not exist without you.

You all have my enduring thanks.

— Jose M. Fraguas

About the Author

Born and raised in Madrid, Spain, Jose M. Fraguas began his martial arts studies with judo, in grade school, at age 9. From there he moved to study karate-do under his teacher, Masahiro Okada Sensei, eventually receiving a seventh-degree black belt in 2009. He began his career as a writer at age 16 as a regular contributor to martial arts magazines in Great Britain, France, Spain, Italy, Germany, Portugal, Holland and Australia. In 1980, he moved to Los Angeles, California, where his open-minded mentality helped him to develop a more elaborated approach to the martial arts.

Fraguas founded his first publishing company in Europe, authoring dozens of books and distributing his magazines to 35 countries in three different languages. His reputation and credibility as a martial artist and publisher became well known to the top masters around the world. Considering himself a martial artist first and a writer and publisher second, Fraguas feels fortunate to have had the opportunity to interview many legendary martial artists. He recognizes that much of the information given in the interviews helped him to discover new dimensions in the martial arts. "I was constantly absorbing knowledge from the great masters," he recalls. "I only trained with a few of them, but intellectually, academically and spiritually all of them have made very important contributions to my growth as a complete martial artist."

Steeped in tradition yet looking to the future, Fraguas understands and appreciates martial arts history and philosophy and feels this rich heritage is a necessary steppingstone to personal growth and spiritual evolution. His desire to promote both ancient philosophy and modern thinking provided the motivation for writing this book. "If the motivation is just money, a book cannot be of good quality," Fraguas says. "If the book is written to just make people happy, it cannot be deep. I want to write books so I can learn as well as teach. Karate-do, like human life itself, is filled with experiences that seem quite ordinary at the time and assume a fabled stature only with the passage of the years. I hope this work will be appreciated by future practitioners not only of the art of Goju Ryu style but karate in general, regardless of the style."

It is clear that every one of us will some kind of leave a legacy behind when we die. The challenge is the same for all of us. For Fraguas, who has authored more than 30 books, the important question is what kind of legacy will I leave? "I believe our main legacy as writers is to educate or even just re-echo those things that we believe are worthwhile - a subjective matter. Even if the idea is obvious or simple, we believe it deserves to be kept alive, and we do that using different ways current with the times; we broadcast our worldview with our family, friends, co-workers, and so on," he says. "Ideally we live by our beliefs so as to lend them credence; the "unfollowing adherent" is just a meaningless mouthpiece - a preacher not following his own sermon. A legacy of values proven out by the bearer's own life would be a very good legacy for anyone. Life is motion, and the real goal of a writer should be to arrest that motion [which is life] and preserve  knowledge [the words of these masters in this book] by artificial means, and hold it fixed so that a hundred years later, when a stranger opens a book and reads it, it moves again since it is life. Since man is mortal, the only immortality possible for a writer is to leave something behind him that is immortal since it will always move. This is the writer's way of scribbling "I was here" on the wall of the final and irrevocable oblivion through which we all must someday pass."

Jose M. Fraguas lives in Los Angeles, California.

Introduction

Some of my best days were spent interviewing and meeting the karate-do masters in this book. There is little I enjoy more than reading a great interview while time slows and sometimes even seems to stop. Having the opportunity to meet and interview the most prestigious Goju Ryu icons of the past four decades is something that every karateka doesn't have the chance to do. Hopefully, in some small way, this will help make up for that. Meeting the masters and having long conversations with them allowed me to do more than simply scratch the surface of the technical aspects of the art; it also allowed me to understand the human beings behind the teachers. Some of the dialogues and interviews began by simply commenting about the superficial techniques of fighting, and ended up turning into a spiritual conversation about the philosophical aspects of karate-do. Although these masters are all very different, they share a common thread of traditional values such as discipline, respect, positive attitude, dedication and etiquette.

For more than 40 years I've interviewed great karate-do masters, one-on-one, face-to-face, with no place to run if I asked a stupid question. Many times it was a real challenge to not just talk to them, but to make the questions interesting enough to bring out their deepest knowledge. I tried to absorb as much knowledge as I could, ranging from their training methods, to their system, to their philosophies about life itself. Their personal cultural backgrounds never prevented them from analyzing, researching or modifying anything they considered important. They always kept their minds open to improving the art and themselves. From a formal philosophical point of view, many of them followed classical philosophies and religions—but they all tempered that with vast amounts of common sense.

They devoted themselves to the art of karate-do, often in solitude, to the exclusion of other "normal" pursuits. They worked themselves into extraordinary physical condition. They ignored distractions and diversions and concentrated on their mental and physical training. They got as good as they could possibly get at performing and teaching the art while the rest of us watched them, leading our "balanced lives," and wondering how good we might have gotten at something had we devoted ourselves to it as ferociously as these masters embraced their journey. In that respect, they bear our dreams.

If you read carefully between the lines, you'll see that none of these men were trying to become a fighting machine, or create the most devastating martial arts system known to man. They focused, rather, on how to use karate-do to become a better person. There are many principles that once discovered open a wide spectrum of possibilities, not only to karate, but to a better existence as individuals.

The interviews often lasted as long as three or four hours. I would begin at their school and finish the conversation at a restaurant or coffee shop. Much of this information had never been published before and some had to be trimmed either at the master's request or edited to avoid misunderstandings. It is not the questions that make an interview. An interview is either good or bad depending on the answers. Considering the masters in this book, I had an easy job. My goal was to make them comfortable talking about life and karate training.

"The great old masters are gone," many like to say. But as long as we keep their teachings in our heart, they will live forever. To understand karate-do properly, it is necessary to take into account its philosophical methods as well as its physical techniques. There is a deep distinction between a fighting system and a martial art. Unfortunately, the roots of karate-do have been de-emphasized, neglected or totally abandoned today.

Karate-do is not a sport, although it can be useful as such in our modern society. Someone who chooses to devote himself to a sport such as basketball, tennis, soccer or football—which is based on youth, strength, and speed—chooses to die twice. When you can no longer do that sport, due to the lack of their required attributes, waking up in the morning without the activity that has been the center of your life for 35 years is troubling and unsettling. In contrast, karate-do can and should be practiced for life—it never leaves you.

All the masters have expressed similar ideas in very different ways. Regardless of the words they used, there must be truth in the philosophies and principles that so many different people have believed in and lived by — and in some cases — died for. The more I interviewed them, the more I realized that those great masters are more like you and me than they are different. They had difficult days and seemingly impossible hurdles, yet they endured and prevailed. Most of what passed as human wisdom is merely the post-examination gabble of excited individuals trying to guess how the new lessons will explain the old questions of life and karate-do training. Anything is fresh on the first hearing … even though others may have heard it a thousand times through a score of generations.

A true karate-do practitioner is like a musician, painter, writer or actor—their art is an expression of themselves. The need to discover who they are becomes the reason for an endless search for the perfect technique, great melody, inspiring poetry, amazing painting or Academy Award performance. It is this motivation to reach that impossible dream that allows a simple individual to become an exceptional artist and master of his craft. Many of the greatest teachers share a commonly misunderstood teaching methodology. They know the words they could use to teach their students have little or no meaning. They know that to try "self-discovery" in quantitative or empirical terms is a useless task. A great deal of knowledge and wisdom comes from oral traditions, which karate-do, like every other cultural expression, has. These oral traditions have always been reserved for

a certain kind of student and considered "secrets," given only to a special few who have the minds and attitudes to fully grasp them. Alexandra David-Neel wrote: "It is not on the master that the secret depends but on the hearer. Truth learned from others is of no value, the only truth which is effective and of value is self-discovered … the teacher can only guide to the point of discovery." In the end, "the only secret is that there is no secret." As Kato Tokuro, arguably the finest potter of the last century, a great art scholar, and the teacher of Pablo Picasso said: "The sole cause of secrets in craftsmanship is the student's inability to learn." To find out what karate-do means to you, what it does for you, and what it holds for you, is a deeply personal process. Each path is different and we all have to find a personal rhythm that fit us individually, according to what surround us.

As human beings, we are always tempted to follow linear logic towards ultimate self-improvement—but the truth is that there are no absolute truths. You have to find your own way in life whether it be in martial arts, business or cherry picking. Whatever path you pursue, you have to distill the personal truths that are right for you, according to your own nature. The quest for perfection is very imperfect, and not in tune with human nature or experience. To have any hope of attaining even a single perfection, you have to concentrate on a single pursuit and direct all your energy towards it. In this sense, perfection comes from appreciating endeavors for their own sake—not to impress anyone—but for your own inner satisfaction and sense of accomplishment. It is important to have a feeling of responsibility; and putting yourself into an art as genuinely as you can, without any sense that you are going to get something back in return, reverberates throughout time and space. We need to honor those who came before us, as well as nurture those who will come after, so the art can grow and expand—you've got to send the elevator back down.

Karate is a large part of my life and I draw inspiration from it. I really don't know the "how" or the "why" of its effect on me, but I feel its influence in even my most mundane activities. All human beings have sources or principles that keep them grounded, and karate is mine. That is when the term "way of life" becomes real. In bushido, the self-discipline required to pursue mastery is more important than mastery itself—the struggle is more important than the reward. A common thread throughout the lives of all the masters appearing in this book is their constant struggle towards self-mastery. They realized that life is an ongoing process, and once you achieve all your goals you are as good as dead. But this process is not all driven by action. Often the greatest action is inaction, and the hardest voice to hear is the sound of your own thoughts. You need to sit alone and collect yourself, free from technology and distraction, and just think. This is perhaps the only way to achieve mental and spiritual clarity.

I don't believe that books are meant to be read fast. I've always thought that writing is timeless and that reading is not a detraction. So take your time. Books are an essential part of our existence and they open new and exciting avenues of life. My goal is to share these interviews with as many people as possible. I hope this collection provides comfort and inspiration for the karate practitioner, the martial artist — regardless of style — and for the casual reader. If you, the reader, find this work useful as both a guide and a reference work and discover some unexpected thoughts and philosophies, the book will have served its purpose. Approach this book with the Zen "beginner's mind" and "empty cup" mentality and soak up the words of these great Goju Ryu karate teachers. They will help you to not only grow as a karateka but as a human being as well.

HISTORY OF GOJU-RYU KARATE-DO

BY LEX OPDAM

People, because of such parlor antics as breaking wood and stone, often wrongly misinterpret the purpose of karate. This is but a small part of the overall art and essence of karate. In peace time karate should be used as a tool to train the mind. In cases of emergency and in times where lawlessness is at hand the practitioner could use one's body to defend themselves against a potential opponent.

It is not easy to define with words what the real nature of karate-do is. Like other forms of Budo, its deep meaning cannot be explained with words. Its essence lies beyond rationality.

The source from which karate originated can be found in Chinese kempo. However, documentation concerning the evolution of Chinese kempo is very poor. There is no hard evidence to prove the origin and development of karate before Chinese kempo existed. One of the theories suggests that kempo originated from Central Asia and with evolution of men spread to India and China. Another theory explains the existence of kempo coming from China more than 5,000 years ago during the time of the Yellow Emperor. Whatever theory, we are only certain that ancient people of combative nature and a sense of rivalry cultivate fighting skills. ~ Chojun Miyagi 1934

The history of Goju-ryu karate-do goes further than this book represents. The most important period concerning the formation of Goju-ryu karate-do is when ryu (style) begins with the legendary Kanryo Higaonna.

Kanryo Higaonna

In 1853, the Okinawan Kanryo Higaonna (Chinese name Shin Zen Yen) was born in the district Nishimura of the city Naha, Okinawa. Kanryo Higaonna was the fourth son of Kanyo Higaonna (1823-1867) who belonged to the Okinawan Shin-clan. Kanryo's father, Kanyo earned his living transporting goods, especially firewood, between Okinawa and neighboring islands. Kanryo possessed a yabarusen (little boat) that he used for his business. He was also a crewmember of a larger ship that ferried goods and passengers between the Ryukyu-islands and China. On these trips to China Kanyo Higaonna heard many stories about China, its culture and its fighting arts from businessmen, traders and public officers who regularly traveled between the mainland and the Ryukyu-islands. Those stories were told from father to son.

As a youth, Kanryo Higaonna's interest grew in the martial arts and he began studying tegumi (wrestling) and to-de (name for the martial arts that was practiced those days). When he was approximately 20 years old, Higaonna began training under the tutelage of Arakaki, Seisho. After a period of time, he traveled to Fuzhou, a providence of China where he started training under kung fu Master Ryoto. Master Ryoto, impressed by Higaonna's rapid progress, introduced him to Chinese Master, Liu Liu Ko (Ryu Ryu Ko). After studying many years in China and learning the martial and healing arts, Kanryo Higaonna returned home to Okinawa. Research has pointed out that he may have trained with other teachers; however, his focus and influence remained Master Liu Liu Ko. Several years after his return from China Kanryo Higaonna began to accept several students to whom he would teach the martial arts from his home. He went on to teach martial arts at the local high school and the royal family of King Sho-Tei-O also observed his teaching and instruction.

Chojun Miyagi

It was at this time that fourteen year old Chojun Miyagi (born 1888 at Higashi-machi, Okinawa) was introduced to Kanryo Higaonna by his martial arts teacher of three years, Ryuko Arakaki. Master Ryuko Arakaki trained in the martial arts described as Tomari-te that stressed body conditioning, makiwara, and hojo undo as preparation and support for the actual practice of karate. Tomari-te name comes from the geographical location of its origin, which is similar to Naha-te and Shuri-te. Chojun Miyagi, son of Chosho Miyagi was of nobility and because of the family's financial means had a lot of time to devout to the study of martial arts. During school time, he participated in Okinawan wrestling and succeeded in almost every physical activity because of his athletic capacity.

Chojun Miyagi kept loyal to his teacher until Kanryo Higaonna's death on October 15; He died in his sleep at the age of 62.

Chojun Miyagi continued his study in the martial arts. In the year 1915, he journeyed to Fuzhou, China where his teacher, Kanryo Higaonna, received his core teachings in the martial arts. This journey was shared with Eisho Nakamoto an English teacher at the Fuzhou City Commercial School. In 1917, upon his return from China

Chojun Miyagi became instructor at the educational center of the Okinawan Police, teacher at several high schools, and was connected to the Prefecture Health Center. In the years that would follow before World War II, he would undertake journeys to research and share his martial arts. An important travel companion on several of these journeys was Master Go Ken Kin. Master Go Ken Kin was a Chinese Master in White Crane Boxing, a tea merchant and a good friend of Chojun Miyagi since 1915 when the two met in China. Go Ken Kin influence on Chojun Miyagi's martial art was significant.

Chojun Miyagi taught karate-do until 1943. He taught mostly in Okinawa, however, he occasionally taught in Japan. In 1934, he spent one year in Hawaii. By invitation of Chinyei Kinjo, president of the Hawaiian newspaper Yoen Jihosha, and with cooperation of the Okinawan society on Hawaii, Chojun Miyagi instructed his Goju-ryu Karate-do. After the Second World War, he resumed his teaching activities. Health problems brought about a decline in his teaching activities and on February 8, 1953, Chojun Miyagi past away from a heart attack.

The Birth and Succession of Goju-ryu

Just before World War II, although not made public, Chojun Miyagi was considering his top student, Jin'nan Shinzato as a possible inheritor of his Goju-ryu karate-do system. Jin'nan Shinzato started training with Chojun Miyagi in 1920. In both words and actions, Chojun Miyagi groomed Jin'nan Shinzato toward stewardship of his Goju-ryu. According to students of

Chojun Miyagi, Jin'an Shinzato was a genius in the martial arts. His knowledge and skill exceeded his fellow students. His role as an assistant teacher, his participation at various meetings and gatherings in addition to performing at many martial arts demonstrations representing Chojun Miyagi, all point towards Jin'an Shinzato as likely successor of Chojun Miyagi.

While demonstrating in Tokyo on May 5, 1930 at the 'All Japan Martial Arts Demonstration' in honor of the Crown Price Hirohito's succession to the Throne of Japan, Jin'an Shinzato was asked what he called his style. He was unable to answer. This prompted him, upon his return from the demonstration, to discuss this query with Chojun Miyagi. Miyagi eventually named his martial art 'te' 'Goju-ryu' and registered this name at the All Japan Martial Arts Association or the Dai Nippon Butokai, the overseeing body of the developing Martial Arts. Chojun Miyagi gave the name 'Goju' to his martial arts because of the meaning Go (hard/external) and 'ju' (soft/internal) as mentioned in one of the most important manuscripts he possessed on the Chinese Martial Arts titled the 'Bubishi', and probably because many Fujian based Kung Fu systems identify themselves as 'soft-hard' styles in relation to the Ki theory (see chapter Sanchin). In the Bubishi, or manual for the art of military science, the words go and ju express the very essence of Chojun Miyagi's karate do in its phrase, "Ho go ju donto" (the way of breathing in and out is a way of softness and hardness).

The new name for Chojun Miyagi's martial art was registered with the Okinawa Kenritsu Taiiku Kyokai (Okinawa Prefecture Athletic Association) on November 21, 1930. This date is significant because Goju-ryu became the first officially recorded karate-style with the Okinawa Prefecture Athletic Association. Jin'an Shinzato's significant role in this historical event provides further evidence of his potential appointment as successor to Chojun Miyagi.

The Second World War interrupted the development and growth of standardizing the karate syllabus and the development of karate in general. Miyagi taught karate for the last time before the war in 1943 at the famous Ritsumeikan University making this a special occasion.

Tragically, however, just before his formal appointment as successor to Chojun Miyagi, Jin'an Shinzato died in 1945 due to heavy bombing of Okinawa and his village Kin-son during World War II. His premature death left a void as to who would be appointed the honorable task of inheriting the Goju-ryu system. As time went on and the war ended and many of Chojun Miyagi's students were busy rebuilding the infrastructure of Okinawa. During and after this post-war reconstruction, karate training slowly revived. Chojun Miyagi passed away in 1953.

Contents

TINO CEBERANO 1

TERUO CHINEN 17

MORIO HIGAONNA 29

TETSUHIRO HOKAMA 39

RON KLUGER 45

DOMINGO LLANOS 53

CHUCK MERRIMAN 63

ANTHONY MIRAKIAN 71

TETSUJI NAKAMURA 103

剛柔流

LEX OPDAM.. **111**

AKIRA SAITO.. **125**

GENE TIBON **135**

TAKESHI UCHIAGE **153**

RAMON VERAS **159**

GOSHI YAMAGUCHI **169**

GOGEN YAMAGUCHI **179**

ONE-ON-ONE WITH AUTHOR **187**

TINO CEBERANO

THE HARD WAY

EVERY MAN, AS HE GROWS OLDER, SEEKS SOME REAL OR SYMBOLIC ACHIEVEMENT WITH WHICH TO CAP HIS CAREER. AFTER RECEIVING HIS 3RD DAN FROM THE LEGENDARY GOGEN "THE CAT" YAMAGUCHI, A YOUNG TINO CEBERANO LEFT HIS NATIVE COUNTRY OF HAWAII TO START LIFE IN MELBOURNE WITH THE PURPOSE OF ESTABLISHING THE STYLE OF GOJU-RYU KARATE IN AUSTRALIA. FROM SMALL BEGINNINGS, THIS STYLE OF KARATE HAS GROWN AND MULTIPLIED, BECOMING THE MOST WIDELY PRACTICED OF KARATE STYLES IN AUSTRALIA.

SENSEI CEBERANO HAS TRAVELED BACK AND FORTH TO JAPAN ON MANY OCCASIONS FOR HIS OWN [REASONS] AND FOR HIS STUDENTS' SENIOR GRADINGS. AND, WITH HIS INVOLVEMENT IN THE INTERNATIONAL KARATE SCENE OVER MANY YEARS AS THE CHIEF REFEREE OF WUKO, AS WELL AS HOLDING THE TITLE OF VICE PRESIDENT OF THE SAME ORGANIZATION, HE HAS CONTRIBUTED TO ESTABLISHING THE ART IN DIFFERENT COUNTRIES AROUND THE GLOBE.

AFTER THE DEATH OF GRANDMASTER GOGEN YAMAGUCHI, THE SENIOR OFFICIALS OF THE GOJU-KAI GRANTED CEBERANO SENSEI HIS INDEPENDENCE AS A PROPAGATOR OF THE GOJU-RYU SCHOOL. THIS DECISION ALLOWED HIM THE PRIVILEGE OF FORMING HIS OWN ORGANIZATION. THE INTERNATIONAL GOJU KARATE-DO (I.G.K) WAS FORMED AND RECOGNIZED BY THE OKINAWAN GOJU RYU RENMEI.

IN FEBRUARY 1992, HIS STANDING AND TECHNICAL EXCELLENCE RESULTED IN AN INVITATION TO BE TESTED FOR HIS 7TH-DEGREE (NANADAN-KYOSHI) GRADING. CEBERANO SENSEI BECAME THE FIRST WESTERNER TO BE GRADED FOR THIS LEVEL UNDER THE AUSPICES OF THE OKINAWAN BUDO INTERNATIONAL.

IN THIS SENSEI'S OPINION, THE ART OF KARATE-DO ADDS UP TO A BASIC ATTITUDE — AN ATTITUDE THAT PLACES THE HIGHEST IMPORTANCE ON SELF-KNOWLEDGE, TRANQUILITY AND RESPECT. "KARATE IS A UNIVERSAL ART. IT BELONGS TO HUMANITY, NOT JUST TO THE JAPANESE AND OKINAWANS," HE SAYS SMILING

Q: How long have you been practicing the martial arts?

A: Since 1951. I started on the island of Kauai, Hawaii. Prior to that, as early as 1949 on the sugar plantation camp where we lived on the island of Kauai, I received an introduction to Filipino arnis from our fathers, uncles and the elders of the village. This got the

youngsters started in an ethnic cultural inheritance that was part of the norm for many of the local boys who grew up in the villages.

Q: In how many martial arts have you trained?

A: I have been involved in arnis, judo, jiu-jitsu, kenpo, karate, kobudo and tai chi.

Q: Who were your first teachers?

A: My father and granduncle were our senior teachers of arnis while we were on the island of Kauai. My uncle's name was Apo Sedong Cabacungan, and he was from Hanapepe. My next instructor, Dr. Rex Glacier, happened to be from the Kalaheo Judo Dojo, and he was associated with the Hawaii Judo Association under Professor Sakabe, who happened to be with the Hongwangji Mission in Honolulu. Next came my first instructor in kenpo … Sensei Fred Imperial. He was under the lineage of the Lone Pine Tree System of Kenpo Hawaii. My next mentor and the most influential instructor leading me into the martial arts proper was Master Masaichi Oshiro of Honolulu, Hawaii. He was the first instructor/pioneer of goju-kai karate under Grandmaster Gogen "The Cat" Yamaguchi. My instruction in kobudo came from many [instructors] in Japan and Okinawa. There was Inoue Mokatsu Hanshi of the Shinken Taira Kaiso lineage Rukyu Kobujitsu Hozon Shinko Kai, Teruo Hayashi Hanshi of the Hayashi Ha Shito-ryu and many others, including the masters of the Okinawa Goju-ryu Federation.

Q: Would you tell us some interesting stories of your early days in the martial arts?

A: As a young boy of ethnic background [Filipino/Spanish] growing up in a multi-cultural society in the islands of Hawaii, the martial arts were evident and saturated well into our lifestyles. As we put it amongst our colleagues or even peers of renown, recalling those days of the 1950s and mid-1960s, we had something special that we all inherited. The mixtures of these passed-on technologies bore special traits, influencing our very nature of compatible fighting skills for what we were then and became as we ventured out into the world beyond our imagination. Mention that [you were] a local boy from Hawaii, and [people knew that] you would were a happy-go-lucky individual who would not back down from any beef [provocation]. We would go "Duke City" (have a go) as a matter of survival or [to] really kick butt. Our service careers often noted that the local boys from Hawaii were the guys who had a bit of something. From that time on, there was a generation of pioneering of those who left Hawaii and went to the states. There was Prof. Richard Kim, master Ed Parker, Prof. Wally Jay, master Gordon Doversola, master Ted Tabura, master Bill Ryusaki, master Ben Largusa, master Ted Lucay Lucay and many more. While [many others] made significant contributions, there are just too many to list. But, having said that, I do have to add one more. This is a pioneer from way down south. Down under, in fact. I am talking about Australia. This [contribution] occurred during the transition. The transition of the martial arts becoming a household word. I can say that it has been an interesting period of time, and it will be even more promising in the future. I am a part of this transitional phase much, just as I was part of the pioneering state from those years during the early 1960s. The person I am talking about, of course, is me.

I will mention some of the old stories from my Hawaii days because these will linger on forever and will be well remembered by those who have experienced what are sure to become legacies.

My first kumite [experience] was at our dojo in the Liliha branch of the goju-kai. My instructor and sempai was Antone Navas. He was a senior student of instructor Masa Oshiro. Navas was a gentle giant. A man in his rightful place amongst the best, he was also a riding companion of the famous Sons of Hawaii, a motorcycle gang known throughout Hawaii at the time. Having come from another style prior to this, I thought that he was going to teach me kumite and take me through the paces, which was the case in the matches before he called on me. In my entire life, I had never encountered anyone with his enormous strength. We started our usual sparring mode, only I was like a little dog trying to hit and run, mainly to avoid this man's strength and skill, as he was as fast as they come. He got hold of me, and I was bounced from one side of the dojo to the other. I lost all momentum, balance and got so disoriented that I felt like a rag doll. He then picked me up, and to my amazement, told me how I should evade and use various tactics to succeed. He then took me aside and said, "Remember this. To fall seven times, is to rise eight. Life begins now." Those words have sunk in well. To this very day, I reflect on [them] in my teaching. Our study in the martial arts is in fact motivational. [In so doing, we must] sustain endurance and develop tolerance and perseverance. Most importantly, we must make spiritual gains that come from the fighting spirit. This is zanshin or internal fortitude. Call it what you may, but it is our power source that we call on instinctively at the best of times. In those years of progress, those beautiful words from my sensei/sempai of the Hawaii Goju-Kai Dojo carried me. They carried me through my days here and throughout the world of which I have served as a student and propagator in this art.

Q: When you started teaching, how did the Westerners respond to traditional Japanese training?

A: Very interesting indeed! I was one of a kind when I arrived in Australia at the time I did. The first time it was in 1962. The second trip was in 1963. I eventually returned to marry an Australian girl whom I had befriended on two occasions while I was on tour as a Marine. Let it be known that karate in those parts was hardly known. As a Marine who had the privilege of doing what I knew best, I had the opportunity to show many people something they will never forget ... goju sanchin and tensho kata, as well as seienchin. In August of 1963, I returned to Melbourne, which is in the state of Victoria, to marry my Australian fiancé. I considered residing there even though I was still a reserve Marine on partial duty.

At one point, I was invited to the Dandenong Judo Club. This is where two well-known exponents of judo were trainees. One was Peter Armstrong, a stuntman in the film industry, and Mr. Malcom Brown was studying to become an accountant. Later, Brown taught tae kwon do and became a sponsor to a very well known instructor in the art. When a person in Australia claims to be the first goju-ryu propagator in the country, we should call a spade a spade.

Now, let me get back to the Westerner's response to the traditional training question. I guess I can sum it up by saying that the students were receptive to the traditional teaching. Or at least the traditional method prevailed. I can also honestly say — for what it is worth — that I would describe [that the whole matter] was a challenge. Our [stereotypical] character trait of an "Aussie" is that he is very liberated, an individual with a lot of freedom who puts on a personalized display and may at times be very skeptical unless proven otherwise. The last statement says it all, as my experience proved only too well what it meant to be a foreign pioneer in this strange country who was tested time and time again. As we say here, "It was my way or the highway." Yes, I am proud to say that tradition prevailed and was accepted. I could go on and on in describing how hard it was to get people to adjust. Instead, let me say that the best of part of this undertaking had been [exposing] the mystery of this hardly known art of the Orient. The only information available was traditional; therefore, it was literally accepted, provided I proved the worthiness of it. The presentation then was ritualistic. It gained momentum when the guest masters of Oriental origin arrived and many more have since arrived. However, there aren't any more or any fewer martial artists here who still adhere to the traditional philosophical state. The motivational attributes that contribute to its select presentation are still here. And most importantly, there is a linkage to why the art remains significant to modern science and a formidable combative technology.

Q: Were you so natural at karate that the movements came easily to you?

A: I couldn't very well consider myself a natural except that I was able to do everything that was asked of me. If natural means that I was able to do things perfectly, then I am fooling myself. I had some memorable lessons, and sometimes it takes a lot of repetition. But I was an eager student and a "sponge" for learning. I've proven myself to others, and it has been a great experience then, now and will still be for years to come.

Q: How has your personal karate changed and developed over the years?

A: In answering this question, I would like to acknowledge the many masters of whom I hold in reverence … their capability, their presentation of their skills in describing the word art as in the martial art, and most importantly, their propagation level in presenting a development format that science presents as the mechanics of training. I believe that my personal karate has changed dramatically because of the many influences I've had from my own father, including in the early years of boxing training. I also became involved in physical education as a teacher. Later, I became a national coach in sport karate, and I had to study the biomechanics of movements in the martial arts. While doing this, I can account for the progression in scientific movements that relate to what had been missing in

my karate of earlier years. Other integrated study of various disciplines in the arts also influenced my standard of creativity and the likes of precision to realistic techniques as well.

In essence, I believe that my training has purpose now, and with that level, there is a maturing consequence that is better, more concise and better understood. A new weapon of this time appears more realistically sound than taking an ancient outdated weapon of yesteryear to fight in this era of today.

Q: What are the most important points of your teaching philosophy?

A: Let me start with my own philosophy as written when I first exposed it to literal recording a long time ago, "It's not the style but the man." The importance of this statement allows freedom for all exploratory measure, as in personal study and the continued interest in the why, how and what for. I choose to go by the following words as my own in the area of teaching. "A teacher with the tools of his trade fires the imagination of his students." We live in a society of advanced technologies. We refer to the availability of many other "ology" and what proves to be the development factor of the individual's quest for the answers that are within grasp of these facility. Do not stop at your expansion. Pursue the thoughts of your roots and origin and seek your truth but be mindful to reality. It is often too much to concede to other ulterior motives for this is the beginning of the end.

Q: With all the technical changes during the last 30 years, do you think there is still pure shotokan, shito-ryu, goju-ryu, et cetera?

A: Considerations of purity are measured on what indoctrination has implied ... believe

what I say and not what I do. This is a way of saying that we know so much, but we must continue to pursue knowledge and progress with the times. To answer your question, let me refer to the goju-ryu system, because that is what I am familiar with, especially now that I have gained insight [into topics], some of which not even many of my senior goju-ryu peers are up to par with on educational development. We modern thinking practitioners have discovered the study of martial arts as a science. It is noted [or comprised] of skill-related subjects that make real the inner functions acceptable or questionable. I would like to mention that the Japanese did not really know — in-depth — what the Okinawans had been concealing for many years from the fold of their sovereignty rulers. And now this plays a major role in the recovery and exposure of advanced technology that we all can appreciate. And that is the linkage of the Chinese styles and their influence on what we find rather valuable at this point in time. So we are advancing, and in doing so, rather that undermining the status quo of our origins in the styles, we are contributing to the enhancement of the technology.

Q: Are different ryu important?

A: In regards to choosing a training center, each practitioner can make that choice. However, to the experienced senior practitioner, he should understand that Okinawa, which is where karate jitsu originated, is but a small island with three specific locations from which the following styles originated: shuri, tomari and naha. It is very important for a practitioner's studies to include the relations and the techniques, which means he must be open to a wider and broader interest in his continued study.

Q: What is your opinion of full-contact karate and kickboxing?

A: Kickboxing is a justifiable practice because it promotes the art of the Thailand, which is muay Thai. In the full-contact karate circuit, knowing that it may be controversial, to say the least, the sport must create what the boxing circuit has done, and that is make safety a priority for amateurs and professionals and [establish] rules that [ensure that] future practitioners can enjoy the sport. This eliminates the untold [number of] promotions to world championships. This [action] may even launch these sports into the Olympics.

Q: In regards to the art of karate, how would you describe the life and dedication of Yamaguchi Sensei?

A: Without question, he was a master in his own rights, an innovator before his time, the figure responsible for creating a respected worldwide organization and the man who brought forward a truly subjective study of karate that many followers to this very day understand only partially. In his lifetime, he was a towering strength of the goju-ryu foundation … without question. I've had the privilege of living under his roof, training with him personally and getting placed in a position of relative importance. I have since gone independently on to pursue further study with the Okinawan masters. These are significant masters who contributed to my continued interest in the arts and have contributed greatly to my level of expertise.

Q: Do you think that Western karate is at the same level with Japanese karate?

A: Yes, at this point in time. However, I'm sure there may be a Japanese master who would say that Westerners lack this or that. It is interesting to note that the martial arts are a worldwide study and the interest in the professionalism and science of the arts are growing. It's just like the wheel that turns in whichever way it advances. This is the nature of progress.

Q: If you were to compare the fundamental differences between Japanese karate-ka and Western karate-ka, can you see any fundamental differences?

A: On a whole, I have not been updated on the development of Japanese karate-ka. Therefore, I will have to base my answer on those to which I am exposed. My opinion is that modern study makes it possible for an individual to make inevitable progress and development in whatever he wants and needs to excel. This stands strongly with today's practitioners … whether they are Westerners or Asians.

Q: Karate is nowadays often referred to as a sport. Do you agree with this definition or do you think it is only Budo?

A: I would like to comment on what is naturally the effectiveness of karate's growth. We are experiencing a transitional point in which sport, if it continues to take over, may bring disadvantages to those who portray or promote this [aspect of karate]. The clarity in practice makes real [or confirms] that Bugei is making distinct gains over the Budo and perhaps a new transition to the karate-jitsu will place karate into a better position of propagation in the Western sector. My comment on this stems from personal observation and experience from international exposure.

Q: Do you feel that you still have further to go in your studies of karate and Budo?

A: Most certainly. This study will go with me to the grave. It is my life, my ambition and my legacy will forever be: "It's not the style, but the man."

Q: At the present time, how do you see karate, in general, and goju-ryu around the world?

A: I do not wish to speculate and then retrieve my statements, but here goes. Karate is a tool, as in other disciplines, that most practitioners see as a motivational activity with a purpose. It will continue — and with proper delivery of its correct technology and with correct teaching—for a long time. The goju-ryu technology will become an influential subject to steer an interested person to [undertake an in-depth] study in culture, skills and compatible techniques. They will also discover a formidable combative technology.

Q: Does kobudo help empty-hand karate?

A: Yes, definitely. It enhances many skills, including balance and evasion, directional power and specific hitting techniques. I recommend this totally.

Q: What's your opinion of makiwara training?

A: I have done this for many years, but I have not reached [a level of] satisfaction from its benefits. With my knowledge of both the biological effects of using this and better ways to enhance my power, I have reverted back to corrective training and proper use of other implements in developing my personal skills.

Q: To progress in the arts, how should a sensei schedule his personal training?

A: Many years ago I had the privilege of training with my other revered teacher and master of Kobujitsu … Inoue Motokatsu Hanshi. He was an astute and very knowledgeable practitioner of many arts. He would practice daily, beginning as early as 5:30 a.m. He worked on various skills and even traveled from one country to another. In his system, he used a miniature calendar on which he scheduled the techniques that he was going to study that day. While traveling, he'd merely turn to his calendar and refer to the item he was going to be working on. Then he would visualize his entire practice. What a remarkable man he was and how he trained us will remain in our hearts for the rest of our time.

Q: Self-defense, sport or tradition. When teaching the art of karate, what is the most important element?

A: The martial arts, as in many other facets, remain integrated largely because of their origin and imbedded items of rudiments and progressive development. In the daily teaching of the martial arts, I see a composite of all [of these items], which can be made presentable by a lesson plan that includes all of them. Of course, there may be variables and interesting progressions of why various items are taught.

Sport and tradition do have their place, but I use them in a different way. I balance them against all of the components in our practice. You see, they all are part and partial of the art. We must not put aside what has been our study, but we must continue to make the study interesting and creative for all to follow.

Q: Sensei, do you have any general advice you would care to pass on to the karate-ka?

A: Take your training and progression seriously. And don't overlook the time factor. We seem to think that we will never get old and that our bodies will always be strong, willing and able. For those who belong to the school that promotes the study of this art for life, pursue this like a daily meal. Sustenance will contribute to the welfare and continuation of the body … similar to your desire to learn more. It never ends. And the mind, the body and the spirit will coexist to bring satisfaction in this practice, if you so choose.

Q: Some people think that it is necessary to go to Japan to train. Do you agree?

A: Definitely not. We have many qualified instructors in the world who can provide quality training. Of course, it should be noted that such a pilgrimage to Japan could be a novelty, as well as visiting Okinawa. By all means, you should do so if you so desire. Obviously, there are cost and logistics to consider, but the trip may "center" you and you may experience innovative training methods. [These benefits have been obvious from others throughout] these past years.

Q: Since you began training, what do you consider to be the major changes in the art of karate?

A: Attitudes and receptiveness to traditional teachings. The manner in which we were taught was accepted as if it were the standard rule. If you did not follow those methods or conform to that way of training, you were told that you would never learn. It is, of course, very enduring to teach that way. The repetition and many hours of physical exercises were strenuous and there were dangerous implications [to the training] that hurt many students. However, the respect and courtesy were exceptional. If you suffered an injury, you'd take it as a mark of honor ... rather than [an incident in which] someone was trying to injure you purposely. We have rules bound by litigation today that make our responsibility in the dojo very restrictive. For most, it is a form of training that caters only to its client rather than teaching the art for what it is and how it will be beneficial to its practitioners.

Q: With whom would you like to have trained with that you have not?

A: In the art of karate, I would nominate Taira Sensei, the weapons master of Okinawa, and, of course, our founder and creator of the goju-ryu, master Chojun Miyagi.

Q: What would you say to someone who is interested in learning karate-do?

A: What do you wish to gain from learning karate-do and how did you decide that it is karate-do that you desire to learn? The reasoning behind these questions is to be certain that we gain a student and not a person of ill repute or someone with ulterior motives who would waste our [the instructor's] time. So it's good to know before hand know exactly where we stand.

Q: What keeps you motivated after all of these years?

A: Someone just asked me this question recently, and I answered it by telling him that I have a desire to better myself through physical conditioning. But there is more to it than meets the eye. Yes, the beginning was a challenge because there was a lot to tolerate, and

it's important to focus on every detail. This literally can make or break someone. In my early years, I was fortunate to have my father teaching me what values were all about. I appreciated what I got, made something of it and considered myself lucky for what came my way. In essence, start what you finish or go until it no longer serves you. Attributes to motivate exist … like a burning cell that activates every muscle in your body. I feel great and see the light of the next day descending upon me as my desire to carry on. I do kokyu breathing to refurbish my energy and life, and this [is motivational]. [Simply] living is motivational, especially when you are happy and positive.

Q: Is it necessary to engage in free fighting to achieve good self-defense skills for a real situation?

A: It would be every now and again, but this is not really a measure of [true] defense. So, the best way to improve your skills and understanding of the mind in responsive action is to spar. Not only will you derive these [aforementioned] benefits, but you will also eventually understand the instinctive relays of energy and cardio threshold. All of these are a specialty of my innovative workout. I will release this when we next meet.

Q: What is your opinion about mixing karate styles? Does the practice of one nullify the effectiveness of the other? Or, on the contrary, can it be beneficial to a student?

A: It is most beneficial. Barriers of style have now been lifted and most certainly bring advantageous results that all students will enjoy and appreciate. Put aside the stigma of "my style" or "my way," as it is everyone's way, and it will open the door to accept the art in its expanded science … ready to explore.

Q: Modern karate is moving away from the bunkai in kata practice. How important do you think bunkai is in the understanding of "kata" and karate-do in general?

A: If one removes the bunkai from kata, it becomes a superficial practice in which meaningless maneuvers simply become a dance and nothing more. The "guts" of kata lie in its bunkai or what can be practiced as kyogi-kumite.

Q: What is the philosophical basis for your karate training?

A: The words that began in biblical times and for those who were seeking the truth certainly precede the common anecdotes of martial arts philosophy. To search is to find. Upon doing so, answers will be granted by virtue of ones understanding or duplication.

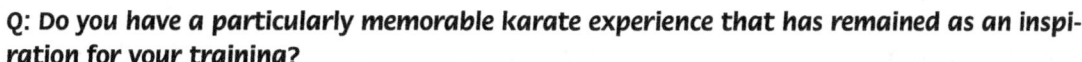

Q: Do you have a particularly memorable karate experience that has remained as an inspiration for your training?

A: Yes, I have a most memorable moment that will never be repeated in all my life. This incident enabled me to share moments of energy exchange with my grandmaster, Gogen Yamaguchi. The year was 1972, and the location was the Adelaide Hills in South Australia. We were at a vintage resort property where we were scheduled to shoot a local television feature of this great master. We were in a cherry orchard in the rear of this beautiful resort. There was mist, and it was a bit eerie. We were in our gi, prepared for a kumite match and the setting was similar to Old Japan. It was the grandmaster and the lowly student. The grandmaster, with his shoulder-length hair, not only looked awesome, but his form was excellent and he was fierce. When the order for hajime was given, it felt like I shouldn't be there, let alone have to face up to our Kaicho, Hanshi Gogen Yamaguchi. It ended as it started ... I was taken for being star struck. Even if I moved to execute, I was checked and there was an answer to everything I delivered. It was the greatest experience that anyone could have encountered. It felt like I was a magnet. I was stopped before even getting started. It will be my story to tell my grandchildren when they too reach a period in time for their lessons. This will be my inspiration to the day I pass on, for what it was and what took place on that morning in South Australia.

Q: After all these years of training and experience, explain the meaning of the practice of karate-do.

A: What karate-do means to me may differ for others. In answering this, I will explicitly refer to my experiences that have influenced my growth in this homogeneous society that can be measured for progress and development. Let me expound on the features of this path — the empty-hand way — that have had a grip on my life and [provided] continued satisfaction and given direction to my ever-growing quest to the attributes by which I follow. It is a unique study, for it encompasses the concern of the elements in life that impose on a serious practitioner the inner depth of mental exploration, the physical energy one puts to test on progressive development, and the soul seeking attributes that lead to the character development and further influence of what evidently becomes a chosen way.

In summary, what I have gained from this study and involvement stays with me as chronological development that I come to recognize as the same thing my dear Sensei Inoue Motokatsu mentioned during one of his lectures to us and that is this journey takes you undisturbed as long as you are on track. Our lives reach a point of cognition to realism or what is known as heiho awareness. In essence, the applications are universal.

Q: How can a practitioner increase his understanding of the spiritual aspect of karate?

A: First, he must have tremendous desire. Personally, I would rather explain what and how this became a venture for me and explain what transpired as I became a spiritual being rather than have someone else explain that based on observances of me. What started as a physical motive for practicing [the martial arts], I [soon] recognized a very unique feeling. I started to feel uplifted and [experience] a power surge of energy during many training sessions. A relaxed state or a state of contentment followed. It was a feeling of having an awareness of everything around me and thinking that I can go on and on with this feeling of control with my senses, my body and mental awareness. Yes, this reality struck me even greater when training in special sessions with masters and other sensei who directed me to search for the inner strength of what comes as spiritual enhancement. I was prepared for change and this became inherent to my studies of religion and other beliefs.

I believe that this is the key to one's search and discovery … being desirous of change. We must consider our belief in the mind, the body and the spirit. When these points or elements of noted existence surface, grasp every opportunity to expand your study, for there lies in it a worthwhile experience that will never set you back and keep you on track with the "Do" of martial arts.

Q: How much training should a "senior" karate-ka be doing to improve at his art?

A: There are several definitions to the term "senior karate-ka." I refer to seniors in terms of ranking in age, maturity and time spent training. Let me advise everyone right now that biological age need not be a deterrent to anyone's involvement in the art. Improvement is not always of the physical nature, but certainly there can be a mastery of skills on a different level, such as theory, correctness of application and philosophical aspirations that bring motivational attributes. It seems like this is the case for many seniors who are no longer able to execute the techniques as easily as they once did in their youthful past. Maturity is the key and hence the practice must be a balanced circuit regime to suit the practitioner's schedule, physical condition and motivational incentive. And, of course, it all highly depends on the individuals desire to maintain the practice.

Q: Is there anything lacking in the way karate is taught today, especially when you compare it with those who were being taught in your early days?

A: In today's teaching, much of the instruction borders on the physical attributes. Unfortunately, the time factor of these workouts limits the intensive motivational and inspirational attributes [that also belong in the sessions]. There's also too much emphasis on sport. Students should realize that the sport element is only a segment of properly learning the martial arts. The sport aspect seems to be the motive most of the time and the attitude [encouraged] is to win at all costs just for the sake of winning. Precedence seems to be on the ego, and it seems like this is the case at most dojo. That is where their priorities are. Understanding the traditional values in practice also lacks details. Ritual exercise means nothing without the understanding and practice of courtesy and respect to the sensei and fellow students, including oneself. Infliction of pain or receiving pain is something that must be suppressed. There are certainly ways it can be corrected and administered with agreeable purpose and positive results. If these changes are met, then things will be better than they were yesterday.

Q: What are the most important qualities of a successful karate-ka?

A: A successful karate-ka must be able to engage, exchange, and enjoy his art and, most importantly, contribute or convey to his fellow man the understanding — coded by our practice of respect, courtesy and awareness to others — when called upon. Once we become involved with the martial arts, we become missionaries to the cause. The cause merely puts us there amongst those who came before us. It engages us as we share this art and for our future existence of surviving the elements that we sometimes take for granted. Let us work together on this, as we do have to sustain this very important study.

Q: If a student wants to partake in supplementary training such as weight training or stretching, what do you suggest?

A: Modern training provides many different modes and circuits of exercise and personal systems that suit every possible development. Yes, I support supplementary training, as I too adhere to physical training with a difference. Your body needs to be nurtured, and you should choose to

follow your desires. This is the modern era of physical fitness, and the technology available certainly surpasses that of yesteryear. Your mastery of the arts must be sorted out as you wish. Past criticisms only led to envy and suppressed motives. Later, you discover the loss of understanding of what it was, what it is and what will be.

Q: What are the most important attributes of a student?

A: To be totally happy and satisfied with his training, to be able to perform and be content with his knowledge and progression of study, and to be able to walk away from any danger when provoked. In a state of higher attributes, a student must also grow in other areas of his life, including health, protection, vocation and motivation.

Q: Why do a lot of students stop training after two or three years?

A: For obvious reasons. First, they lack the foresight to reach the levels to which they once strived. In other cases, they are an undefined subject because they are essentially just a puppet in training … rather than absorbing and relating to the studied technology. In other cases, they become bored because they do not improve. As I mentioned earlier, the mind, body and soul must all be on track. Otherwise, a student's career is going to be shortened.

Q: There is very little written about you in magazines. Unlike some martial artists, you obviously do not thrive on publicity. Why?

A: I have had write-ups in all of the Australian magazines, the European magazines and several American publications, such as Black Belt. Among other things, there has been a word or two mentioning my participation in some of the tournaments in the 1980s and the

1990s. I am honored indeed for your interest in this interview and this may launch my existence in a manner that I will be most proud. My role has been known amongst many from the many years of worldwide service in karate-do. I take pride in my work and contribution to our martial arts. It is not a lack of desire to [have stories] published about me. Instead, it's been circumstances. While I was in Australia, I was a leader, propagator and a senior practitioner who created for those who wished to learn. I have had my day in competitions, my role as a top worldwide adjudicator and an executive for many years that put me well into the driver's seat, headed in the right direction. Perhaps now that I am in my maturing years and still active in teaching and propagating this opportunity will launch new, creative innovations that will be a subject for exponents worldwide. As I reiterate, my role out there has been that of a player. I did not exist to be highlighted or grandstanded but to be innovative and productive. I have produced world champions from Australia, worked with movie celebrities, provided security for prominent people and worked with heads of State from many countries. Still, I remain humbled by the fact that I've been there done that and am still going enjoying everything that has been given me. So, again I am indeed grateful for this opportunity, not only for myself but also for my colleagues, because this is a start for us all.

Q: Have there been times when you felt fear in your karate training?

A: Yes, I suppose we [all] may — from time to time — encounter such experiences, particularly when on duty and having to engage in the inevitable. [Let me now] reflect on what my instructor once said to me, "To fall seven times, is to rise eight. Life begins now." Choice words.

Q: What are your thoughts on the future of karate-do and what's your opinion about karate entering the Olympics?

A: I am happy to answer that with convictions of pro and con that will reveal the many reasons that provoked conditions of today's karate-do, as well as respond to the many conditions that play a role in the sport's participation into the Olympics. First, the future of karate-do lies basically in its propagation and creative interest to combative technology, as it was an art. Our directions changed over the times and created ulterior motives that caused the climatic conditions of politics in sport-oriented training. If we are to follow the

"Do" of karate, then it should be concerned with defense first — not attack. The competition mode totally destroys the ideals of the karate way. Second, in the event of karate-do being admitted to the Olympics, I dare say that our competitions would be a drawing card for the spectators. This is proving itself as a low-scaled version of karate in its origin.

Now, I want to comment about something from the earlier years of WUKO's development commission. This pertains to the kumite rules for shiai. At the time, there were only three foreign members of the elite Referee's Council that had been privy to these meetings. That was Sensei Frank Nowak and Jerry Thompson, as well as myself. Our chairman was Sensei Teruo Hayashi of the FAJKO. The subject was the inclusion of sanbon shobu, a replacement for ippon shobu. All technicalities aside, we were involved deeply in the concepts of other shiai. These other items would have been more conclusive and definitely would have brought credit to karate-do in its implementation should they had been introduced and applied as rules. However, that was not the case, so the game continued with progressive changes [implemented] to highlight the current style of competition rule to suit all participants. One major but very sad and controversial system [that had developed] had been the start of political conflict from all groups and all styles. This eventually led to fragmentations too wide and broad. Thus, the objective of unity died. The biggest thing that it [the fragmentation] created is egoism. Ideals and the code of a karate-ka [were not important]. Instead, winning at all costs and at all risks became important. I regretfully expose a long kept feeling of remorse and disappointment because of the disservice that it [this whole process] had done to many. My role is, as I said, to teach. Hopefully this lesson will not go unmanned for its corrective nature and still may be reinstated to bring again a resurgence of the karate-do that we knew of the past. For the future, I can think of another alternative to the Olympics, but I will reserve that for a well-planned program that is now on the drawing board.

Q: Is there anything else you would like to add for the readers?

A: They should understand that there is a beginning to all of this. Karate-do evolved not only from our humble masters from Okinawa but also for many years outside of Japan. Today, it has developed into a major household word, and it's important in regards to physical education and cultural attributes. Furthermore, it continues to grow with so much interest that motivational experts recognize it as a formidable practice both for the body and the mind.

TERUO CHINEN

A PEACEFUL MAN

He was one of the world's leading instructors of Okinawan goju-ryu karate.

Only a lifetime dedication could have produced such awesome skill and power that was Chinen Sensei. Very few around the world could match his dynamic and powerful techniques and actions. A retired schoolteacher, he was not a believer in too much mysticism or any other form of "ism." He believed — as a Buddhist — in the capabilities of the mind to enhance an individual's potential but not from a cryptic or inexplicable perspective. For him, the connection between physical technique and thought was of the outmost importance. His knowledge and understanding of Chinese culture and philosophy surprised many. For him, however, it is a simple way to understand the roots of karate. As a master of karate-do, Chinen Sensei was around long enough to have seen most things, and that's probably the reason why he was a man who really was at peace with himself.

Q: What would you tell us about your family involvement in the martial arts?

A: My family has a long tradition of martial arts. I was born in Kobe City, Japan, in 1914. My father was a Navy career man in Okinawa. In 1945, we moved there, and this is where I met Miyagi Sensei years later. My father was a shorin-ryu practitioner. My grandfather was a shorin-ryu instructor, and my uncle was an expert in the bo. In fact, he had kata named after him, such as Chinen-no-kou. I was the first member of my family who took the goju-ryu style of karate. My family accepted it well, but my brother gave me a hard time for a while because he thought I should have stuck to the family tradition of shorin-ryu.

Q: Sensei, what is your relationship with Chinen Masami Sensei of yamanni-ryu?

A: Yamanni-Chinen-ryu has always carried two arts. One is the weapons system and the other is shorin-ryu karate as I mentioned in the beginning. Masami Chinen was my granduncle.

He lived in Shuri, Okinawa, and worked at the Shuri City Hall, as did my brother. I used to call him granduncle Shobi. My father adopted the Japanese ways and did not use the Masa name for his children. Later on, my brothers and I all received Japanese names, and they are as follows: Akira, Hirokazu, Teruo and Toshio. No more Chinese names and no more Masa line!

Q: How did you come to live near Miyagi Sensei and how do you remember him?

A: My mother's younger brother was a police officer in the Naha district, and his chief happened to be Chojun Miyagi, who was providing instruction at the police academy. He had several houses, and one of these was three blocks away from Miyagi's. My uncle, being a single man, didn't need the spacious house and gave it to my mother for us to live there. We were a large family (six brothers and sisters), and there was no father. As far as the training concerns, I was just a kid, much too junior to receive serious attentions from Miyagi Sensei. Of course, I didn't know who he was, but I remember Miyagi Sensei was a stern and quiet man. His movements were very soft but extremely powerful, limber and flexible. The combination of such power and flexibility was incredible. His hand strength was incredible and his movements very precise. Only those actions required to do the job were executed. There were no unnecessary movements whatsoever. His reputation was that of a humble man and a kind individual. Of course, at that time there were challenges, but Miyagi Sensei never did this out of a bravado attitude.

He came from a very wealthy family. Because he didn't have to worry about money, he put all his time and energy into karate. He could simply afford to do that. His group of students was comprised of different levels of skill, and he treated them according to their specific skill and understanding. He personalized the instruction for each student. This is the main reason why you see students of Miyagi Sensei doing the same things but slightly differently. He personalized the instruction and gave each student what he really needed at that period of time. Another factor was the stage of his life that Miyagi Sensei was at that time. It is not that anyone is doing it wrong, but they learned it differently at different times.

I have heard really silly stories about Miyagi Sensei, such as the one that he could leave his footprints on the dojo ceiling because of his ability to do a back flip so high that he kicked the ceiling. To begin with, the dojo was outside. It didn't have a ceiling! Miyagi Sensei was way too intelligent to risk damaging his body that way. He was very powerful man, but he was only human.

Q: Who introduced you to him?

A: My uncle took me to his dojo one evening. He told Miyagi Sensei that my family was practitioners of shorin-ryu and asked him to accept me. He said yes and that was it. No paperwork!

My first class involved standing basics and front kicks, deep knee bends, stand-up [techniques] and kicks. That kind of stuff.

Q: How was the training afterwards?

A: It was a quiet. There was no yelling or loud kiai. In fact, the kiai we practiced was very internal. The reason for this is the dojo was located in the middle of a residential area, so yelling was not really appropriate! He was a police officer. Therefore, the last things he wanted were screams and yells coming out of his place.

Q: How did he direct the classes at that time?

A: Well, he was not in a good health, so he sat down a lot and directed the classes. He observed and gave instruction. We did a lot of kata. Kata and supplementary training were the basics of the training. The supplementary training included the makiwara, chiisi (stone lever weight), nigiri game (gripping jars) and many other [traditional items]. There were not a lot of students and the assistants always took good care of every disciple. Miyazato Sensei was one of them.

Q: Did Miyagi Sensei choose the assistants personally?

A: It was not that kind of structure. There weren't "assistants" as we understand today. They were "seniors" taking care of the "junior" students. Miyagi Sensei would say, "Go help this student." And they did.

Q: How do you remember the death of Miyagi Sensei?

A: From a historical point of view, I was too young to really understand what was happening. I remember that police agents were all around Miyagi's house. I realized that he was a very important individual, and I believe everybody knew the end was near because he had been sick for a long time.

Q: When did you start your training under Eiichi Miyazato Sensei?

A: Miyazato Sensei was Master Miyagi's senior student. When Miyagi Sensei died, Miyazato Sensei received all the training equipment and established his own dojo to continue the teachings of Master Miyagi. Of course, I went with him. I remember we had to move the equipment from one place to another, and I took the makiwara and the chiisi. It was a nice walk. It was only two miles or so! At that time we didn't care about rank of promotion of any kind. We simply cared about karate. We didn't need a belt to know who was good and who wasn't. Belt ranking came later, and it originated from the art of judo. They were using only three belts: white, brown and black. Additional colored belts came afterwards as instructors experimented with introducing incentives for regular training.

Q: How was it at Miyazato's dojo?

A: It was a typical Okinawan building. It had a household Shinto shrine with the statue of Busaganashi. The dojo had an open door ... Japanese style. It was beautiful, and I really liked it.

Q: From where did the word Jundokan come?

A: It was Miyazato Sensei who gave birth to Jundokan. There is an old Chinese poem called Jundo Seisho. Translated, this means, "Do the right way." Miyazato Sensei took a quotation from it.

Q: When did you receive your rank from Miyazato Sensei?

A: It was around 1958 when I was going to Tokyo to teach. Master Miyazato presented me with a black belt. There was no rank designated or certificate presented. In 1974, when I was dispatched to South Africa to teach, Miyazato Sensei gave me a certificate proclaiming the rank of rokudan – 6th Dan.

Q: How different are the Okinawan and Japanese teaching methods?

A: They are very different. In Okinawa, the training is more individualized and personalized. Of course, the teacher corrects your mistakes, but the class structure follows the Chinese example in which students work on their own. At a certain moment in time, the whole group can go through drills or kata at once, but most of the training is individually done. In Japan, the training follows a more militaristic approach. This training structure is very good for young and talented students because you can truly create great karateka … if they survive this kind of structure. Everybody does the same techniques over and over again. Many schools in Japan use this approach, and the technical level [of students] becomes really good. Everybody is cut by the same mold so the individual doesn't receive personal attention as in the Okinawan approach. As I said, it is good for young people who are physically strong and who have a decisive mind.

The Okinawan counterpart is more subtle, more tailor-made for the individual student. The teacher treats each student, taking into consideration the ability, age, and physical make-up and peculiarities of each individual. People are quite different — different body structures, philosophies, customs, and ways of expressing themselves — so it is natural that their karate will develop differently. The Japanese approach is more like, "Let's go to train very hard for two hours." When the time is up, they just get on with it and do it. Okinawans follow the Chinese way more. They have a 24-hours martial arts mind. When they feel like training, they just do it. They don't care about the time. The Chinese are more relaxed about it; therefore, I think it is more natural. From my point of view, the art has more possibilities of blossoming this way. If you don't understand how Chinese people think, you may never understand the philosophy behind your karate. The Chinese are very dramatic and exaggerated … maybe because the country is so big geographically. Chinese history is 10 times longer than Japan's. The Chinese mind goes with the Tangtse and Hwan Rivers … slowly but surely. Even conversations between Chinese people are a little mystic; they never reveal their entire mind.

Q: Is your Jundokan International organization separate from the Jundokan in Okinawa?

A: Yes, it is separate. The reason that it is separate is that you must adapt the art to the country where you live and teach. Kata, for example, must stay the same, but the concept of the form must change in relation to the culture of the country where the instructor is teaching. Some may think I am saying something stupid, but that is exactly what the old Okinawan masters did when they learnt kung fu and shifu from the Chinese masters who brought the art to Okinawa. These Okinawan practitioners (who later became masters of karate) took the teachings and adapted it, giving it an Okinawan flavor and creating the birth of Okinawan karate.

Q: Do you advocate training in other disciplines?

A: I do. I have grades in kendo, judo and Okinawa weaponry, too. I think that the study of other martial arts forms may assist the students to gain a better understanding of their main art.

Q: You acknowledge that goju-ryu has a strong influence from Chinese arts. This is very unusual for an Okinawa teacher.

A: Well, I don't know if it is unusual or not, but I always give credit where credit is due. For the astute observer, the relationship between goju-ryu and some Chinese styles of kung fu — especially pa kua — is quite obvious. You can see those influences in the circularity and the footwork. We can also see similarities in kakie and tui shou [pushing hands] from tai chi chuan or the chi sao of wing chun.

Master Kanryo Higaonna, Miyagi's teacher, traveled extensively to China's Fukien Province and trained strenuously for more than 15 years under the legendary Ryu Ryuko. Higaonna Sensei returned to Naha, Okinawa with a great number of kata and knowledge that he passed onto Miyagi Chojun. Miyagi Sensei refined these techniques and kata. In 1931, he named the system goju-ryu. The name (hard and gentle style) reportedly came from an amalgam of some of the Eight Precepts of Chinese kenpo found in the ancient Bubishi manuscripts. There is a particular verse that translates as: "Everything in the universe is controlled by the opposing principles of yin and yang and the way of inhaling and exhaling embraces hardness and softness." Everything is breathing ... hard and soft.

Q: When did you come to the United States?

A: I came to the United States in 1969. Between 1958 and 1969, I was in Tokyo at the Yoyogi dojo, helping Mr. Higaonna Morio teach gaijin at his school. My first intention was to go to Brazil to teach because there had been an outpouring of demand for goju-ryu teachers in Europe, South Africa and South America. However, because the situation was unstable at the time, I ended up in the U.S. I was ready to go to Brazil because Miyazato Sensei called me and told me his wife's brother had company in Sao Paulo, and he was thinking about sponsoring me so I could open a dojo to teach goju-ryu. Then, the country had a coup d'etat, and the political situation was inappropriate, so I did not go at that time. I decided to accept the offer to visit the U.S.

I only wanted to stay in the United States for a short period of time, maybe three months or so. However, when I came to Spokane, I saw the low technical level of karate there, and I decided to stay longer. I knew it wasn't anybody's fault. I understood there had been many teachers before, many bridges, and the messages often got crossed. There was such a gap between the practitioners and me! I didn't want to make any instructor uncomfortable, so I offered to help correct what they were doing and establish some kind of foundation on which we could build. To be honest, it was harder to work with the instructors than with the students. I believe it was a mix of ego and the difficulty of changing what they were doing for so long. I totally understood the situation and gave them as much private instruction as I could. I knew it would take time to fix the problem, and I also knew that sometimes it is better to start from scratch instead of trying to rebuild the whole thing. Because things were still chaotic in Brazil, I figured I might as well stay in the U.S.

Q: When did you form Jundokan International?

A: I believe it was around 1980 when Higaonna Sensei formed his own organization, and I decided to stay with Jundo Seisho under Miyazato Sensei. My idea was that Jundokan International would be a foreign office of Jundokan Okinawa. I wanted to support Miyazato Sensei, and that's why I chose the name of Jundokan International.

Q: What are the characteristics that set goju-ryu apart from other styles of karate?

A: As an art of Budo, all styles and systems of karate-do lead to the same goal. So, in the spiritual goal ... there are no differences. Technically, goju-ryu uses the duality of hard and soft to deal with any technical approach. We use the circular movements in most of the actions because it is more natural and it dissolves the incoming energy from the aggressor more fluidly. The fighting distance is shorter than in other styles, and this simple fact effects the chambering position of the fist in hikite, the targets we hit in combat, et cetera. For instance, because the fighting distance is shorter, the fist usually is chambered higher than in other karate methods. Why? There is not enough room to punch. Furthermore, there are many fast and short circular techniques. Some of these techniques involve the snapping of the wrist to increase the power at the moment of impact. When the distance is short, speed is not that important but power is. The technique does not have to travel that far, so the practitioner needs to be able to generate a powerful blow. At this short distance, speed is not relevant. Instead, it's how powerful your strike is, especially if you hit each other simultaneously. The training methods used to develop power in short distances are circular. Because using your whole body produces maximum power, goju-ryu stylists need to shift their body in circular motions to get an added advantage.

Q: Is this the reason why goju-ryu stylists do some of the kata that other styles practice with slight changes in direction?

A: It is. In goju-ryu, everything is very subtle. Things are not so obvious like they are in other karate styles in which you can see through the techniques clearly. In goju-ryu, everything is in some kind of disguise. A technique may look easy, but it may actually be difficult to master. For instance, goju shares some kata with shito-ryu. However, in goju, the angles in some of the techniques are different. We also stress tension and proper breathing — at all times — in the techniques and kata.

Q: Like in sanchin and tensho?

A: Yes. Sanchin teaches the student how to properly use oxygen and send it to all the parts of the body. This kata also helps to judge the student's level when practicing other forms. I do believe that strong basics are the secrets to becoming a good karateka. Tensho is one of my favorite kata because it deals with breathing, and breathing is the key of life. If you are capable of focusing on one thing for an extended period, that [ability] can translate to something else. In the Western world, students don't like to spend too much time repeating the same technique. Thus, instructors should adapt and change their teaching approach. Sometimes this creates problems in the long run. People train for different reasons, and those [reasons] should be respected. I have changed my teaching methods in some ways, but the essence of the training is the same. I may change with times, but the quality of what they receive is the same. Chi or ki comes through breathing. Breathing comes from the tanden and promotes the smooth flow of energy throughout the body. The amount of benefit you derive from this varies; it depends on the practitioners. All styles rooted in Chinese systems practice this, along with stimulating chi through movement ... and goju-ryu does this also.

Q: You mentioned tensho kata. Does it have roots in Chinese kung-fu?

A: Yes it does. Tensho represents the kata of white crane kung-fu. A woman created this style. In Okinawa, tensho kata is considered to be at the same level as pechurin [suparimpei], but I always teach it to beginners so they can develop the proper breathing pattern and greater lung capacity.

Q: Sanchin kata is an important part of the goju style of karate. What can you tell us about it?

A: It is true that sanchin is one of the pillars of goju-ryu, and its importance and meaning go beyond the well-known translation of three battles. It also goes beyond the body-mind-spirit principle. This form is the basic training form for many Fujianese [Fukien] styles of chuan-fa [kung fu], primarily those with the animals, as the system's white crane. Sanchin seems to have originated some 300 years ago and is considered to be a white crane kata. This form was the basis for the breathing method, strength, stance and strategy in the Southern Shaolin temple. The training in sanchin takes place in three stages, which are training in the form, training the chi [ki] and training the spirit [shen]. Training the form is learning the pattern of the kata and the moves along with their applications. The training of the ki is the training of the principles behind the moves. This involves the study of how the principles are used to give the correct energy application and the flow of the energy throughout the sequence of the moves. This understanding can be then applied to other kata or forms. The training of the spirit is the final and most difficult phase of sanchin development. This means the ability to direct ki and to use it as the will directs. It also involves achieving the correct state of mind required for combat. These arise only after a very long time of dedicated training. Finally, the idea of the number three goes beyond all these things we have talked about. In sanchin, the number three symbolizes a three-dimensional approach to the form, but this is extremely difficult to explain in written format without the proper physical explanations of the technique.

Q: What is your opinion of karate being a sport?

A: Karate is not a sport, but some aspects of karate can be used as a sport activity in competition. Budo is the most important thing I teach. Sport makes a student focus on speed and not the power behind the techniques. Everything evolves around who is the one scoring faster and not necessarily the one who is more powerful. Your opponent in a real confrontation will fall because of power — not strictly because of speed. It is not that speed is unimportant, but you want to make sure that you don't throw away power for useless speed. Karate was never designed for sport. Yes, you can use the front kick and the reverse punch to score a point, and that may be enough for tournaments. However, self-defense is a different thing altogether. You can't build a house with just one tool; you need a number of tools. And to protect ourselves, we need a variety of tools. Today, sport karate is very good and it [has reached a] high level all over the world, but there is a great danger [in that] because true karate spirit and attitude can't be maintained in sport karate training. This can be achieved only with the correct approach, and that is up to the instructor. Karate should be for everybody from children to older people. Everybody can derive benefits from proper karate training, regardless of their age. Perhaps when the students are young they can focus on competition. When they get older, they will need more than that. That's when the art and true karate-do comes along. You have to cultivate the art and the true karate when you are young. You can't think that it will be there when you are older if you haven't taken care of it before.

Q: Why haven't you been an advocate of the tales attributed to the old masters?

A: I'm trying to steer clear of that mysterious approach to karate training. You know those claims. "My punch is so deadly that I can't go to tournaments." Or, "Meditation brings the ultimate enlightenment." That type of stuff. I'm tired of hearing that sort of thing. Speed and power in karate come from correct training methods, strong conditioning and endless repetitions. I believe conditioning is one of the most important aspects of training, and I ask my students to do the same.

Q: What are your recommendations for makiwara training?

A: My first advice is that a student should only start under the supervision of a qualified instructor. Makiwara training is not a joke because it can ruin your hands if it is not done properly. I have always been attracted to it because of the view of those bloodstained, straw-padded posts in Miyagi's backyard dojo. Training with a makiwara is very important in the development of proper impact and kime in the techniques, but, as I said previously, it has to be properly taught. Otherwise, it can cause arthritic problems later in life. Remember, your hands are a wonderful piece of physical engineering, and you can cause irreversible damage to them. Treat your body with respect. Calluses are just a byproduct of the training. Training with a makiwara improves your timing, impact, and coupled with properly taught footwork, can greatly enhance your dexterity in striking on the move. To me, training with a makiwara represents the last hope in maintaining the essence of the original spirit of traditional karate. It's [makiwara training] the kind of karate that — unlike others — doesn't promote hands and feet as soft as a baby's because there isn't an emphasis on sport competition. The feeling for self-protection has been lost, and makiwara training keeps this feeling.

Q: What do you mean by treating your body with respect?

A: We all want to live well and have a long and happy life. To do this, we must take care of our body and provide it with the utmost respect. During my 20s and 30s, I carried a wounded body. But as a teacher, I don't want my students to suffer the same injuries. I have done my best to develop good teaching skills that are physically harder but safer. We no longer practice some of those conditioning exercises that may not be so good.

Q: How important is bunkai in the understanding of karate?

A: Very important. Miyagi Sensei broke the different kata into a wide variety of applied physical situations that could be used in self-defense scenarios. He explained the bunkai by having an attacker perform an aggressive move and then — using the move from the kata. My way of teaching is geared towards continuing Miyagi's interpretation of the different kata in goju-ryu. What it is interesting is the fact that the true meaning of the techniques may not at first be evident. Sometimes the real bunkai may be very difficult to detect and has some kind of secret meaning behind it. Sometimes you find that the bunkai is applied in a different direction or using other principles to make it effective in combat. If you don't know how to unlock these principles and techniques, you may never find the real reason behind the technique. As I said previously, Chinese philosophy is very mystical, and in many ways, bunkai is also mystical. If kata movement goes to the right, you must think the answer is to the left. If one looks at the sky, then the enemy may be on the ground. Leave 10 percent of your karate a mystery and enjoy it. Use your imagination.

Q: How important is the concept of style in karate training?

A: Nowadays, people talk about different styles and peculiarities of this or that particular method. When I started training, there were only three in the town of Naha. They were shorin, goju and uechi. When I moved to Tokyo in 1958, there were more than 10 different styles. They

referred to them as styles, but they were very similar. I never thought that there were that many differences. It was mostly a way of calling the school after the sensei's name.

Q: You are residing in the United States. What is your opinion about the level of martial arts in that country?

A: I truly think that the technical level in the U.S. is very high. Sometimes, from the outside, people only see some "watered down version" of karate, but you should look at the top Japanese masters teaching there. There are great traditional instructors, and their students are very good. The U.S. is a melting pot because you have top instructors from Korea, Japan, China, Okinawa, et cetera. The intense competition has meant that the instructors of the various arts have really had to polish up their skills. And they have "borrowed" techniques and ideas from other styles and systems to make what they are practicing and teaching better. This has always been always a feature in martial arts history. Not even goju itself was a pure one-family style.

Q: What is your opinion about kickboxing and other similar fighting events?

A: I don't object to the full-contact karate or kickboxing scene, but for dojo training they should stick to one style and teacher. "Window shopping" is not good for martial arts. I believe that these kinds of events and activities have their place, but they are not Budo.

Q: Do you think it is a good idea to have one single federation that controls all karate styles?

A: My opinion is that karate is an individual or private thing. An organization overseeing distinct and separate martial arts, such as the Okinawan systems, would eventually hurt the quality of those methods. Culturally and traditionally, the Okinawan martial arts are too individual and distinct to be grouped together arbitrarily, so I don't think that approach is positive for karate or any other martial art style.

Q: It is obvious that your approach to training is more Chinese than Okinawan or Japanese. Why?

A: Basically, your body tells you when it wants you to move. In me, that response is through kata. The psychological response in me is due to my major field of study, which is the history of China. My need for training is spontaneous, and I will do so anytime and anywhere.

Q: What are your hopes for the future of the art?

A: I hope that the next generations will not only improve technically but also know how to share their knowledge. People must pass on the traditions and not lose them. In the old days in China and Okinawa, the teaching was done behind closed doors. Now, thanks to the media, karate-do is no longer a secret and it is within everybody's reach. It is up to us to preserve its value in the world. I feel strongly that the future of karate-do is still very positive, but hard practice is the key.

MORIO HIGAONNA

THE MASTER, THE WARRIOR

HE IS A MASTER, HE IS A WARRIOR, HE IS ONE OF THE MOST CHARISMATIC KARATE INSTRUCTORS IN THE ENTIRE WORLD. BORN IN 1940, THE SON OF A POLICEMAN, SENSEI HIGAONNA'S AMAZING KNOWLEDGE OF BOTH KARATE AND GOJU-RYU HISTORY HAS CONFOUNDED PRACTITIONERS FROM ALL STYLES AND DISCIPLINES. THE CHIEF INSTRUCTOR AND FOUNDER OF THE INTERNATIONAL GOJU KARATE FEDERATION, HE HAS SPREAD THE TEACHINGS AND TRADITIONS OF ORIGINAL GRANDMASTER CHOJUN MIYAGI TO ALL CORNERS OF THE WORLD. HIS POWER, SPEED, AND QUICK SMILE ARE SECOND TO NONE, AND THE CALLUSES ON HIS HANDS SHOW HIS LETHAL DEVOTION TO KARATE-DO.

FROM OKINAWA TO JAPAN, FROM JAPAN TO CALIFORNIA, AND THEN BACK TO THE FAR EAST AGAIN, HIGAONNA'S SPIRIT HAS BEEN FORGED IN THE FIRE OF TRADITIONAL KARATE TRAINING AND SHAPED BY THE HAMMER OF HIS INTENSE WILL AND DEDICATION. MANY OTHER TEACHER DON'T HESITATE TO SAY THAT HIGAONNA'S STUDENTS ARE THE BEST ALL-AROUND KARATEKA IN TERMS OF RESPECT, TRAINING SPIRIT, AND SAMURAI COOPERATION. HE IS A LIVING EXAMPLE TO ALL KARATE PRACTITIONERS OF HOW THE ART CAN SHAPE A MAN INTO A WARRIOR. HIS GOAL, THOUGH, HAS NEVER BEEN TO GLORIFY HIMSELF, BUT RATHER TO PRESERVE AND PERPETUATE THE TRADITIONAL TEACHINGS HE LEARNED IN CHOJUN MIYAGI'S FAMOUS GARDEN DOJO.

Q: When did you start to train?

A: Well, it was a long time ago! My father taught me the basic techniques of shorinji-ryu, but he didn't feel very comfortable doing so. Later on I went to train under Shimabuku, not the famous isshin-ryu master, and other teachers until I end up with An'ichi Miyagi.

Q: There are some wild stories about you as a teenager.

A: I used to skip school and steal food. I'd rather spend the day at the beach than go to school. I was really shy, but also a difficult child.

GOJU RYU LEGENDS

Q: How you were introduced to goju-ryu?

A: It was Shimabuku who recommended goju-ryu. He thought that me being stocky would fit very good into the style. So I started under An'ichi Miyagi who was running Grandmaster Chojun Miyagi's school – the original garden dojo. I felt in love with goju-ryu on the very first day. I started to train up to six hours a day!

Q: What was Aichi Miyagi like?

A: He started to train under Grandmaster Miyagi right after the war in 1948. He joined the school with other three boys who, considering his weak body, expected him to quit right away. Yet An'ichi was the only one to stay and keep training at the dojo! Grandmaster Miyagi used to teach the history of the art to An'ichi – the oral traditions and the philosophy – but not before Aichi had finished the chores of fixing the house, cleaning the garden, et cetera. After the grandmaster's death, his wife decided to keep the dojo open with An'ichi as the instructor. Later on, the garden dojo was closed and everyone moved over the new dojo named the "Jundokan" operated by Eichi Miyazato.

Q: Why did you leave Okinawa and go to Japan?

A: Master An'ichi joined the Merchant Marines and left the dojo to travel all over the world. I decided to move to Tokyo in order to study at Takushoku University and teach karate. A teacher there was one of my old classmates named Ryujo Aragaki. When he left I took over the teaching. It was a great time for me – just teaching and training the whole day!

Q: Sensei, I would like to ask you about some facts about yourself and your teacher, An'ichi Miyagi. Specifically, it is said that An'ichi sensei was only a child when he trained with Chojun Miyagi Sensei, that he learned only part of the system, and that his character is, shall we say, flawed.

A: If it wasn't so funny this would make me very angry. It's also very ironic, but please let me explain this in detail and clarify it once for all. People seem unwilling to accept my word that my teacher is the little-known An'ichi Miyagi, but willing to accept the claims of one of my former students that his teacher was Chojun Miyagi the founder of goju ryu. This despite the fact that he would have been barely more than an infant when Chojun sensei died. They ignore the truth but accept the ludicrous. The fact of the matter is very simple. When, full of nervous excitement and with the money my mother had given me clenched in my fist, I first went to the garden dojo of Chojun Miyagi sensei as a boy of sixteen, I was told by Koshin Iha, a student of Chojun Miyagi sensei, "If you want to train seriously An'ichi will teach you." He has taught me every since; I only have the one teacher. At first I was not particularly impressed by An'ichi sensei. Although his movements were very smooth and powerful, I was more impressed by the naked power of the younger students, Saburo Higa particularly. You could feel the rush of wind when he kicked and punched and the physique he developed from sanchin training was awe inspiring. It was only as I progressed and began to understand Chojun Miyagi Sensei's goju ryu that I became aware of An'ichi Sensei's mastery of it.

People should check their facts before they speak publicly. When Chojun sensei died on October 8th, 1953 An'ichi sensei was in fact twenty-two years old; his birth date is February 9th, 1931. His formative years, from 1948 until 1953 were spent in intense personal training with Chojun sensei on a daily basis, at times he was the Founder's only student. How better to learn goju ryu karate than to acquire it from the founder at a young age and spend the rest of your life perfecting your skill!

I know other instructors have claimed to be my primary teacher and this is ridiculous. I know who taught me and even now, when I need my kata checked, I return to the same source, An'ichi Miyagi. There is no doubt in my mind, so why would there be doubt in the minds of others. Of course when I started karate all the sempai taught us. Training was very different them, it was more like an extended family arrangement, older brothers helping younger brothers. If you really stretch the point, all of them could say that they taught me. However, it's true that others would offer their advice from time to time even as I got older. For example, Miyazato sensei checked my sanchin perhaps two or three times in all the years I was at the Jundokan, but my teacher was, and is, An'ichi sensei. I have to say that Miyazato sensei was always kind to me personally but had a habit of saying unkind things about people behind their backs which always made me feel uncomfortable.

Q: I was hoping that you would address the question of your training at the Jundokan after the garden dojo of Chojun Sensei closed.

A: It seems like only yesterday that An'ichi sensei would call at my house and ask me to help him repair makiwara at the Jundokan dojo, or clean up the yard and the equipment. It was at the Jundokan that An'ichi sensei really started to teach me seriously. He explained to me every tiny detail he had learned from the Founder about our method and I was fascinated by his knowledge.

When I think of it I experience the thrill and excitement again of my training in those days. An'ichi sensei gave everything he had when training, and expected us to do the same.

GOJU RYU LEGENDS

Unfortunately this led to disagreements with Miyazato sensei. Miyazato sensei felt that An'ichi sensei was much too tough, and his iron discipline, together with the physical demands he made on students, would lose us members and therefore income.

Q: Why did you leave the Jundokan?

A: There were a number of reasons for leaving the Jundokan. An'ichi sensei was not shown the respect he deserved. Also, when Miyazato sensei would change details of the kata, An'ichi sensei would protest and a heated discussion would then take place which was very unpleasant. I didn't like the board that was displayed publicly with the names of those who had not paid their dojo fees. I thought this was demeaning. And then there was the matter of the loan that was taken out to build the Jundokan. An'ichi sensei paid for the Jundokan building lot to be cleared with his own money and didn't expect to recover anything. However, the actual building costs were paid for by a loan guaranteed by Harno Kochi and this, I understand, was never repaid which angered An'ichi sensei a great deal. He left to join the merchant marine and the Jundokan changed a lot for me as a result but I stayed on even after that, for a while at least.

Q: Is this where the accusation came that An'ichi left Okinawa to avoid paying his debts?

A: Exactly! In fact things were the other way around. He spent a lot of his own money on the Jundokan then left to join the Merchant Marine in order to earn a decent living—life was still very hard in Okinawa at that time. When the source of this allegation—that An'ichi sensei had left Okinawa to avoid paying his debts—was confronted recently he denied saying anything of the sort!

Q: This allegation seems to have become something of a cultural tradition in Okinawan karate society. Gichin Funakoshi's critics claimed, also in the absence of any credible evidence, that he left Okinawa to avoid paying his debts. Perhaps this is an inevitable result of being a successful karate master, particularly if you train students that became internationally famous.

A: You may be right. An'ichi sensei told me that Miyazato sensei was upset when he heard that my Yoyogi (Tokyo) dojo was busy because he assumed that I was making a lot of money. In fact, all the fees went to the owner of the dojo and I only received a small salary and a place to sleep. The salary was only paid for the days I taught. If I went away for a gasshuku, for example, I was not paid. I didn't realize what the problem was, or that there was a problem about money or anything else until in July 1981, when Ryosei Aragaki asked me to come back to the Jundokan. I told him that I had made up my mind and I couldn't change it. Then in August 1981 at the championship in Osaka I was asked to attend a meeting and was surprised to find Miyazato sensei there.

He complained that when I went home to Okinawa I never went to see him. I really didn't understand what he was talking about as I had no reason to go and see him. While I respect him as a student of Chojun sensei, he wasn't my teacher or anything like that, and I really didn't know what to do under the circumstances. Mr. Arimoto who was also at the meeting said that I should apologize to Miyazato sensei, so I did, and thought no more about it.

Q: I know that you have rather strong views on the subject of dan grades, but have publicly said very little. May we hear your opinion?

A: Dan grades have only become important because they cause so many problems. Chojun Miyagi sensei refused to award dan grades and the martial arts didn't have dan grades until judo adopted them. I was given third dan by Miyazato sensei at the first grading I attended when I was little more than a kid and it meant nothing to me, then or now. I never wore the belt. I agree that for students they are a way of measuring progress, but at a high price. They cause discontent, squabbles, and lead to excessive pride in self, which is the opposite of what martial arts training should develop in a student. Every one has different standards so, inevitably there are differences between the level of students from different dojo even when they have the same grade, and then the politics start. I believe that there should be black belts and white belts only, and that the focus should be on training, not on accumulating rank.

Q: On the subject of training, could you please tell me something about your own?

A: I am pleased to say my training has hardly changed over the years. Recently I started to study meditation with Sakiyama sensei who is a famous Zen priest. Every day I run, practice hojo undo, kata, and also meditation. My family is as supportive as ever so I am free to train for at least six hours each day.

Of course, you must remember that physical training is just the gateway to mastery of the mind. That's why you must strive to achieve true humility through training. If you don't, it's difficult, if not impossible, to rise above the purely physical because your mind is forever clouded by thoughts of material things, pride and scorn for others, and similar negative feelings. Good karate makes good people, and I feel a responsibility to pass on what was given to me as a way of thanking my teacher, An'ichi Miyagi, and, hopefully, produce more good karate people by doing so. Because I teach so much I have a responsibility to train as hard as I can to pass on my knowledge in as pure a form as possible. If you do not train hard you should not teach!

Q: How is your training these days?

A: Good. I train quite a bit. When I was in Okinawa I didn't train as much as I would have liked to, but now I'm back to a lot of training and I feel really good. I do a long warm-up using some conditioning drills. Then I move into the hojo undo which are special exercises named chisi, sashi, and onigi game. I train on the makiwara for over an hour, then move to kata training and the heavy bag. Three days per week I meet my instructor and we practice kakie and free-sparring using gloves and headgear. I practice around three a hours of kata per day.

Q: Do you teach what you train?

A: Karate teaching and training is not something easy. Everybody starts very passionately, with a lots of illusions, but due to the hard training only a few people continue. In the mid '60s karate was so popular that my classes were literally packed with students. I used to drill these students through kihon (basics) – but after a while not very many were left. In karate training, those who stick with it go through a process of self-analysis. They start questioning a lot of things about themselves and their reasons for training. The answer become a reflection of themselves. As a result, this leads to more focus, determination, and overall inner peace.

Q: As a teacher, did you have any problems adapting from the Japanese students' mindset to the Western world students' mentality?

A: Not really, but it is true that you have to know how to properly communicate to the different cultures. For instance, in Japan or Okinawa, people don't ask questions, they just repeat what you tell them to do. In the West, everyone want to know "why," so you have to explain. That's the reason why I teach more applications in the West than I do back in Japan or Okinawa. Of course, once the student reaches the black belt level he doesn't need an explanation for everything. The problem in the West is that many people think of themselves as masters because they know kata applications when, in fact, they can't properly perform the kata itself because they waste too much time asking instead of doing.

Q: You traveled extensively in China in order to research the original training. What did you discover?

A: A lot of very interesting things! I contacted different Chinese masters who helped me to dig into the roots of the goju-ryu system. In one of my trips, the city mayor invited 15 or 16 old masters who performed katas from sanchin to suparimpei. We all agreed that our techniques had evolved from the Chinese white crane and tiger styles.

Q: Are the katas the same as the original Chinese?

A: Pretty much. I'm against changing kata. I believe that kata is not just something that someone made up. They are hundreds and thousands of years old. There is a lot of information in each one of them. Few people know that there are certain kata to be practiced in the morning and others to be performed in the evening in order to get the most from them. I understand that a lot of knowledge has been lost through the years but it is my responsibility to keep this important information alive for the generations to come.

Q: So you are against personal interpretations of kata?

A: I'm against changing the essence of kata. I always say that kata is like a printed letter. The are portraits of the basic techniques and history. If you change the essence of kata, you loose all this.

Q: Sensei, please tell us about kata training.

A: A kata is a pattern of movements which contains a series of logical and practical attacking and blocking techniques. In each kata there are certain set or predetermined movements which the student can practice alone, without a partner. These kata have been created by previous masters after many years of research, training, and actual combat experience.

The applications of the techniques in these kata have evolved from and have been tested in actual combat. In this way each kata has been improved and refined, and has evolved into the kata we practice today. Because of the time and the kata's complex evolution it is impossible to trace the exact development that the kata underwent, but it is known that the old masters studied the combative techniques and movements in the fighting between animal and animal, animal and man, and man-to-man. They also studied the physiology of the human body and its relationship to combat, taking into account such factors as the circulation of the blood in a twenty-four hour day, the vulnerability of the vital points in relation to the time of day, and other cyclic laws of nature such as the rising and setting of the sun, and the rise and fall of the tides. All of these elements are incorporated into the kata.

Q: What is the purpose of kata in karate training?

A: The purpose for developing kata also varied with the times and with the people who developed them. For example, in China over 1600 years ago kata was developed and practiced for the purpose of self-defense, whereas the Buddhist monks would practice kata for the purpose of strengthening the spirit as well as the body.

To practice the kata correctly every movement must be repeated over and over again. Only through constant repetition can the techniques become reflex action. Fortunately to that end, an important aspect of kata is that it can be practiced alone, anytime and anywhere. When kata is performed by a well-trained person, its dynamic power and beauty of movement become almost aesthetic in quality.

Almost all of the Goju Ryu kata were handed down from Higaonna Kanryo Sensei. Higaonna Sensei had studied and trained for many years under Ryu Ryuko Sensei in Fukien Province, China. The following kata were handed down by Higaonna Sensei from Ryu Ryuko Sensei: Sanchin, Saifa, Seiyunchin, Shisochin, Sanseru, Sepai, Kururunfa, Sesian, and Suparinpei. The original creators of these kata are unknown.

Q: Sensei what can you tell us about the kata practiced in the Goju Ryu style?

Many of the kata names are Chinese numbers symbolizing Buddhist concepts. For example, Suparinpei (the number 108 in Chinese) has a special significance in Buddhism. It is believed that man has 108 evil passions, and so in Buddhist temples on December 31st, at the stroke of midnight, a bell is rung 108 times to drive away those spirits. The number 108 in Suparinpei is calculated from 36 X 3. The symbolism of the number 36 is given in the explanation of Sanseru which follows. The number 3 symbolizes past, present and future.

Sanseru, written in Chinese characters, is the number 36. Symbolically it is calculated from the formula 6 X 6. The first six represents eye, ear, nose, tongue, body, and spirit. The second six symbolizes color, voice, taste, smell, touch, and justice.

Sepai, similarly, is the number 18. It is calculated from 6 X 3. The six here is the second six of Sanseru. The three represents good, bad, and peace.

The four kata, Gekisai Dai Ichi, Gekisai Dai Ni, revised Sanchin, and Tensho are relatively new, having been created by Miyagi Chojun Sensei. Gekisai Dai Ichi and Dai Ni were developed by Miyagi Sensei in order to popularize karate among young people. These two kata, performed with exaggerated movements, are relatively easy to understand.

Miyagi Chojun Sensei's Sanchin preserves the essence of Higaonna Kanryo Sensei's Sanchin, of which it is a variation. Miyagi Sensei developed it particularly to balance the former one. Its performance requires a different use of the muscles, leading it to a more symmetrical development. This is important for optimum use of the body, and especially in the prevention of injury to the back and other areas. A detailed explanation of Sanchin will be given later.

Whereas Sanchin kata can be considered an aspect of the "go" (hard) of Goju, Tensho kata represents the "ju" (soft). One of the purposes of Tensho kata is concentration on shifting focus points while performing the soft hand movements, Moreover, within these soft hand movements tremendous power is generated.

Q: If kata is a printed letter, what is kumite?

A: Kumite is handwriting, and everybody has their own penmanship! In sparring, you have an opponent and it's a little bit easier because you adapt to the movements of your adversary. In kata there is only space and time and you. There is no opponent – nothing to grasp – you have to imagine and aim for a spiritual opponent.

Q: Do you consider karate an art or a sport?

A: Karate is a martial art that uses no weapons. This doesn't mean that I reject the sport aspect since I feel that's one part of the whole art. However, karate is deep. If you simply retire after doing only competitions, and have strictly focused only on winning against an opponent, then karate has no meaning at all. Karate is for all your life. We can continue training until we are 70 or 80 years old. The real purpose of karate is not to beat someone or to win against someone. Karate is a pacifist philosophy of self-discovery.

Q: Why did you create the Okinawan Goju Ryu Karate Federation?

A: My whole idea is to preserve the teachings and philosophy of Grandmaster Chojun Miyagi and spread them all over the world. That is why. It was not a matter of ego or power. I only want to protect and pass-on these teachings.

Q: You are very much into physical conditioning. Is the traditional method better than modern approaches such as weight training?

A: Not necessarily, but the traditional conditioning methods allow the practitioner to work the muscles in the body as a unit, not in an isolated way as weight training does. The traditional way was developed to help karate technique, so the training methods fit the karate structure and the way of moving the human body.

Q: Why do you train so much on the makiwara?

A: When we punch the makiwara, we are not only conditioning the knuckles but developing power, speed, and body coordination and punching mechanics. Everything comes together in makiwara training. On the other hand, if your body is not conditioned, it is very easy to hurt yourself when you hit someone. Just don't forget to start slowly and add power and increase speed as you improve in kihon.

Q: What does the term "do" mean to you?

A: Do is the way for the men. I never let passion or feelings rule my behaviour. I try to stay clam and face problems like Grandmaster Miyagi did in the Second World War. He didn't have any food at all, but yet he stayed calm. This is very hard to do, but it shows a lot about your spirit. Karate is spirit. Karate is life. Karate, for me, is like a cloud with nothing substantial to grab onto. You can do karate all your life and still find new meanings and new answers – that's why I practice every single day.

Q: Do you practice zazen and meditation?

A: Yes I do. For me, being focused on what I do every day is very important. I don't think about tomorrow when I train. I train today, I do my best today – then I'm happy. If tomorrow I'm alive when I wake up, then I will do the same thing. I try to be extremely concentrated on the "now."

Q: What do you expect from your students?

A: Everybody has different reason to train karate. Some look for health, others for the sport, and some for self defense. There are many things yet to be discovered in goju-ryu. So I expect my students to keep researching the art so one day they can find the answers through their own personal investigation. Karate training has to be done with heart and sincerity. It brings your body and mind together. That's the real karate.

Q: What is the real meaning of karate practice for you?

A: The true meaning and spirit of karate are imbedded in the kata and only by the practice of kata can we come to understand them. For this reason, if we change or simplify the kata either to accommodate the beginner or for tournament purposes, then we also will have lost the true meaning and spirit of karate.

In karate there is no first attack. Every kata begins with a defensive movement, which exemplifies this spirit. Not only is there no first attack, but the best defense is to avoid the fight altogether. That is why it is said that karate is the art of a wise man.

TETSU HIRO HOKAMA

MASTER OF THE OLD WAYS

Tetsuhiro Hokama is 10th Dan Hanshi, President of the Okinawa Goju-Ryu Kenshi-Kai Karate-do, Kobudo Association and founder of the first Karate museum in the world. Although he is not as well known in the United States as are other Okinawan Goju-Ryu teachers, Hanshi Hokama is one of the most knowledgeable Goju-Ryu Karate masters in the world. His speed and power is inspiring and his knowledge of vital points is vast. He is a researcher of the history of the indigenous Okinawa art of self-preservation known today as Karate and Kobudo. Hanshi Tetsuhiro Hokama is truly a master of the "Old Ways".

Q: What can you tell us about your beginnings in the art of karate-do?

I was born in Taiwan in 1944 to Okinawan parents and began karate training as a child in 1952. My grandfather Seiken Tokuyama taught me the fundamentals of Shuri-te Karate. In 1961, I began my formal training at the Naha Commercial High School Karate Club. That same year I began training with the legendary Seiko Higa (1898 -1966) a student of Kanryo Higaonna (1853-1915) and Chojun Miyagi (1888-1953). It was at Higa's Dojo where I met Kobudo teacher Shinpo Matayoshi (1922-1997) and began learning Kobudo, Hakutsuru-ken (White Crane fist) and Kingai-Ryu, a martial art that my father, Shinko Matayoshi (1888-1947) learned in Manchuria.

Q: What happened when Sensei Higa passed away?

Upon the death of Seiko Higa in 1966 I continued my training with one of Higa's top student Seiko Fukuchi (1919-1975) who was Seiko Higa's assistant instructor. It was both of these great masters that taught me the "Kakushite" (hidden hand) referring to the secret techniques in kata. To be honest, I was not convinced with the 'bunkai' that I was first being taught, and kept asking questions and even doubting the kata applications. I think that seeing my sincere desire to learn, they began to teach me the "Old Ways". Higa Sensei eventually gave me a copy of the 'Bubishi', an ancient martial arts text and told me to study it deeply.

Q: What is the material you regularly teach in your classes?

In a class at my dojo you will see a very complete system of Goju-Ryu Karate being taught. Tuidi (grabbing hands), Kyusho-jutsu (vital point's art) and Kobudo are a part of the daily regimen as well.

Q: What is karate for you?

Karate is many different things. We have the Budo karate, the sport karate, karate for physical health, karate for self-defense, etc. It is important to understand this and to have an open mind since society and human being change. What we can't forget no matter how we practice karate, is that it has a traditional and philosophical base that it is essential to its practice.

Q: What are your feelings about tournament karate?

I understand that in order to promote karate we had to hold tournaments since this brings attention to the art. When I began karate there was no protective gear. The protective gear allows a student to further his sport kumite techniques. We should not just train in karate but to try other arts such as judo and kendo as well. If your body is strong from training in other arts and hojo-undo you will be able to withstand any strikes or kicks to your body.

Q: How the war altered the art of karate?

The war changed a lot of things. Many of the seniors had stopped practicing for a long period of time and did not want to become involved. A lot of them forgot several kata or were never taught all of them in the first place.

This was a very difficult period of time for the art of karate in general. Chojun Miyagi had died suddenly, and we had no water, electricity, and in many cases, no home. It was a survival period where our primary concern was for our families, and providing food for them – it was not a good time for karate.

Q: Was kata taught differently before the war?

Yes, very much so. I think it was more of a Chinese influence in the open-hand techniques.

Q: What was the relationship between Miyagi Chojun and Higa Seiko?

Chojun Miyagi trained under Kanryo Higaonna. Seiko Higa was also a student of Kanryo Higaonna until Higaonna's death in 1917. Higa then became a student of Miyagi Sensei. He trained mostly with Miyagi Sensei before the war.

Q: Do you think it is necessary to engage in free-fighting to achieve good fighting skills in the street?

You need to experience the random nature of free-fighting, but the sparring should not always resemble that seen in tournaments. Sometimes competition free-fighting is over-refined from a self-defense point of view – that kind of sparring is a highly specialized skill used in a very artificial environment. I think that engaging in dojo sparring is of greater benefit. Simply sparring against one opponent is not enough; you need to face two or three opponents at once to get a realistic understanding of the chaos of real fighting.

Q: What can you tell us about the Karate Museum?

I did set up a Karate museum in my dojo in 1987 to help people understand the history, culture, and philosophy of Okinawan Karate and Kobudo. More than 300 items are displayed. We must remember that karate is one aspect of Okinawan cultural pride, so I put great effort in teaching and building this museum collection, helping to spread the way of Okinawan Karate throughout the world. My goal is to eventually get a building for the museum.

Q: Sensei you talk about slow motion training to develop the right "feeling", is this solely applied to kihon training, or do you feel it is useful in kumite and kata too?

It can be applied for everything in Karate. The ideal training to develop instant or instantaneous power comes through training the body with slow movements. In order to be able to develop the body so that it can accelerate, you must be able to understand how the body moves, and this understanding can be developed through slow motion training. Human body is a perfect machine, bones are hard, muscles should be soft and tendons are like "ropes". Understanding this perfect engineering will provide the foundation for the right movement.

Q: What are your thoughts on the future of karate do?

I hope that Olympic recognition does not mean that karate will go the way of sport only and turn totally into a competition sport where winning Olympic, or other medals becomes the be-all and end-all of the training.

Q: How do you perceive the art of teaching? How you do teach?

That is a very difficult question to answer. The main idea is that we need to "change" and "adapt" to the times and the circumstances. We [teachers] can't teach the same all the time because people change, students change, society changes, etc. It is not possible to set yourself in a way of teaching for all the time and all the students.

Q: Can you elaborate more Sensei?

Think of an orange. When you look at an orange you "see" only an orange but a Master Chef "sees" an orange, juice, jam, a cookie, wine, etc…and many other possibilities than come with that orange. A professional understands the subtleties of that particular "orange". The same is true for the art of karate-do. There are many different aspects to a very simple basic technique or application approach of a fighting movement. This is what a karate master is.

Q: How this principle applies to the bunkai or application of the techniques found in kata?

We all know that there is a "simple and direct" application of the kata movement...using the same body action but there are also many other ways of applying the principle of that technique in a different environment. That "deeper" bunkai requires a higher level of understanding not only of the karate technique but also of the "reality" of a street encounter. In the end, it is not the "superficial" aspect of the techniques what is important but the intrinsic principle that you can use and apply under many different circumstances. That is the true mastery of the kata. Memorizing a kata is fine but knowing the bunkai gives you a better in-depth knowledge of what every movement is about. Every different style has a different interpretation of their bunkai. The main thing is to know there is something else to just doing the kata. The concentration is deeper when you understand the bunkai behind each kata movement.

Q: Goju Ryu only has 12 kata – small number compared to other styles? Why is that?

Because you don't need a big number of kata. Karate mastery has nothing to do with the number of katas that you "remember", please note that I didn't use the word "know". To know a kata you have to go deep into the form, its principles, its applications in many different circumstances and understand its "essence". There is a lot of work to do with one single kata... imagine if you try to do that with 40 or 50 kata.

Q: What is your favorite kata and why?

Actually I don't have a kata that I particularly like more than others. The number of people who really understand how to perform kata in the way they should be performed is now very limited. Of course, there isn't a single kata I can myself perform perfectly. But I still continue to study all the kata that I learned during my years of training.

Q: Finally, if you could give one piece of advice to all practitioners, what would it be?

I would ask you to thoroughly study the techniques at the heart of Karate – regardless of the style. Strive for a deep understanding of the technical foundations of the art, doing this by learning about the fundamental mechanics of how to use your body and training as hard as you can to improve this understanding. Always have motivation to train and practice the art.

RON KLUGER

THE HARD AND SOFT WAY

HE IS ONE OF GOJU RYU'S OLD GUARD. HIS TECHNIQUES AND WORDS ARE DIRECT AND TO THE POINT, WITH NO BEATING AROUND THE BUSH. SENSEI KLUGER KEEPS ALIVE THE TRADITION STARTED BY CHOJUN MIYAGI MANY YEARS AGO, WHEN HE FOUNDED THE GOJU RYU SYSTEM.

RESPECTFUL OF OTHER ARTS, SENSEI KLUGER DOESN'T HESITATE TO CLARIFY SOME OF THE MAIN ASPECTS OF THE ART. HE ADVOCATES THE "HARD AND SOFT WAY" OF DOING THINGS. HE IS AN STUDENT OF THE LATE EICHI MIYAZATO SENSEI. HIS TEACHINGS COME FROM THE BOTTOM OF HIS HEART AND HIS WORDS LEAVE NO ROOM FOR MISUNDERSTANDINGS.

HIS DEDICATION AND LOVE FOR THE ART OF GOJU RYU KARATE-DO IS EVIDENT IN HIS EVERY SENTENCE. AFTER ALL HIS YEARS OF TRAINING AND TEACHING, SENSEI RON KLUGER IS STILL ONE OF THE FEW OLD MASTERS WHO CAN SHOW THE NEW GENERATIONS THE RIGHT WAY.

Q: How long have you been practicing karate?

I started training at 1965 with Judo and in 1970 started Karate Do.

Q: How many styles (karate or other Martial Arts methods) have you trained in and who were your teachers?

I started Judo at age of 13 and in 1970 started Shotokan Karatedo (Oshima linege) in 1972 started Okinawa Gojuryu. Judo I trained with the best of those days in Israel: Gadi Skornik, Dennis Hanover, Yona Melnik, Amos Gilad…..Karate Do started with the late Meir Yahel Sensei, of Shotokan, and in 1972 met the late Leon Pantanowitz Sensei of Karate Do South Afrika from Okinawa Gojuryu (Jundokan linege). I spent 1974 -1975 in South Africa as Uchi Dechi at Karate Do South Africa, Cape Town HQ Dojo under the fine teachings of the late Denis St, John Thomson Hanshi. Since my return to Israel I am teaching educating Budo, full time, professionally. Since 1984 I am officially a student of Eichi Miyazato, Sensei and following his

GOJU RYU LEGENDS

teaching with close cooperation of the historic Jundokan Dojo of Okinawa. Throughout the long years I met, trained with many great Sensei of Goju: (Eichi Miyazato Sensei & all Jundokan Sensei, Higaonna Sensei, Goshi Yamaguchi Sensei, Hokama Sensei, Toyama Sensei), Okinawa Kobudo - Yamanni Ryu: (Nishime Sensei) Shotokan: (Kanazawa Sensei, Kase Sensei, Stan Schmidt Sensei, Dorfman Sensei), Shito Ryu: (Kotaka Sensei, Kenzo Mabuni Sensei, Demura Sensei, Saito Sensei) Wado Ryu: (Suzuki Sensei) experienced: Tai Chi, Iaido and Aikido....all, to deepen my understanding of my own Okinawa Gojuryu and Budo in general.

Beside the Budo aspect, since 1971 I am learning and teaching Israeli system of military self-defense – Krav Maga.

This two sides of the same coin giving me and my students an excellent balance between classical Martial Art and practical street reality.

Q: How were your beginnings in the art of karate and your early days in karate competition?

My first experience in Karate Competition was 1975 in Cape Town, the rules where very different, Ippon Shobu with very easy on control, broken nose, teeth or ribs where part of the game. Between 1977 – 1982 I was part of our National Team and competed in all National and International events I could. By 1984 I stopped competing and started to Referee. I become National Chief Referee, WKF Judge and by 2000 removed myself from all duties of Refereeing nationally and internationally. Since, I am fully concentrating on educating & teaching the next generation to classical Karatedo and Budo.

Q: Were you a 'natural' at karate – did the movements come easily to you?

Since I am training systematically from age of 13, training, self-discipline is part of me; I had great Teachers....so I use to training regulations. The training is in my nature, so the movements become natural, but no question working very hard not only to keep them, but to improve them.

Q: What can you tell us about your teachers?

I had the privilege to train under the watching eyes and care of the best Sensei. In my Judo days I had the best of the best, I have been trained from early days the importance of not only hard training but correct training! As for Karate Do also had great Teachers, Denis St. John Thomson as my sensei during the my time at his Dojo as Uchi Dechi, thought me very tough, old school! I was living during 1074 -1975 at his Dojo in Cape Town (those years he was part of the Jundokan Dojo). It was typical old school Okinawa Goju, seven days training; it was a very traumatic but strangely positive experience. I learned dedication, focus and correct way o my future students. As from 1984 I am visiting annually the Jundokan Dojo of Okinawa, had the privilege to train most of the time with Miyazato Eichi Sensei individually, one on one. This is the most valuable quality times. Throughout the long years I trained and spent time with Koshin Iha Sensei, Hichiya and Minei Sensei as well as all the Seniors of Jundokan all product of Miyazato Sensei. I had the pleasure to meet Shihan, Nishime Kyoshi who teaching us Okinawa Kobudo of Yamanni Ryu, a great Sensei with true knowledge. He is truly a Master Teacher, inspiring and willing to teach!

Q: What attracted you to the world of karate kumite competition?

In the early 70ties competition scene was very different, I went for championships as a natural path to all Yudansha at my Dojo, however it was clear at all times that this is a youngster's game, fun, you doing your best, but after there is a lifelong journey ahead. Classical Budo is the real think! I enjoyed the competitions it's atmosphere, excitements, winning, losing, the game was a game!

Q: What do you think are the most important characteristics of your style of karate?

My main subject is Okinawa Goju Ryu as thought by Miyazato Eichi sensei and the Senior staff of the historic Jundokan Dojo of Okinawa.

Miyazato Sensei explained me many times, we teach you the original Kyhon and make sure you keep the original Kata as we learned, what you do with it, which treasure, value you discover and dig out of your Kata is upon you. You demand to research your Kata, your way of Gojuryu Karatedo, the outcome will be your fingerprint, your own handwriting of Karatedo. I believe it is all about strategical and tactical principles. I am keeping the principles of Okinawa Gojuryu and taking it to today's day to day reality. It means, that we giving up to date interpretations to the waza and using it as a real self-defense tool.

I use Karatedo as most important educational tool to all my practicing people. The Dojo is a laboratory to experience and face daily life's challenges: focusing, determination, will, priorities, decision taking, strategy, sensitivity, empathy, ability to face and overcome life obstacles and many more factors to strengthen and educate fine human character.

Q: Karate is nowadays often referred to as a sport... would you agree with this definition or is a martial art?

I am standing quit far from this definition. Sport is a game! Great for youngsters, it is fun! However live or die is for sure not a game! In my humble opinion Martial Art is Budo, its unique value is most serious real all around Self Defense, physically as well as mentally. spiritually. At all times and age we may play games but a grown up person most of the time needs to act mostly maturely with responsibility. I have also a most doubtful view on the Olympic movement and their goals, economics. I truly believe Budo is in opposition to their goal.

However, there is a huge place for Sport Karate, but this is not Budo. The choice and the responsibility of each and every Karateka, (or parent to a Karateka), to make the right decision, to be on the right path to satisfy their aims.

GOJU RYU LEGENDS

Q: Do you think Kobudo training is beneficial for a Karate practitioner?

As a Karateka/Budoka, who following an Okinawan path, I believe Kobudo is part of my Karatedo. At our Karate Do International Renmei, throughout the 45 years of our existence, we practiced as part of our syllabus Kobudo. I see it as an extension to our Karatedo waza into the weapons. Kobudo is most enjoyable and beneficial to all Budoka.......

Q: When teaching the art of karate – what is the most important element for you; self-defense or sport?

Teaching Martial Art for me is mainly to give my folks an all-around self-defense system, an art of mobility/flexibility and a clear philosophy based on well-structured strategical/tactical principles.

All the above mentioned is based on the ground of Okinawa Goju ryu and developed upon my life experience.

My aim is to give our students a lifelong path for self-development, ability to defend themselves and their people, to develop personality and character to face life challenges during a person's lifetime.

To make it clear, in my view the statement that "all starts and ends with courtesy" is most important!!! The very same hand that may need to kill, will cure, help, assist full heartedly, always!

Q: Kihon, Kata and Kumite, what's the proper ratio in training?

My view is that the three "K" are all equally important! Kyhon are like the letters, the ABC, you must make sure you have them. It is clearly a pre order; we must perfect it exactly as it has been thought.

Kata is moving, combining, learning the principles of the specific Ryuha. Kata teaches discipline, perfection and a life long investment to explore it's meanings, it's secrets. Kata too, like Kyhon is pre-arranged according to the regulations of your style. If Kyhon is the letters, Kata is the grammar to enable perfection in using the letters, the style's specific language.

Kumite, is your free expression, your own way to use Kyhon and your consequences from the deeper study of Kata. Kumite is expressing your skill, your knowledge and your understanding of the practical use of your Karatedo. As an analogy, this is your very personal hand writing.

In my eyes, if you learn a bit deeper than just kicking and punching an drawing a Kata, your Kumite should show a clear picture of your style and it's characteristics.

Again, as an analogy: we all know reading, writing, however not all of us are Shakespeare in using our own language. I feel, it is the key factor in understanding Martial Art, as deeper you dig, as more you invest in widen horizons to found answers, you will better and rise above the average.

Q: What is it that keeps you motivated after all these years?

I am still excited to work with people, to research the ART to learn and develop new up to date teaching methods. Throughout the long years of learning, practicing and teaching I was able to do my Martial Art in a few dimensions: practicing and teaching classical Okinawa Gojuryu, teaching Military Self Defense, developing and running our governmental program of training and qualifiying Instructors, Coaches, Teachers and Master Teachers in the field of Martial Art at my government recognized and approved Institute according to our Sport Law. I regard all my activities as a Student, Sensei, Lecturer, researcher, as one! 21 st. Century Budoka !

Q: How important is competition in the evolution of a karate practitioner?

I see the importance at the early, young age. Developing physical abilities, athletic skills, building character to be able to take winning and losing as part of life, sportsmanship...with clear understanding that is a game with clear rules. I am teaching my people to realize that is only the playing stage and right after is a lifelong path of the real Budo !

Q: What really means "Ikken Hissatsu" and how it applies when used in sport Karate?

You have one chance to finish the job! This is generally the case in reality, but often you need more than one blow, because of the ever changing situation. However the modern WKF karate rules killed this aspect! The Ippon shobu rules are a bit closer to it!

Q: How do you see the art of Karate evolve in the future?

In my opinion, Karatedo is an ever developing, changing ART! I can see that sport karate will take its place and classical Karatedo will continue to flourish according to the various Ryuha and Sensei's direction. There is plenty of space and followers for both directions.

Q: What advise would you do to those who want to focus on becoming a Karate teacher?

Invest seriously in studying your style and don't neglect the art of teaching! Both professions are equally important! Never cut yourself off from an advanced tab of knowledge in your way of Karatedo, always seek for continue to study and strive full heartedly to uncover the unknown.

Invest your best at all times to advance your studies, never stop learning!

Always remain a most curious and devoted student!

Q: What advice would you give to students on the question of supplementary training?

Hojo Undo is most important! You must understand clearly the difference between General Fitness and Specific Fitness! Our investment mainly Specific Fitness which means I can do my Sport discipline the best, all training should be focused to improve your real ability to be the best physically and mentally according to the needs of your specific field of activities. Hojo Undo is providing this! All supplementary training program, should be the outcome of professional analysis of your discipline. Not enough to train hard, you should train according to a most professionally structured training program.

Q: What advice would you give to an instructor who is struggling with his or her own development?

Instructors must train under the supervision and guidance of a higher authority. If there is no input you dry out your ability to give out!

Teaching yourself is a very limiting stage!

You should seek knowledge and widen horizons at all times equally in your karate and also teaching methodology, pedagogy.

Q: What are the most important points in your teaching methods today?

Step by step development. Each and every class, term, year is a measurable educational process to the individual. I am teaching a class but connected and deal with an individual. Each grading is a main for the Sensei to measure his ability to forward objectively the student. Doing my best to make sure a clear balance between fitness, physical well-being and mental training to strengthen personality!

Q: Do you think that Olympics will be positive or negative for Karate?

Sport Karate lovers will enjoy Karate at the Olympics if it will succeed. Me personally, giving very little credit to the Olympic movement and its dealing with Karate. However I will be happy for my Sport lover friends.

As for the Classical Karatedo people, it will not change much.

Q: Please tell us about your experience and training in other Martial Arts.

I have trained, Judo, Ju jutsu long term, experienced Tai Chi, Aikido, Iaido off course Military Self Defense – Krav Maga. All those are supplementary for my Okinawa Gojuryu, to deepen and widen my understanding of my Martial Art.

Q: What is your opinion about the format "Shobu Ippon" division in Karate competition?

I like it, much closer to ideas of Budo than WKF rules. It is much closer to real self-defense.

Q: What karate can offer to the individual in these troubled times we are living in?

Lifelong body& mind conditioning. All around self-defense (physical as well as mental). Keeping you fit, flexible and well-conditioned. Teaching you self-confidence and self-esteem. Character building, and education you systematically to real time decision making. Working

toward giving you the right tools to face, day to day obstacles. Karatedo designed to give you the best material and mental preparation for real life, tailored to you individually.

Q: Finally, what advise would you like to give to all Karate practitioners?

Karatedo is well balanced between the physical and the spiritual studies. Keep this balance at all times.

Regulate your training, keep it as part of your average, normal routine throughout your entire life.

Always keep up your deep desire to understand each and every move of your Karate. It is all upon your desire to discover the hidden from your eyes.

Search for the Sensei you feel he is able to fulfill your hunger for knowledge, look for the Sensei who is a role model of his teachings, when you found it stick to him!

DOMINGO LLANOS

WINGS OF FIRE

Domingo Llanos was born in the Dominican Republic. In 1971, he moved to Haverstraw, New York. In 1973, at the age of sixteen he had his first Goju-ryu Karate experience through a friend of the family. Two months later, he was introduced to Black Belt Hall of fame member Sensei Chuck Merriman, from whom he received his 4th Dan, and still trains with today. Sensei Llanos has also trained under other famous Goju-ryu Karate teachers such as Teruo Chinen and Morio Higaonna. As a member of the organization presided by Sensei Morio Higaonna, he was awarded 5th Dan. In 1997, he visited the island of Okinawa to compete in the Okinawa Karate and Kobudo Tournament and to train at the Jundokan under Eiichi Miyazato and some of his most prominent student. At the end of his stay in Okinawa, Llanos was awarded the rank of 6th degree black belt by Eiichi Miyazato. In August of 2010, he was promoted to 7th Dan and on April 17th 2016 to 8th Dan by his lifelong teacher Sensei Chuck Merriman. Llanos began training karate primarily for self-defense, but in 1975, it all took a different turn when he was invited to compete for the first time at the Latin American, Caribbean, and United States Championships held in El Salvador. This was the turning point of his competition career that lasted more than two decades. In 1977, Llanos extraordinary ability earned him a place on the National AAU Karate Team. While competing for AAU, Llanos set and broke many records. His accomplishments included being a five-time National Kata Champion, 4 times overall Champion (Kata, Kumite & Weapon) and being the light weight Kumite Champion.

He competed in the AAU until 1983. Llanos also competed professionally with the "Transworld Oil Karate Team" (formerly known as Atlantic Oil Karate Team).

He competed successfully in most major USA National open tournaments. Some of his international victories included the World Union Karate Organization (WUKO) Championships in Tokyo, Japan (5th place in Kata), 1981 World Games in Santa Clara, California (3rd place Kata) and 1982 World Championships in Taipei, Taiwan (silver medal).

A highly respected teacher, as well as competitor, Domingo Llanos is the head instructor for Karate International in Haverstraw, NY. His school has consistently turned out students who are champions not only in Karate but also in life.

Q: How long have you been practicing karate-do and who were your teachers?

I started practicing karate in 1973 at the age of 16 years old, at the house of a brown belt student of Sensei Chuck Merriman. After two months of training, he decided it was too much for the house to take (we practiced in a small room on the third floor) so he took three of the people training including myself to the dojo in New City, New York where he had trained under Merriman Sensei. I have been a student of Sensei Chuck Merriman since 1973. Although, I have had the pleasure and privilege to train on different occasions with some excellent Sensei such as; Morio Higaonna, Teruo Chinen, Masaji Taira, Eiichi Miyazato Sensei and most of the senior instructors of the "Jundokan" dojo in Okinawa, I have remained loyal to my first karate teacher. Chuck Merriman Sensei has been a teacher, father figure, coach and a mentor.

Q: Why did you start competing and how were your beginnings in competition?

Chuck Merriman Sensei once said, "prepare yourself and wait for the opportunity because when the wagon comes if you are not ready, it leaves without you." I had no idea what he was talking about at the time, but it stuck with me. I was only a green belt at the time with no clear vision of where karate training will take me other than loving the training and learning. I trained any where I could, including cleaning people's basements to allow a few of us to have a place to practice. Competition was never something I aspired to do or even thought of. I was in love with karate from day one and all I wanted to do was practice every day. In 1975, after about a year and a half of training Merriman Sensei took a team to El Salvador to the Latin America, Caribbean and USA Championships. As a brown belt, he invited me to be part of the team, I thought it would be exciting to travel to another country so I jumped on the wagon. We were missing one person to complete the black belt team, our team captain Sensei Ron Martin chose me for the spot. As it turned out I won my first ever competition match and continue to perform well throughout the tournament. As a result of my performance I was promoted to my 1st degree black belt. Upon returning I attended another AAU tournament in New Jersey and won both kata and lightweight black belt fighting. It was only at that moment, I realized this was a path I wanted to follow. For many years I successfully competed in kata, kumite (no-weight division) and weapons. In those days the hardest part was coming up with the funds to travel to a competition. 1977, I earned a spot on the United States AAU Team to the World Championships in Tokyo, Japan. I believe it was the first time kata was introduced to the world championships. I was excited until I was find out I had to come up with the funds for

the trip. With the support of my students and the community, we raised the funds for the trip. Thanks to Merriman Sensei's lesson of being prepared, his guidance and teachings combined with dedication, hard work and my passion for karate, I was able to compete in three world karate championships WUKO (1977 Tokyo, Japan, 1980 Madrid, Spain and 1982 Taipei, Taiwan) as a member of the AAU Karate Team. In addition, I also competed and won a bronze medal in the 1981 World Games in Santa Clara, California. In 1982 Taipei, Taiwan, I won a silver medal in kata and finished top 10 in kumite. I did some full contact karate in its inception as well as competed in open karate tournaments as a member of one of the greatest team ever assembled, the "Transworld Oil Karate Team" formerly known as "The Atlantic Karate Team" also coached by Sensei Chuck Merriman. Karate gave me the opportunity to travel the world and experience wonderful people and cultures.

Q: How different from other karate styles are the principles and concepts of the style that you practice, Goju Ryu?

Goju-ryu deals with universal principles, hard and soft as does life. One can never be too hard or too soft because by going in either extreme you will be at a disadvantage. You must know when to give in or yield to a situation and when to say no or stand your ground, a balance between the two is an appropriate concept for life or combat. One has to adapt to different situations and opponents; some opponents you can beat by attacking, others by countering or a balance of both depending on the situation. Goju-ryu uses both linear and circular techniques where as some other styles are more straightforward. In my opinion and speaking from experience (fighting with no weight divisions) evasive movements (body shifting) and quickly closing the gap instead of force against force gives a smaller opponent a much better chance to survive or defend the attack. In this respect the principles and concepts of goju-ryu are a bit different than other styles. The techniques are gear towards opening and closing the opponent, it is more of an in close fighting style.

Q: How did you structure your personal kata training when you were preparing for a competition?

Kihon is an essential part of the training. No building can stand the test of time without a strong foundation. I learned that early on from my karate teacher and understood the importance of basic training. I started my daily routine with building what I stand on, my legs, so I ran 3 to 6 miles a day for at least 6 days a week for as long as I was competing, I still do some running just not as much. The training continued at the dojo with strength training, almost always using my own body (very little weight training) and then on to kihon. As for kata training, some days I would break the kata into very small parts (just like kihon), other days 3 parts or just doing half of the kata as well as performing the full kata until I was satisfied with the results. The key is repetitions and paying attention to details. Something I think is very important is the transitions between movements. I am well-disciplined so I did not have issues with doing the same thing over and over. The week of competition, I would try to peak by Thursday if I was competing on Sunday. Thursday I would always perform as if I was competing and if on my first try I performed at competition standard I leave it alone to take with me the feeling and visual of the performance for the event. If not, I would continue doing it until I got the results I was looking for. I rested for about a day or two by doing light stretching and slow movements.

Q: Do you think training in karate can help the young generation in becoming successful as individuals in the future?

Absolutely, I personally come from a generation where respect and discipline were part of growing up. Karate strengthen those value taught to me by parents. Growing up, you were taught the value of hard work and to be respectful in order to be admired by others as good person. The basic foundation; the family structure has changed. Now a day with both parents working the values have changed in part because of the lack of supervision. Karate is a substitute or a vehicle for students to learn these values, if taught correctly. Classes should be gear towards character building. The physical movements should be taught with a correlation to a mental benefit. Students will grow up understanding these values and applying them to become successful as individual in life. It is a great contribution to society in general.

Q: What do you think are the most important qualities for a student become proficient in any art of karate?

Each person thinks differently and people do karate for different reasons. A person's character will determine how far they will get. The level of proficiency depends on the interest of the practitioner, but I think the most important thing is always self-discipline, passion combined with hard work. Some people train when they are constantly being coached and supervised by others or train with partners, which is fine. This group of practitioners will reach a certain level, but probably not achieve a high level of proficiency unless they continue to have support. They lack self-discipline and that is ok if you enjoy karate as a hobby or a way of defending yourself or to just want to keep fit. To really excel in karate, you have to have a strong character, be disciplined, dedicated and willing to work hard; do repetitions of techniques until they become a part of you. Each day of training is like another day in life, you look for new things to make life more exciting and better. Live and train enthusiastically. As a competitor you need to wake up on your own and get yourself going before the competition wakes up, you need to train when the competition is resting. On rest days, I had the habit of doing push ups and sit ups while watching TV when a commercial came on, just to try to keep ahead of the competition. Constant training will lead to less injury and a much higher level of proficiency.

Q: With all the technical changes during the last years, do you think there still are "pure" styles of karate?

I don't know about pure styles of karate because all styles have gone thru some form of transformation over the years. It may be because a lot of information was passed down thru word of mouth or simply because of student's misinterpretation of what was being conveyed in the lessons. I like to think there are authentic styles of karate that can easily be identified by looking at the kata. I have only practice goju-ryu all my life and I think if I did a kata from another style with a goju-ryu flavor it wouldn't exactly represent that style. There are many differences that would show; goju-ryu does "gedan-barai" in a circular manner where as other styles do the same move much more linear and also the chamber of the hand is held in a different position. Other styles have adopted versions of goju-ryu kata while goju-ryu itself has remained with just twelve kata, of course with slight variations depending on the dojo or organizations. A lot of these changes stem from competition. The competitors are looking for an edge to impress the judges so they are doing kata from other styles because they're longer and just seem more difficult to perform and as a result the authenticity of their style is disappearing. A building structure is designed a certain way for a reason. If you change the supporting structure it will have an effect on that building and possibly cave in. You may be able to give it a facelift as long as don't change the supporting structure. The same can apply to karate styles. Too many changes and additions can affect the authenticity of the style.

Q: Karate nowadays often is referred to as a sport... would you agree with this definition or is "only" Martial Art?

I think there is the sport aspect of it brought on by competition. As a competitor, I had a clear mind as to where I was going with competition and karate as a martial art. I played to the rules I was competing under, I never lost track of what was real or not. I started karate to defend myself not to compete. If you just treat it like a sport, I think you will end up like most well known athletes; you will shine for a while and then when you can no longer compete it is all over. I don't agree it should be referred to as sport because in sports you have rules for fighting, in a real fight there are no rules so students of karate will get the wrong impression of what is real or not real. What works as a sport may not necessarily work in a real situation. A martial artist will train for life even if not with the same intensity level because of age and other difficulties one may encounter. Regardless of age you can continue grow your mind by training, teaching and improving the self defense aspect of the art in order to maintain the original purpose of the fighting arts.

Q: How do you see karate in North America and around the world at the present time?

I have gotten away from competition and I mostly keep to my dojo so it is very hard to judge the current climate in karate in North America and around the World. When we talk about karate in North America, we have to make a distinction between the more modern form (open or some times referred to American Karate) or the more authentic or traditional karate. The former has developed into more of a show of martial arts movements combined with gymnastic and other acrobatics moves with without much substance in terms of applications of techniques, it is more of a spectacle. I don't want to minimize the hard work or the athletic abilities of the competitors in this area, but it seems to be losing the essence of the art. It seems to me authentic or traditional karate continues to flourish and maintain in a positive direction in terms of spreading all over the world. While other forms of martial arts come and go karate-do is rooted in its basic foundation. In North America as in other parts of the world karate is still very popular; specially amongst young people. It is up to the older generations to continue to keep and pass on the values and traditions of karate-do.

Q: Do you think that the amount of Kata in the style is relevant in the mastery of the art of Karate?

Not at all, it is better to know one kata and do it well or have sufficient knowledge of it than to have many kata without understanding. Probably not different than filling up your plate with food you are not going to eat, it becomes a waste. In goju-ryu we only 12 kata and that is a lot when it comes practicing and perfecting them. Just doing the embusen is not enough, properly training with intensity to develop proper balance and speed takes a lot of time to break a kata down into parts and really work on it. People are always looking for more because they become bored with the old. Day to day living it is not that exciting, but somehow we have found the fun in each day. Kata should be the same. More is not always better.

Q: When teaching the art of karate, what is the most important element: self-defense or sport?

I guess it all depends on the school and interest of the practitioner. Some schools focus more on the sport aspect of karate and again I think that is ok if that is where you want to take your training. The reality is that while it helps with reflexes and movements, it is totally different than a street situation. Teachers should make clear to students the reality of both sport and self-defense and address those differences in classes. The element of self-defense should be much more important as the arts were created to protect yourself and love ones.

Q: Kihon, Kata and Kumite: what's the proper ratio in training?

In general, Kihon should be practice for about 20 to 25 minutes in the beginning maybe spent more time on individual techniques than move on to combinations. Kata and Kumite... it depends on the individual preference; these days I spent most of my time focusing on kata. Of course, if a person is involved in competition and being that most if not all specialize in one event, they should practice according to their preference. It is important to practice all three specially at a younger age.

Q: What do you consider to be the major changes in the art since you began training?

In terms of training, when I started you enter the dojo to train or follow directions and didn't ask too many questions, if any. No one questioned what was being taught, you just follow directions in the class. Back when I started training you didn't ask about rank, it came as result of your training and attitude. Nowadays students want to know why they do everything and if it works or doesn't work before they even have an understanding of what they are learning. The rush to be promoted is constant, just because they know a kata pattern for a rank they think they are ready for the next belt. In Those days not many kids did karate so now you also have parents asking about testing for the child. I guess because of the pace of life these days; patience is overlooked so people want to have everything in a blink. Students don't want to put the time and effort to train and want everything the easy way.

Q: Who would you like to have trained with that you have not (dead or alive)?

Being a goju-ryu practitioner and having only concentrated on one style, I was lucky to have trained in seminars and some times for extended periods of time with some of the better known goju-ryu teachers living, but I definitely would have liked to have known and train with the founder of goju-ryu Chojun Miyagi Sensei. I love the stories of the old days and what practitioners had to go through just to be accepted in a dojo as a student. The training was very challenging according to the stories I have heard and I would have liked that.

Q: What that keeps you motivated after all these years?

I get ask this question a lot and my answer is very simple; I have a passion for karate. I tell people I found a toy when I was 16 years old that I felt in love with that never got old and I am still playing with it. I never get bore or tire of it, the constant search to improve myself and to understand the mechanics of the techniques keeps me motivated. For me in some ways is about conquering myself, not allowing my thoughts to defeat me. One hour of training is less painful than spending a whole day fighting with yourself thinking you should train or should have trained. Procrastination is something a majority of people live with and that is no way to make yourself happy. When you really think about it, is a lot easier to just do it.

Q: How do you think practitioners can increase their understanding of the spiritual aspect of the art?

Through the training of techniques one will develop a sense of strength, confidence, courage, control and patience. If one trains hard enough to develop the above, it will set free their ego to develop into a better person. Strength to stand up for yourself and others, confidence and courage to succeed in life, control to avoid unpleasant circumstances and patience to understand and treat others with kindness. It is for this reason most of us will train their whole life for a

fight that may never happen. The thinking has to transcend techniques, once you have an awareness of your talent and physical abilities, you than have to figure out how to apply to everyday life for the good of mankind, it is a core belief you practice day in and out. In goju-ryu breathing techniques ("Sanchin" and "Tensho" kata) are a major part of training. Thru this type of training the practitioner learned to connect with their inner self by focusing on coordinating breathing and movements, tension and relaxation, amongst other things. It is a form of meditation, a student has to try to free their mind from other thoughts and just focus on proper breathing coordinated with the movements of the kata. The breathing is done by deeply inhaling thru the nose and exhaling thru the mouth with the focus on the lower abdomen. Like techniques one should be consciously working on practicing the spiritual aspect of the art in daily life. This is Do, the way.

Q: Is anything lacking in the way Karate is being taught today compared to how they were in your beginnings?

Now a day we probably have better methods of training. A lot of people are cross training and implementing new ways to improve. Karate training it is probably not as strict as it used to be and the discipline is lacking in some ways. People have adopted the gym mentality which didn't exist in those days. Of course, the market is different today, the majority of schools are teaching young children so the teaching methods have changed to satisfy the population. There are a lot of exercises we used to do that we cannot do these days because you may be liable if someone got hurt. The legal area has changed the way classes are run because one can find themselves in a legal mess if not careful.

Q: What do you consider the most important qualities of a successful karate practitioner?

Discipline, passion combined with hard work and perseverance! A person can be talented but if you lack the discipline, desire and willingness to work hard until the right results are acquired the talent means nothing. These are qualities important in all aspects of life.

Q: What advice would you give to students on the question of supplementary training (running, weights, et cetera)?

I would say not just to do supplemental training, but to think in a way the supplemental training can enhance their karate techniques. Running is great because it helps with your leg strength, but you may want to do distance for endurance as well as sprint to develop more speed. Weight training is the same, I do a little of it, usually to strengthen certain techniques. In goju-ryu we have many tools we use to supplement our goju-ryu techniques. There are many methods and ways available these days for practitioners to better their techniques, you just have to be creative. Over all I think it is great to supplement the training just be mindful of what you want to accomplish.

Q: What are the most important points in your current personal training methods?

I have continued to train very much the same as when I competed, I am just more cautious in the way I train because of knee surgery and the fact I want to train for longevity. I do about three to four days of running combined with strength training (push-ups, sit-ups, squads and dips), I then focus my dojo training between supplemental exercises, kihon and kata. I also incorporate bag training on some days. Kata is the most important thing and what I dedicate most of my time to. For me, it all starts with creating a feeling and let the feeling take me through the training.

Q: What is your philosophical basis for your karate training today?

I believe in constant never ending improvement so every day I train to be a little better than the day before. I have a battle with myself everyday which keeps me going. I believe in the mind of a beginner, so every day is a new day and a new technique to work on. It is the thought of knowing it all, I am too old and no longer need to practice that makes people complacent and eventually lazy.

Q: Have there been times when you felt fear in your training?

The fear of not being able to train due to illness or injury has crossed my mind from time to time. So far god has been on my side and I am thankful for it.

Q: Do you think that Olympics will be positive for the art of karate-do?

Competition has always played a roll in the spread of karate throughout the world; specially among young people. So yes, I think it would give karate a bigger stage for the public to view the art. I just hope it doesn't lose the essence of the Do, the way. Karate-Do, as a way of life is beautiful, I hope it doesn't become just the way of competition.

Q: What are your thoughts on the future of karate?

Karate will continue to grow in popularity. It is such a great tool to build character by developing young minds into capable, strong, confident adults. If taught properly, in a fun an educational way, it will be of great benefit to the communities. My concern is that we may lose the essence of Karate-Do in exchange for popularity.

Q: What final advice would you give to all karate-do practitioners regardless of style?

We as practitioners and teachers have the responsibility to continue to spread karate-do as much as we can all over the world and to teach it in a manner that benefits the communities we live in. We have enough violence in the world so it will be detrimental to arm students with weapons they cannot control; it will only cause more harm than good. Of course, we must teach self-defense as a last resort. It is more important to educate, build minds from the inside out; teach the mental benefits of the art. The better a person feels about themselves, the more productive they will become in life. My advice is to teach and practice karate-do in it's most pure form to preserve what has been passed down to us with the effort of so many great teachers before us.

CHUCK MERRIMAN

WISDOM OF THE AGES

CHUCK MERRIMAN'S KARATE CAREER BEGAN IN 1960 AND WITHIN A FEW YEARS HE HAD BECOME ONE OF THE LEADING FIGURES IN AMERICAN KARATE AND THE PERSONAL BODYGUARD FOR STARS SUCH AS DIANA ROSS AND THE ROCK GROUP "KISS." HE MANAGED THE FIRST PROFESSIONAL, CORPORATE-SPONSORED KARATE TEAM, WHICH COMPETED ACROSS THE GLOBE IN THE 1980S. MERRIMAN HAS COACHED THE BEST COMPETITORS IN THE UNITED STATES AND WILL SHARE HIS 40 PLUS YEARS OF KARATE EXPERIENCE AND TRAINING SECRETS ONLY WITH THOSE WHO ARE TRULY SERIOUS ABOUT LEARNING THE ART.

HIS EVOLUTION AS MARTIAL ARTIST LED HIM TO TRAIN WITH SENSEI MIYAZATO EIICHI FROM OKINAWA, IN THE TRADITIONAL GOJU-RYU STYLE. MERRIMAN'S GOAL IS NOT ONLY TO PRODUCE GOOD KARATEKA, BUT RATHER BETTER HUMAN BEINGS IN THE PROCESS. SENSEI MERRIMAN IS ONE OF THE ICONS OF AMERICAN KARATE AND AN ORACLE OF KNOWLEDGE FOR THE YOUNGER GENERATIONS.

Q: How did you get started in martial arts?

A: I started judo in 1960 in Norwich, Connecticut. I then moved to New York in 1961 to continue my training in karate under Sensei Chris DeBaise. At that time I was living in the dojo of Bernie and Bob Lepkofker, the so-called "Judo Twins," who were 6-foot-4 and weighed 225 pounds. Living at the dojo was not all that different from the hard, disciplined training in Japan. Anyway, the judo classes were held on the fifth floor and on the third floor Sensei Chris DeBaise was teaching shito-ryu karate. The karate studio had a shower in it and I was allowed to use it. After observing the classes for a long time I went to DeBaise and naively asked if he could teach me kata. He agreed, and so I found myself practicing judo and karate 7 days a week! I used to compete and for a long time I was one of the top kata competitors in the country.

Q: What sparked your interest in martial arts?

A: Martial arts always appealed to me because it was an individual effort and accomplishment. In school I was always too short for basketball, too skinny for football, and too slow for track. But martial arts just seemed to fit me naturally – it clicked for me.

Q: Did you receive instruction from Peter Urban?

A: Yes. But only after DeBaise decided not to teach anymore and gave me a recommendation. Urban's policy was that even the black belts from other schools had to wear white belts and line up in the back of the class. It was interesting because if you wanted the right to sit with the black belts you had to earn it. One day I decided to take a spot with the shodan, and that meant I had to justify it. After the warm up, Sensei Urban lined up all 15 black belts and I had to go through them all! It was not a matter of winning or losing but a case of survival. I have good memories of Sensei Urban. Some people criticize him but he was very truthful and ahead of his time. He was not cut out of a mold. There was only one of him. Some of the things he said at that time nobody understood, not even me…but with today's perspective he was terribly right.

Q: What happened next?

A: I amicably left Urban in 1967 and I never had a feeling of belonging to goju-kai every since. After I disassociated myself from Urban, I always felt outside of it. It is true that Yamaguchi Gosei was a great man and a great karate teacher but I couldn't relate to him much. So when Gonnoyoe Yamamoto, who was another of my teachers, started his organization, and broke away from Yamaguchi Gosei, I moved with him. This was from the mid-'60s to the early '70s. The last time I trained under Yamamoto was in 1972. For many years I was pretty much on my own. By this I mean I didn't belong to any organization. I did not change anything but I had to adjust certain things to being by myself. I was teaching my students exactly what I was taught by my teachers. I never created, invented or developed a new style.

Q: Did you enjoy your experiences under Sensei Higaonna and the International Okinawa Goju-Ryu Karate Federation?

A: I knew Sensei Higaonna since 1975 and he always gave me a lot of advise even though I didn't belong to his organization. He never put me off or had a bad attitude because I wasn't his student. Because of this I enjoyed being around him. So after some years I decided to join with him. I gathered all my students and told them what I was planning to do. I don't like to tell people what to do because I don't like to make decisions for anybody. This way I don't have to pay for a wrong decision. Anyway, everybody agreed and we went full force with IOGKF. It was a great time. The atmosphere, the people, the training – everything. No chips on the shoulders or wrong attitudes by anyone. This was a reflection of Higaonna's behavior and personality. Budo is a "warrior way" and in Okinawa the word "bushi" means a "gentleman warrior." Gentleman is the important word here. It means the character of the person. You are a guide and example to follow and you do what you say. People judge you more by what you do than by what you say. In karate, with rank comes responsibility. This is what "do" means.

Q: Did you train and study in Japan?

A: In Tokyo I trained under Sensie Yonemoto (Okinawan goju-ryu) and I used to go train in Okinawa at the Jundokan, where Miyazato Eiichi Sensei used to teach. At the time of his passing, he was a 10th dan hanshi and successor to the founder of goju-ryu, Sensei Chojun. It is interesting you mentioned two different words: "training," and "study," because they are completely different. Studying is much more than showing up for practice, just like studying in college is not just showing at the school and then sitting there. Study is a learning process which entails research about philosophy, technical aspects, physiology, and other related matters. It is much deeper than just training.

Q: So you had different teachers all these years, right?

A: Yes. I must say that during all my years of practice I have been extremely fortunate to have such a great teachers as Sensei DeBaise, Sensei Peter Urban, Sensei Yamamoyo Gonnoyoe Sensei (Goju-kai), Sensei Higaonna Morio, and Sensei Miyazato Eiichi of the Jundokan in Okinawa. My judo teachers were Bernie Lepkofker, Nakabayashi Sadaki and In Soo Hwang.

Q: Do you prefer kata or kumite?

A: At this point in my life I prefer kata, but in order to be a complete karateka you need to strike a balance between both, since one doesn't exist without the other.

Q: How important is the sport aspect of karate in your teaching and coaching?

A: I don't stress any aspect of how students should apply the knowledge and ability that they've gained through their training. It's up to them to apply all this information in as many beneficial ways as possible. As far as coaching, the first important thing is to know the rules. As a coach, you must know the rules because those apply to everybody and they might be decisive in sport competition. On other hand, a coach doesn't need to teach technique to the competitors since they already know it. The whole thing is more about bringing out their talents, and knowing what buttons to push to make them believe in themselves – in short, to make them do what they do best. A coach is a motivator, a helper, an advisor – and not just a technical teacher. You must treat every member of your team equally, no favorites. Never lower your standards to treat someone special. Set an example to the players with your attitude and behavior because you have to find a common ground to bring everyone together. Compared to other sports, in karate everybody competes individually – they are a team but it's not like basketball or football where they play all together. So the psychology and the approach has to be a little bit different. Just remember that karate was never designed to be a sport.

Q: You coached a professional karate team, right?

A: Yes, I did. The object was to upgrade the level of professionalism in karate and to try to make karate a regular professional sport. But martial arts people are very different than athletes in other sports. Getting paid is a residual benefit of being a professional. Professionalism is an attitude, a way of behaving and relating to the people around you – and some of them didn't have a clue. Few people understood that their role had changed and they had to conduct themselves in a different way. Therefore, certain attitudes were a major factor in disbanding the team. But it was a very educational experience anyway.

Q: What are the good and bad sides of competition?

A: A desirable aspect of competition is that it is an area where a student can place themselves in a stressful situation with an unknown quality and quantity of opposition. Then they can evaluate themselves in light of the final outcome. An undesirable aspect is that competition is strictly subjective in judgement and is someone's opinion of your performance, not necessarily what actually took place. Many people confuse tournaments and competitions with reality and by doing so gain a false impression of their true ability and knowledge.

Q: If karate becomes an Olympic sport, could it lose part of its purity and spirit?

A: I don't think the Olympics did much to preserve the purity and spirit of judo! In my opinion, it did exactly the opposite. In my logical mind, why would the outcome for karate be any different? And don't forget that the Olympic Organizing Committee is experiencing it's own purity, spirit, and ethics problems at present.

Q: What styles have you studied other than goju-ryu?

A: Originally Sensei DeBaise taught shito-ryu, but it was for a very short period. I did attain sandan in kodokan judo and shodan in hakkoryu jiu-jitsu.

Q: Do you recommend that your students study other styles?

A: Not really. Okinawa goju-ryu is an extremely deep style of karate which requires a great deal of time and effort. I don't think it is necessary to study another style of karate if the karate style you choose provides the proper self-defense structure within its framework of teaching. The old phrase "jack of all trades, master of none" immediately leaps to mind.

Q: What is the ideal relationship between student and instructor?

A: An ideal student/teacher relationship should contain the same qualities as any other successful relationship – mutual respect, concern for each others welfare, consideration, patience, honesty, integrity, and openness.

Q: How has karate changed in the last 30 years?

A: Authentic, traditional karate hasn't changed – just the people in it and their perception of what karate really is!

Q: What is the importance of kata?

A: Kata, and its components of kihon bunkai and oyo bunkai, is the very essence of traditional, authentic karate. You can practice kata alone, in a small area without the need of training aids. Kata affords a serious student an opportunity to analyze – kihon bunkai –and put to use – oyo bunkai – the training, knowledge, and experience that the student has gained through years of training. Oyo bunkai – to apply what you have analyzed – allows the student to develop the kata (pattern or form) and the kihon bunkai (basic or standard analysis) on a more personal level without restrictions.

Q: What do you think about full contact karate and kickboxing?

A: In my opinion, full contact karate and kickboxing are essentially the same sport, with some rule variations. I have a great respect for the courage and commitment to the rigorous physical training that these athletes exhibit. I think it is an exciting spectator sport. I have coached and trained real world champions in every category of sport karate, including WUKO/WKF, Pan American Games, AAU, Open Circuit, PKA, PKC and WAKO. My son, Chad, is a national and international competitor and champion in all aspects of sport karate and is also a silver and gold medallist in Golden Gloves boxing. He is also an excellent judo player.

Q: How did you coach karate?

A: I analyzed everything and found that there are three things that a competitor needs to score a point: distance, timing and target. If you look at the professional players in any sport they don't play a game every day, they do drills. Many people in karate were sparring constantly and I realized that drilling was the key. I believe in drills, therefore I devised drills to develop coordination, lateral movement, and timing. These drills helped to instill muscle memory in the fighter to react in a certain way. They instill programming into your muscles to react before you think. If you have to think you've been already hit. I used drills to develop stamina, awareness, and kime. Later on, you put all the elements together to make them work in kumite. On a mental level, I always stressed that every fighter should find their exclusive routine or ritual in order to build up their energy and spirit. This is something very personal. Something similar to what actors do.

Q: What is your personal training like now?

A: My personal training at present is centered on developing a better understanding of the kata of goju-ryu. Oyo bunaki is my main point of study presently. I have also started Zen training at Kozenji Zendo in Shuri, Okinawa under the watchful eye of Zen Master Sakiyama Sogen Roshi. In his years as a young man, Sakiyama Roshi was also a student of Sensei Miyagi. It is very important to understand that you retain what you practice frequently, not what you practice intensely. I try to stick to a well-rounded program since it's the key to well-rounded development.

Q: Do you think the art of karate has to change accordingly to the practitioner's age?

A: Absolutely! Karate doesn't change, we do. I don't think it's a case of "has to change," but being aware of the natural process of physical and mental changes normally associated with

aging. In you want longevity in your karate life, then the training in your younger years should be geared toward enhancing your ability to train in your later years.

Q: What's your opinion on the qualities and rank an instructor should have before starting to teach?

A: The standards for rank in karate are nationally and internationally different and vary from style to style, dojo to dojo, and teacher to teacher. Because of this, I don't think rank, as such, should necessarily be a factor in determining teaching ability. Qualities of a good teacher, on the other hand, are more easily outlined. I think a primary talent a teacher of any kind should possess is the ability to communicate knowledge and experience to each individual student on their level of understanding. The coach needs patience to allow each student to develop at their own pace, but with the encouragement to develop to their fullest potential. Mutual respect, courtesy, consideration, mutual welfare, honesty, integrity and openness are all desirable qualities for a good teacher. It is essential to develop these qualities and not just pay lip service to them.

Q: What is your philosophy in the dojo?

A: That's a hard question to answer. Westerners don't understand Japanese or Okinawan culture so it's kind of difficult to import it to the United States. But I do believe that traditional karate and traditional martial arts are good for society because they're based on respect – which is what our society needs. In traditional martial arts you learn these values. As far as the dojo philosophy is concerned, I would say that I use a benevolent dictatorship. I know it may sound a bit harsh but that is the way to do it. Everybody has a lot of opinions about everything but in my dojo you train under my circumstances or not at all. Too many young people are making their own decision when they don't have the ability to make good decisions yet!

Q: And your philosophy in life?

A: Karate is something a person is, and not so much what they do. You can't cut all the different aspects into pieces since they are all one thing. You learn from your teachers and your coaches, but in the very end it is all about you. You have to try to be the best you can be and take responsibility for your success or failure. Karate is a tool that we use to train our mind, spirit, and bodies.

Q: What do you feel is wrong with karate today?

A: Nothing is wrong with karate! But maybe those of us who profess to practice and teach karate should examine ourselves more closely as to what our perception of karate is, and if our intentions and motives are correct within the context of that perception.

Q: Do you use meditation on a regular basis as part of your training?

A: No, I don't use meditation as a part of my training or my teaching. I am presently pursuing a study of Zen but I don't consider Zen a meditation in the strictest sense. Roshi said, "Zen and karate are not the same, but can compliment each other."

Q: Is there a particular message you want to share with the karateka and martial artist in general?

The proper study of karatedo should be for the purpose of developing yourself to your highest potential – mentally, spiritually, and physically. It's essence is to learn how to live correctly and to be a positive and beneficial influence on those who rely on your guidance.

ANTHONY MIRAKIAN

THE LEGENDARY PIONEER

ANTHONY MIRAKIAN IS CURRENTLY THE MOST ACTIVE SENIOR MEIBUKAN INSTRUCTOR. HE STARTED HIS GOJU TRAINING UNDER MASTER TOGUCHI AT THE SHOREIKAN DOJO IN THE EARLY 1950S WHILE STATIONED AT THE KADENA AIR FORCE BASE IN OKINAWA. HE ALSO TRAINED THERE WITH OKINAWAN KARATE MASTER RYURITSU ARAKAKI. WHEN ARAKAKI SENSEI NOTICED MIRAKIAN'S PASSION AND COMMITMENT TO THE ART, HE ADVISED HIM TO TRAIN UNDER THE FOREMOST GOJU-RYU KARATE MASTER ON OKINAWA, GRANDMASTER MEITOKU YAGI, THE TOP STUDENT AND SUCCESSOR OF THE LATE FOUNDER OF GOJU-RYU KARATE, GRANDMASTER CHOJUN MIYAGI. MIRAKIAN WAS THE FIRST WESTERNER GRANDMASTER MEITOKU YAGI TAUGHT AND THE FIRST TO RECEIVE A BLACK BELT FROM HIM. MIRAKIAN SENSEI LEFT OKINAWA AND RETURNED TO THE U.S. IN NOVEMBER OF 1959. ONCE HE GOT ESTABLISHED IN THE EARLY 1960S, HE STARTED TEACHING MEIBUKAN GOJU-RYU IN THE PUREST FORM IN THE BOSTON AREA. IN 1990, DAI SENSEI YAGI PROMOTED MIRAKIAN SENSEI TO KU-DAN [9TH DAN] HANSEI. HE IS THE ONLY NORTH AMERICAN OUTSIDE OF OKINAWA THAT HOLDS THIS RANK AND TOP HONOR.

SENSEI MIRAKIAN'S ACADEMY IN WATERTOWN, MASSACHUSETTS, IS THE NORTH AMERICAN HEADQUARTERS OF THE MEIBUKAN GOJU-RYU KARATE-DO ASSOCIATION BASED IN KUME, NAHA CITY, OKINAWA. IN 1972, GRANDMASTER YAGI APPOINTED MIRAKIAN SENSEI THE OVERSEAS GENERAL MANAGER OF THE MEIBUKAN ASSOCIATION. HIS DOJO OFFERS OKINAWAN GOJU-RYU KARATE TRAINING IN ITS PUREST FORM. MIRAKIAN SENSEI IS A TRUE AND EXCELLENT EXAMPLE OF THE BENEFITS OF LIFE-LONG KARATE TRAINING.

Q: You arrived in Okinawa in the early 1950s. How would you characterize Okinawan karate in that era?

A: This was "The Golden Age" of Okinawan karate. It was during this time that karate training first became available to Westerners, which caused a great impetus in the propagation of Okinawan karate to the Western world. During these years, Okinawan karate was taught in a traditional way as an art form of self-defense. The karate masters upheld the old karate values and standards and placed great emphasis on dojo kun (etiquette). They took pride in patiently teaching their national art to Westerners, as well as Okinawans. Karate was presented in a dignified, strict manner. To a Westerner, it appeared fascinating, challenging and mysterious.

Q: Do you think something has been lost, as karate has been modernized?

A: Yes. Unfortunately, much of the essence and spirit of traditional karate has been lost. Since the advent of karate championships, many practitioners are competing to win at any cost. This approach is not the traditional aim of Okinawan goju-ryu karate-do.

Q: Why Okinawa? How could an island so small and remote have produced the world's best-known martial art?

A: That's a very interesting question. Okinawa had the perfect chemistry to develop the art of karate. The Okinawans had the time to devote to the martial arts. Theirs was a quiet and simple agrarian and fishing society, without distractions. Because Okinawa was alternatively dominated by China and Japan, Okinawans were forced to develop unarmed martial art techniques to defend themselves against larger and stronger armed foes. Also, they were forced to look inward and develop an inner strength that characterizes the art. Okinawans are a civilized and peace-loving people, and these traits are reflected in the unique moral foundation of their art.

Q: How long has karate been practiced in Okinawa?

A: For well more than 1,000 years. Certainly, Chinese martial arts were practiced in Okinawa during the Tang Dynasty, and this was from 618 to 906 AD. By the 14th century, oral traditions say that a karate-like art was being practiced there.

Q: When you first arrived in Okinawa, how did you find a karate school?

A: Accidentally. A friend and I hired a taxi and asked the driver to take us to a karate school. He took us to a judo dojo. One of the students there directed the taxi driver to take us to the district of Nakanomachi. When we arrived, the school turned out to be the Shoreikan goju-ryu karate dojo of Grandmaster Seikichi Toguchi.

Q: What was Grandmaster Toguchi's school like in those days?

A: The training at Grandmaster Toguchi's school was intensive. We trained six days a week. The only day off was Monday. The training started at 6 p.m. and lasted until 10:30 p.m. The calisthenics alone lasted an hour and a half. These were hard, demanding calisthenics that were performed in 85- to 100-degree heat and extremely high humidity. We would do all sorts of stretching, loosening-up exercises and strength training. The assistants to Toguchi Sensei were very demanding. They expected 100 percent effort from us. There were about 40 students in the dojo. The school was perhaps 25 feet wide and 45 feet long, and it had a patio where we could work out. The makiwara (striking posts) were all outside. Toguchi Sensei supervised all the workouts. He was the only black belt in the dojo, but he was assisted by some of his advanced brown-belt students. They led the calisthenics and the basic drills.

Q: I take it that a brown belt in those days was the equivalent of a higher rank today?

A: Yes. At that time, in the 1950s, a brown belt was a highly respected rank. Some of the Okinawan brown belts were powerful and very skilled. I would say that many of the brown belts that I saw then would have to be considered the equivalent of fourth- or fifth-degree black belts today.

Q: Describe the physical condition of the Okinawan students.

A: Most of the Okinawans, even the beginners, were in excellent physical shape. They didn't begin karate training to lose weight or to get in shape; they were physically fit to begin with.

Q: What was the training for beginners at Grandmaster Toguchi's dojo?

A: The beginners were trained at a very slow pace. Black footprints, extending 15 or 20 feet, were painted on the dojo floor. There were two sets; one for Okinawans, and one for the larger American servicemen. For three or four months, we trained by walking back and forth on the footprints, trying to learn sanchin stepping. We also learned basic techniques like punching, blocking, kicking and striking. The training was very repetitious. The kata we practiced were basic gekisai ichi and gekisai ni. We practiced these for a long time. The pace was slow, but it was physically intense. No idle talk was allowed, no socializing, no taking it easy.

Q: Did the seniors "lean" on the junior students and push them around, as one often sees in dojo outside Okinawa today?

A: That wasn't allowed. Advanced students weren't allowed to take advantage of a lesser student. They were there to help the junior students in a strict but friendly environment. There was a feeling of mutual respect and brotherhood in the dojo. In later years I noticed that this was part of Okinawan culture. They take great pride in the teaching of karate. Karate is their national art and heritage, their cultural contribution to the world. They take pride in presenting it in a civilized and dignified manner. There was no reason or excuse for needless injuries, brutality or reckless wild actions.

Q: What kind of kumite did you practice?

A: We practiced prearranged sparring [yakusoku kumite]. We practiced one-, three- and five-step sparring, as well as kata-bunkai-kumite. There was no free-fighting. When you practiced with the advanced Okinawans, you had to remain alert, because they were fast, strong and skilled; they also had control. The attitude was very serious. The students practiced kumite as if their lives depended on it, as if a mistake could be fatal.

Q: Was makiwara training part of the regular workout?

A: It was optional, but most students did a lot of it. It was common for Okinawans to have a makiwara in their back yards. The makiwara were very abrasive. The hitting surface was made of rice straw ropes and it frequently would cut your knuckles. One of Grandmaster Toguchi's most advanced students was an Okinawan named Sakai. He wasn't large, but he was extremely powerful. He used to work out seven days a week. He would get up at 6 a.m. every day and punch the makiwara hundreds of times. During practice one day, he cut his knuckles and bled so profusely that he fainted. His wife had to come and throw a bucket of cold water over his head to revive him. He developed thick calluses on his hands, and he had devastating punches and strikes.

Q: Were you given tests for promotions?

A: Yes. From time to time we were asked to perform kata and kumite in front of Toguchi Sensei. No compliments were ever given. If we didn't meet his high standards, we would simply fail the test. I remember once a serviceman didn't get promoted, and he went to Toguchi Sensei and asked him what part of his kata was wrong. Toguchi Sensei said to him in a very abrupt manner: "Everything was wrong."

Q: Was there a moral code you were supposed to abide by?

A: Yes. Toguchi Sensei was very strict in not allowing his students to misuse the art. There was an American student there who got into a fight with three other servicemen in a bar. He beat them up badly. Later, he bragged to one of the Okinawan brown-belt students that goju-ryu karate techniques were very effective in actual combat. When Sensei Toguchi heard of the incident, he became very upset. The serviceman was told to never show up in the dojo again. Also, there were a couple of skillful Okinawan karate students who fought with some Okinawans in the villages. Toguchi Sensei expelled them for misusing the art of karate.

Q: Did Toguchi Sensei ever perform kata for the students?

A: Yes. On the eighth day of every month, Toguchi Sensei would have a ritual commemoration in memory of the founder of goju-ryu karate, Grandmaster Chojun Miyagi, who passed away on October 8, 1953. He would have all of us, from white belt to brown belt, get up on the floor one by one and go through one kata. At the end, he would get up and demonstrate an advanced kata. We were amazed at the beauty, precision, power, fluidity and control of his movements.

Q: Are any of your fellow students at Grandmaster Toguchi's dojo still practicing karate?

A: Yes. Today, several are masters in their own right. Masanobu Shinjo Sensei and Zenshu Toyama Sensei were both green belts at that time. Today, both are highly ranked, highly respected masters. And Katsuyoshi Kanei Sensei , president of the Jinbukan Goju-ryu Karate-do Association, was also a student there. He is a very strong goju- ryu karate and kobudo master and a fine gentleman.

Q: Who was your second karate master?

A: Ryuritsu Arakaki Sensei. We met for the first time in Toguchi Sensei's dojo. He was an architect, a man in his mid-forties. He was a seventh-degree black belt master who had studied with Chojun Miyagi and Seiko Higa. I was fortunate that he befriended me, and he treated me as a protégé. I would visit his house on Sundays and eat dinner with his family. It was a great privilege to be invited into an Okinawan home. We would talk about the history of Okinawan karate, Chojun Miyagi and his training in China, and the old masters. He took me around to various dojo and introduced me to many great masters. I would never have had the opportunity to meet them on my own. One day he took me aside and said, "I can see that you have a great passion and desire to train in goju-ryu karate. You should train with the foremost authority on goju-ryu in Okinawa, Grandmaster Meitoku Yagi; he is the top, senior student of Chojun Miyagi." I was reluctant to do that, as it was at least an hour's bus ride from my base to the Yagi dojo, but Arakaki Sensei was insistent. He said, "You must train under him."

Q: How were you introduced to Grandmaster Meitoku Yagi?

A: Arakaki Sensei approached Grandmaster Yagi and recommended me to him. We visited him on a Sunday afternoon. I remember that day vividly. When we arrived, Grandmaster Yagi was in his dojo drilling holes in the wooden nametags that he hung on the rank-tag rack. His dojo was next to his house and there was a small fenced patio for outdoor workouts. He offered us tea. My first impression was that he was a very serene master. I said to myself immediately, "Here is a man of great physical, mental and spiritual powers." I sensed that I had met a great master. After asking me questions for an hour, with Arakaki Sensei interpreting, Grandmaster Meitoku Yagi asked me to demonstrate a kata. When I finished, Grandmaster Yagi turned to Arakaki Sensei and said that I had a build like the great Chinese kempo masters ... like a spider. At that time I had a very sinewy body. I weighed about 150 pounds and I was 5 foot 11. He said, "I will accept Mr. Mirakian as a student, and all I expect in return is a few words of gratitude." I was immensely happy. It was a great honor to have been accepted by Grandmaster Yagi, because Grandmaster Meitoku Yagi was highly respected among the inner karate circles in Okinawa.

Q: Did Grandmaster Meitoku Yagi have other Western students at his Meibukan dojo?

A: No. I was the only one, and I was the first Western student that he taught. There were about 15 or 20 Okinawans. As soon as I started training in his dojo, I could sense that the karate techniques and kata were practiced in a very natural way. Each student did kata according to his own physique and abilities. It wasn't as if someone handed you a suit and said, "Wear it, even if it doesn't fit you." Although the karate students were not allowed to change the basic techniques, there was more flexibility than in other dojo. A tall student, for instance, wouldn't be required to go so deep into kiba dachi or zenkutsu dachi that he lost mobility.

Q: What was the training schedule at the Meibukan dojo?

A: Grandmaster Yagi held four-hour karate training sessions Monday through Friday. Although the formal workout started at 7 p.m., the students would arrive earlier than that to work out on their own. I would arrive two hours before the workout to stretch, do calisthenics, hit the makiwara and work with traditional Okinawan training equipment. Grandmaster Yagi

was the superintendent of the Custom's House. He would come home from work in a suit. If you saw him in the street, you would take him for a university professor. He was about 5 feet 8 inches tall, he weighed a solid 180 pounds, and he had broad shoulders and very powerful hands and arms. He would come home at seven — and without eating supper — put on his gi, and the formal training would begin.

Q: What kind of training equipment was used at the Meibukan dojo?

A: There was a makiwara, chishi (strength stones) of about 5 to 10 pounds, stone jugs for developing a strong grip, free weights and a heavy punching bag. There was a homemade barbell, which was made from two railroad wheels that weighed perhaps 100 pounds. These wheels had probably been used years before on the small railroad cars that ran through the sugar cane fields. But in the honbu (headquarters) dojo, there wasn't an emphasis on lifting heavy weights. My impression was that Grandmaster Yagi felt that excessive weight lifting would cause flexibility and speed loss. He stressed that punching against the makiwara was the best way to develop devastating power.

Q: What was the atmosphere like at the Meibukan dojo?

A: A very subtle spirit pervaded the dojo. When you stepped inside, it was as if you stepped into another era or another time. It was as if you were going back to the Shaolin monastery 1,000 or 1,500 years ago. There was something mystical there, very difficult to express in words. A person had to be attuned to perceive this mood. There was also very little speaking allowed. There was no socializing, no idle talk, no ego, no flexing of muscles or physical vanity. That would have been contradictory to the concept of the dojo, and none of it was allowed. The karate training consisted of a blending of physical, mental and spiritual elements harmonized in a very smooth way. There was no harshness. The grandmaster led the class in a strict and disciplined way, but he did it with a friendly attitude. The karate students felt very comfortable being taught by Grandmaster Meitoku Yagi.

Q: How was the formal workout structured?

A: The formal training started at 7 p.m. and ran to 11 p.m. Grandmaster Yagi would lead the workout with the assistance of his senior student, Sensei Yushun Tamaki, one of the finest karate instructors I have ever met. To begin, all of the students would line up in complete silence. We would begin by going through all the goju-ryu kata to suparimpei, one after the other. This practice was done very seriously, with tremendous concentration; the mind wasn't wandering, and there was no wavering of the eyes. Once the student was training in the dojo, he had to be in command of his mind and in complete control of himself. Everybody responded to the commands at once. Everything was a drill in unison. There were no stragglers. We would always end the training with sanchin kata and tensho kata. Sometimes we would begin with sanchin as well.

Q: Would the junior belts step aside for the advanced kata?

A: No. Everyone, even white belts, did all the kata. But you must remember that the beginning Okinawan students had some awareness and appreciation of karate before they began training, because it was their national art. The beginners knew that just because they were allowed to go through the advanced kata didn't mean that they had mastered them. They were only familiarizing themselves with some of the movements. Okinawan masters told me that to perfect a single kata takes two to three hours of training a day for three to five years. In some cases, it could take as long as 10 years. Okinawan students understood this.

Q: How were you taught the kata at the Meibukan dojo?

A: Grandmaster Meitoku Yagi would usually take me aside and teach me the movements of the kata once. While he was performing the kata, I would follow him. It was a great honor to be taught by the grandmaster, and it was taken as a sign of respect that you would give absolute concentration and learn the basic movements on the first try. I watched like a hawk. There's a saying in Okinawa that the master speaks only once. The kata were taught in a systematic and logical way in the Meibukan dojo. Yushun Tamaki Sensei led the karate class in the practice of the kata, and the students followed him. When we went through the kata for the first time each evening, no corrections were made. But as we kept practicing the kata over and over, Grandmaster Meitoku Yagi and Yushum Tamaki Sensei would make the necessary corrections to each karate student. The kata were taught slowly and patiently, step-by-step to the karate class. Generally, once a student was shown the kata, he was expected to correct the movements himself. When I was learning the tensho kata, I didn't realize it but I had been practicing a wrong move for one to two months. Finally, after paying closer attention to some of the advanced students practicing the tensho kata during one of the workouts, I noticed the right movement of the hand and corrected it myself. This was a very difficult technique to learn, because it was performed fast. Leaving a person to discover and refine techniques by himself has a great built-in value. A student who has to do this becomes highly observant, one of the most important factors in mastering karate. You must remember that there is a Buddhist tradition in Okinawa: To make spiritual progress, you must search for yourself.

Q: Were the students asked to perform kata in front of the class?

A: Twice a week or so Grandmaster Meitoku Yagi would have us sit down quietly on the sides of the dojo, and one by one we would perform kata. The atmosphere in the dojo was so calm that you could hear a pin drop. We would get a chance to see every student's kata and see the strengths and flaws. We benefited from the relaxed contemplation of each other's kata. There was never any praise given.

Q: Did Grandmaster Yagi perform kata in his dojo?

A: On occasion. They were the finest kata I have ever seen in goju- ryu karate. It was beauty in motion. The perfect balance of hard and soft. He had tremendous power, control and speed. I remember his sanchin in particular. It didn't have the extreme tension you see in some practitioners, but when he tensed his body, it was impressive and deceptive ... like tempered steel covered by velvet.

Q: What followed the kata in the workout?

A: After we finished going through the kata, we would practice many different types of kumite that had been adapted from the breakdown of the kata. We would also practice combinations of striking, punching, kicking, blocking and counterpunching. We would practice many patterns, such as jo-chu-gae, chu-gae-jo and gae-jo-chu, and do many different techniques in a very fast, sequential manner back and forth across the dojo floor. Then we would practice ippon-kumite at close range. When we did this, there was one arm length between the attacker and defender. At this range, given the skill and speed of the students, there was no margin for error. We paid close attention. We had to develop lightning-fast reflexes or we would get hit. The emphasis was on watching the pupils of the opponent's eyes. We watched closely enough so we could always see the punch telegraphed by the eyes. This was a form of active meditation, and this is much better than sitting meditation. The outside world did not exist, and we couldn't worry about the past or future. Only the split-second counted. This made the mind very strong; it developed tremendous power of concentration. We practiced against various students, so we constantly had to adjust and readjust according to the makeup of the opponent. I was a weapons technician in the U.S. Air Force. Every day I had to move three to five tons of heavy equipment by myself. And then I trained in karate four to six hours per night, five nights a week. This schedule made me very strong. But even with my strength and good training I had difficulty in blocking the punches of some of the Okinawan students. In three-step sparring against Mr. Tamaki, I was able to block his first punch and his second. On his third punch, however, he had so much momentum and power that most of the time I had to just get out of the way or get hit. There would be many repetitions of techniques, hundreds of punches, strikes, blocks, kicks. The workouts varied from day to day, but we always did the basics, covering the same techniques again and again and again. There was a heavy emphasis on fundamentals, such as kata and sanchin. To develop a good stance, strength and balance, we practiced kake-uke on most evenings. This was not practiced as a full strength tug-of-war, as seen in some dojo today. Instead, it was done in a softer, systematic balanced way. I believe this is one of the best goju-ryu karate exercises. I remember many times practicing against Mr. Tamaki. When I tried to exert too much strength on the palm of his hand, he would sense that I was rigid and off balance and sweep me to the floor. I had apprehension at first, and my mind wasn't as calm as it should have been. Eventually, I learned that if I remained calm, without any preconceived ideas, I could sense when he was going to try to sweep me and just lift my foot. This taught me a fundamental principle that you have to relax both your body and mind to detect changes in your opponent. Kake-uke was originally used to pair highly skilled practitioners for kumite. If one student could not move the arm of another student in kake-uke or could not hold his stance, he would not be allowed to engage in kumite with that student. The feeling was that if he couldn't handle the other student in kake-uke, he would not be able to block his punches either. Thus, he could be seriously injured.

Q: Your students practice the arm-toughening drill called kotekitai. Was that practiced at the Meibukan honbu dojo?

A: No. That has been introduced in the Meibukan dojo in the past 20 years. This arm-pounding exercise originated in Taiwan, from Taiwanese kempo. Before that, the students would

toughen their arms by practicing forearm strikes on the makiwara, by hitting their forearms against the trunks of the banyan tree and by blocking each other's punches.

Q: How did the workouts end?

A: Every workout ended with sanchin. Before sanchin, however, we practiced the exercise that I call the flexible horse. Each of us would count to 100. Usually there were 20 or more students, so we did at least 2,000 flexible horses. It was hot and humid there, especially in the summer. So, by the time we finished, we were soaking wet. Sweat would run down our faces, into our eyes and cover the floor. I wouldn't dare wipe the sweat from my eyes. If I did, all of the Okinawan students would give me dagger looks as if to say, "You are doing something that is improper. Can't you take a little physical punishment? Don't you have the mental fortitude to ignore discomfort?" After zazen (sitting meditation) and bowing to the master, we would take off our uniforms and go outside to dry off. The China Sea was only a half a mile from the dojo, and sometimes there would be a cool breeze. In about 10 minutes, it would dry our shorts and we would be able to put on our clothes. Then I would walk three miles to the bus terminal and ride the bus home.

Q: You are known for conducting hard, demanding workouts in your dojo that lasted many hours. Were the workouts in Okinawa harder when you trained there?

A: Although the karate workouts at my dojo are very intensive, the training in Okinawa was even more rigorous. They were continuous workouts. There was rarely a break. When karate practitioners talk about the training in Okinawa in that era, they always talk about how hard it

was physically. They talk about the many hours of daily training, the relentlessness of the workouts, the endless repetition of techniques. But many students never grasped that it wasn't the physical element that was most important. It was the way the training was conducted; it was the mental intensity that counted. When you trained in the dojo, nothing else mattered. The emphasis in the dojo was on developing tremendous powers of concentration in a relaxed environment. The goal was to develop the mental concentration and physical power to be able to move in and stop an opponent with a single technique — one punch, one kick.

Q: What was Grandmaster Meitoku Yagi's approach to makiwara training?

A: Grandmaster Yagi felt that makiwara training was the best method to develop a devastating punch. The makiwara were on the patio of his dojo, which was surrounded by a seven-foot fence for privacy, so no one could view the workouts from the outside. There were six makiwara. How much you hit them was left to your own discretion, but most of us practiced diligently. The makiwara were about three feet from the fence. One of the students would tie a stick to the top of the fence and suspend a string with a stone attached to the end of it, like a plumb line. The makiwara all had a certain amount of give ... usually a few inches. The student would position the string so the stone hung perhaps three inches behind the makiwara. Then we would hit the makiwara and try to move the stone. When we were able to move it easily, we would move the string farther back. Then we had to put more power in the punches.

Sometimes Grandmaster Meitoku Yagi would practice very short punches on the makiwara. He would stand with his feet parallel in front of the makiwara and throw one-inch punches. That makiwara was made of seasoned pine and it had little give. I punched this makiwara on occasion, but I had difficulty in bending it. One night I was going to hit it, and I couldn't find it. When I noticed it, I asked Mr. Yushun Tamaki, Grandmaster Meitoku Yagi's top student, what had happened. He said that Dai Sensei had come out the evening before just as it was getting dark. He positioned himself in front of that makiwara, made a loud sound like "Unh!" and broke the makiwara with a blow of just one inch. Still I wonder all these years later what sort of an awesome punch that must have been to break off the makiwara from that very short distance. When Grandmaster Yagi's son, Sensei Meitetsu Yagi, visited my dojo in Watertown, Massachusetts, several years ago, he said that his father had developed 100 percent of his internal power over his many years of training.

Q: Is it necessary to develop callused hands in makiwara training? Some old pictures of Grandmaster Chojun Miyagi, for instance, show that his knuckles were unblemished.

A: You can practice on the makiwara and not develop callused hands. However, the tops of most makiwara in Okinawa were wrapped with 8 to 10 inches of rice straw rope and this would cut into the knuckles, leading to heavy calluses. But there are other ways to construct a makiwara. Sometimes they would cover the top with a blanket and this arrangement would not cut into the knuckles. It is possible to have normallooking hands and still develop a powerful karate punch. Many people misunderstand makiwara training. They mistakenly believe that the goal is to beat the hands and develop huge calluses, but the real emphasis is on strengthening the hands and wrists, so the wrist will not buckle if you have to hit someone. Also, makiwara training encourages good stances. If your stances are weak, your punching techniques will also be weak. The makiwara exposes this. We did not hit the makiwara an equal number of times with each hand. I was told that if you are right-handed, you should hit the makiwara three times as often with your left hand and viceversa for left-handers .For example, being right-handed, if l hit the makiwara 500 times with the right fist, I would strike the makiwara 1,500 times with the left fist. This way a student develops ambidextrous power.

Q: In the practice of kata, was there much discussion of the meaning of particular moves and their applications?

A: There was very little explanation of the meaning of the kata, and there was no discussion of terminology. There was very little talking at all. The emphasis in the training was on doing rather than discussing. Some of the simple applications of the kata were obvious to us. Sometimes Grandmaster Meitoku Yagi would ask Mr. Yushun Tamaki to attack him, and then he would demonstrate an application. Many times, however, the applications were left to the student's imagination and inquisitiveness. This is a logical approach that forces students to think. Some of the techniques in the kata are obvious: a strike here, a block there, a counter there. However, many of the applications are very difficult to figure out and are sometimes the opposite of what a karateka thinks. There can also be many applications from a single technique. I was told that masters in China would intentionally keep the advanced applications of their techniques secret, so masters from other styles would not learn their hidden fighting techniques. Someone once asked Grandmaster Yagi if gojuryu karate had any gokui or hiden as other martial arts did. Gokui are the deep innermost secrets that can be understood only by those who have been training for a long time. Hiden are those secrets passed down and taught only to special students. The grandmaster replied that there were no formal gokui or hiden in gojuryu karate. He did say, however, that every kata had nanjiru gokuden or secrets that you learned yourself. These could only be understood by trial and error. He said that the effort was more important than anything else. The long repeated efforts are the secrets. You learn by yourself, under your teacher's tutelage, little by little, through long repetitive training and hardship. He also pointed out that a beginner and an advanced student, when seeing the same technique or application, will understand completely different things.

My feeling is that an inexperienced student (with only a few years of training) should not worry about applications. Instead, he should work on basics. For someone who has been studying longer, say eight or 10 years, it is healthy to ponder the meaning of the karate techniques. But one shouldn't lose any sleep over it. In an actual fighting situation, it is not the conscious applications that count; it is the spontaneous subconscious reflex reactions that count.

Q: What do you mean by that?

A: Karate is not a purely physical art. It has physical, mental and spiritual aspects. The philosophy of Okinawan karate — and gojuryu in particular — is that in training the body the practitioner is also subconsciously training the mind. This is the tremendous richness that exists in true karate. As the body trains naturally, so does the mind. For a beginner, all the movements are mechanical and must be done consciously by repetition. The conscious and subconscious minds clash with each other. The student has to learn by highly repetitive efforts. There are no short cuts. The student has to think about keeping the footwork right, the body straight, the shoulders down, the eyes looking forward and the breathing regular. After two or three years of this training, the movements become less mechanical. After 10 or 15 years, the movements become effortless and automatic. In the case of an attack, the practitioner will react spontaneously. The subconscious mind will take over, and the movements will be lightning fast. If the reactions of the practitioner are conscious, they will be too slow and to the point of being mechanical. In the advanced practitioner, there is no differentiation between blocking and striking or offense and defense. It is all included in one movement. This is the by-product of years of training the mind as the body is conditioned.

Q: What was Grandmaster Yagi like when he was in the dojo? Was he approachable?

A: I would say that he had a certain amount of approachability, but — out of respect — I would not approach him often. If I asked a question about an application, for instance, he would often stop and call his senior student, Mr. Yushun Tamaki, and explain the particular movement. But sometimes he would not explain anything at all. Everybody respected him. There was a great esprit de corps, and there was also a sense of good, harmonious human relations. The dojo was not run in a highhanded manner. In some other dojo, I noticed, the masters kept aloof from the students and would get highly annoyed if someone asked about an application from a particular kata.

Q: Was freefighting practiced at Grandmaster Meitoku Yagi's dojo?

A: No. Grandmaster Meitoku Yagi was, and is still, very much opposed to free-fighting. There has never been free-fighting in traditional Okinawan gojuryu karatedo. There have been some experiments, but they have been dropped. Chojun Miyagi himself tried the idea of freestyle sparring with protective equipment more than a half century ago, but he cast the idea aside because he felt there wasn't any equipment that could cover all the vital areas.

Grandmaster Meitoku Yagi felt that the emphasis in gojuryu karate should be karatedo … karate as a way of life. He said that there was a spirit of Budo in karate that is different from the spirit of sports. Grandmaster Yagi felt that free-fighting takes the true essence away from karatedo. In free-fighting, karate becomes a sport, and true karatedo is not a sport. That is why free-fighting was taboo. It detracts from karate-do, brings bad feelings into the dojo and students suffer injuries. We practiced very spirited pre-arranged kumite in Grandmaster Yagi's dojo, but

we did not engage in free-fighting.

Q: Don't you think it is necessary to engage in freefighting to achieve good fighting skills in the street?

A: No. Let's say a person has been practicing karatedo very diligently for five to 10 years. After so much practice, a student should have developed good strong techniques, fast reflexes and he should be able to defend himself against any unprovoked attack. Free-fighting can hinder the development of good karate techniques, especially in Okinawan gojuryu in which the emphasis is on ending a fight with a single devastating technique. Fighting in a ring and fighting in the street are different situations. Many techniques are not allowed in free-fighting. Because of this, freefighting can actually limit the practitioner. Okinawan karate is meant to be a lifetime practice. Grandmaster Meitoku Yagi still practices everyday at age 78. A student who regularly engages in free-fighting is unlikely to be able to practice karate for more than a few years. I don't allow freefighting in my dojo.

Q: Are any of your fellow students at Grandmaster Yagi's school still practicing today?

A: Yes. Several have become distinguished masters. The most prominent student in Grandmaster Yagi's Meibukan dojo was Yushun Tamaki. Today, he is a ninth-degree black belt master. He has retired from the dojo, but he still practices daily. He is the true embodiment of what a karate master should be. He is highly skillful, he is tremendously powerful, and he is polite, humble, unassuming and hard working. His kata and technical skills are exceptional. Both of Grandmaster Yagi's sons were students at the dojo when I was there. The younger son, Meitetsu Yagi, was about 9 or 10 years of age in those days, but he was already a highly spirited student. He is an eighthdegree black belt master today ... a strong, skilled and energetic karateka. He has a dojo in the village of Nagata. He came to teach in my school in Watertown, Massachusetts, several years ago. My students became familiar with his favorite English word: "Endure!" He would repeat this throughout his demanding workouts. The older son, Meitatsu Yagi, was in his early teens when I first trained with him. He was slender, and his movements were fluid and strong. Today, he is a ninthdegree black belt master and was inaugurated as the chairman of the AllOkinawan Gojuryu Karatedo Association on June 25, 1989. He is a powerful master with beautiful kata. He also came to teach at my dojo several years ago. Sensei Meitatsu Yagi has always been a very strict and powerful karate master. In addition to being the chief instructor at the Meibukan Honbu (headquarters) Dojo in Kume, Naha City, Okinawa, he is also the president of the Okinawan Meibukan Gojuryu Karatedo Association. Sensei Meitetsu Yagi is the vice-president and Grandmaster Meitoku Yagi is the chairman of the Association.

Q: One reads a lot of conflicting information about the practice of sanchin. No other kata seems to cause as much confusion. How was sanchin presented to you in Okinawa?

A: Sanchin is the kihon kata, the basic kata, of Okinawan Gojuryu. It has many purposes. One of them is to train the practitioner in bringing forth strength. According to Chinese masters, the human psychic/psyche center dwells in the tan tien, one and a half inches below the navel. This is referred to in many Chinese Taoist texts as the spiritual cauldron. Sanchin emphasizes strengthening of the jan tien. The karateka who practices sanchin for many years will develop a strong physique and tremendous power through enhanced flow of ki, the immaterial substance of life and energy. Sanchin will calm a student, develop composure and enhance selfcontrol. It also has many physical benefits, such as controlled breathing and the ability to withstand an opponent's attack. It's very important in the development of fighting skills. If a person pants and loses control of his breathing, he will lose control of his techniques and ultimately of himself. Another purpose of sanchin practice is to harden the entire body through dynamic tension breathing. I remember a demonstration in Okinawa more than 32 years ago by a master who had an extremely powerful sanchin. His breathing sounded like the roar of a lion, and he exuded tremendous vitality and power. I asked an Okinawan friend who he was. It turned out that he was a master who only practiced sanchin … no other kata. He was in his late fifties and had been practicing sanchin eight times in the morning and eight times at night for 35 years!

In my opinion, sanchin is of the utmost importance for a karateka trying to master gojuryu karate. If a person neglects sanchin, it will affect his entire gojuryu karate training. The teachings of gojuryu are founded on the sanchin principles of proper inhalation and exhalation and the expansion and contraction of the lower abdomen. At Grandmaster Kanryo Higaonna's dojo, the students performed nothing but sanchin and basic techniques for the first three to four years of training. This kata is normally practiced with three steps forward and three steps back and then one step forward and one back. At Grandmaster Kanryo Higaonna's dojo, it was sometimes performed with 15, 20 or 25 steps forward and the same back. This karate training based on sanchin was very intensive and demanding.

Q: Do you think a practitioner can damage himself through improper practice of sanchin?

A: Yes. If a student doesn't practice sanchin properly, he could hurt himself. A practitioner must have good sound instruction.

Q: You saw many grandmasters perform and teach sanchin. Have you ever seen it performed silently, with no audible breathing?

A: No, never. The level of breathing varied from school to school, but I've never known it to be performed silently.

Q: Was there more than one version of sanchin practiced at Grandmaster Yagi's dojo?

A: Yes, there were two versions. Originally, the sanchin that Grandmaster Kanryo Higaonna brought back from the Fukien province in China was done openhanded. On various occasions, Grandmaster Meitoku Yagi would have us perform this version. But the sanchin we practiced most was the closedhand version Grandmaster Yagi learned from Grandmaster Chojun Miyagi.

Q: Was the sanchin testing similar at the respective dojo of Grandmasters Seikichi Toguchi and Meitoku Yagi?

A: No. Sanchin testing at Grandmaster Toguchi's dojo was harder and more dynamic. There was a lot of pounding on the shoulders to keep them down. Also, the testing of the legs was more intense. On the other hand, the testing at Grandmaster Yagi's dojo was slightly softer and more natural. There was more emphasis on posture and the proper positioning of the arms relative to the body. The hitting of the shoulders and legs was a little lighter. Great emphasis was also placed on proper breathing control, as well as tensing of the whole body.

Q: From your description, there seems to have been a powerful, unspoken etiquette in these Okinawan dojo. Did your masters discuss this?

A: Yes. My second gojuryu karate master, Ryuritsu Arakaki, told me that if we take the morality, the ethics and the meditative aspects out of karate, we're left with only animal skills. In karate, he said, we learn to fight like lions, tigers, monkeys, cranes, bears, dragons and the other animals from which we have adopted our fighting techniques. What balances this knowledge is the moral training imparted with the fighting skills. If you take the morality away from karate training, then you're left with something dangerously close to brutality. This is why dojo kun is so important. No unseemly behavior, no rudeness, no harshness and no brutality was allowed in any of the Okinawan dojo I visited. The true philosophical concept of Okinawan gojuryu karate is to seek the way of virtue. In karate, through training the body and mind, we strive to cultivate the ideal human nature of physical, mental and spiritual unity. The Okinawan masters felt that students should strive to be virtuous and pursue the ultimate goal, which is to win any situation with any skills but fighting. Grandmaster Kanryo Higaonna was the leading Confucian scholar on Okinawa. In the Confucian Analects, there is tremendous emphasis on filial piety. Grandmaster Kanryo Higaonna stressed that his students should have respect for themselves, their fellow students, families and life in general. Dojo kun reflects this aspect of karate training.

Q: You mentioned that the atmosphere in Grandmaster Meitoku Yagi's dojo was peaceful and relaxed. This sounds quite different from many modern karate schools, where the training is held in a stressful, almost militaristic environment.

A: Yes. We trained with a very relaxed but alert state of mind. The master conducted the training with a soft, subtle hand. There was no militaristic atmosphere, no rudeness, no harsh commands. You were expected to train with the attitude of a hawk that was ready to pounce on its prey. You needed a heightened concentration stemming from a relaxed state of mind. The most important aspect in karate training is the student's mental attitude. If the student entertains fear, apprehension and rancor, his movements are likely to become stiff, rigid and slow. Nervousness and a disturbed emotional state will cloud judgment and perception of an opponent. The training at the Meibukan dojo cultivated a calm, tranquil, alert state of mind.

There is a story about Yatsusune Azato, the famous Shurite master who lived in Okinawa in the late 19th and early 20th centuries. Some say his skills in karate and swordsmanship were unsurpassed. He once fought a duel against the most famous swordsman in the Ryukyu Islands, a tremendously powerful man named Yorin Kanna. He chose to fight unarmed, even though Kanna was armed with a long sword. Azato surprised Kanna by parrying his initial attack with a turn of the hand and then — with a lightning-fast karate technique — drove Kanna to his knees and ended the duel without killing him. He later told his students that Kanna was a swordsman of great skill who, because of his fearsome reputation, was able to terrify his opponents at the very beginning of duels. In every match, he immediately would go for the kill. Azato explained to his students that victory is possible if a practitioner refuses to be terrified and remains calm. It is not easy to remain calm and unperturbed in stressful situations. To develop a calm, undisturbed mind requires many years of training.

Q: Did you have a chance to view non-Okinawan martial arts during your years in Okinawa?

A: Yes. I traveled extensively in Japan, Taiwan, Korea and Hong Kong. I have an avid interest in the history of the martial arts. I visited many martial arts schools, observed a variety of styles and met prominent masters. I still keep in touch with many of them today. For instance, I met the eminent Hung Master and famous Chinese actor Dr. Kwan Tak Hing in Hong Kong in 1968. I still keep in touch with him today and value his friendship greatly. He visited and demonstrated his Hung style of Chinese martial arts in my dojo. His demonstration was so impressive that my students still recall his outstanding techniques and forms. He demonstrated all of the Shaolin Monastery animal movements.

Q: Detractors of Okinawan karate maintain that Okinawa was a cultural backwater and that it was the Japanese who breathed life into Okinawan karate. How would you respond to this?

A: I would say that this is not true. These claims are based on a limited knowledge of Okinawan karate. Sure, there is merit in what the Japanese and other outsiders have done for Okinawan karate. They have helped make karate popular, and it is now practiced all over the world. And yes, there have been some external changes in Okinawan karate attributable to outside influences. But the essence of Okinawan karate has not been changed. It was and is

extremely rich and powerful. Karate is a pure Okinawan traditional art. It is part of the Okinawan culture. Throughout the world, Japan is called the "Home of karate." But in Japan, Okinawa is called the "Home of karate." In Okinawa, karate has been practiced for more than 1,000 years. Outside of Okinawa, karate has been practiced since 1923.Now where do you think the vast store of knowledge would be?

The Okinawans are the true masters of the art and they have a deep knowledge and repertoire. Okinawans are humble, peaceloving people. Like the Chinese, they refrain from ostentatious display, wild claims and ego trips. They do not brag about their knowledge or skills. These traits are assets in most cases. But they can also be liabilities, in that the Okinawan karate masters often don't bother to refute the excessive claims of others. There are many karate masters making great claims for themselves who have far less skill than the great Okinawan karate masters such as Juhatsu Kiyoda, Seiko Higa, Meitoku Yagi and Shinken Taira. These masters were not interested in promoting themselves. As for those who would say that 19th-century Okinawan martial arts were not of a particularly high standard, this is based on hearsay from the reports of travelers and old photographs. Did these people ever stand in front of Ankoh Itosu, Kanryo Higaonna or Yatsusune Azato in combat? Nineteenth century Okinawan karate masters were extremely powerful. Their skills were highly sophisticated and deadly. But until 1902, the art was taught in complete secrecy, and it was taught only to a select few. Outsiders traveling to Okinawa obviously wouldn't be shown these secret arts. And you can't judge the skills of masters by photographs. The only way to find out about the history of Okinawan karatedo is by going to Okinawa and studying with the masters. The history of Okinawan karate-do is not in books. I was fortunate to be in Okinawa during the golden era of karate, when karate was slowly being presented to the outside world. I lived there in an era when Okinawan karate masters were beginning to selectively teach their unique art of karatedo.

Many outsiders went to Okinawa to study karate. But many of them studied Okinawa karate for a relatively brief period, sometimes for as little as a few months. They might have learned a small part of the art and then gone back home. Many of them, because of their limited knowledge, eventually came to a stumbling block and could progress no further. This does not mean

GOJU RYU LEGENDS

that the art is not sophisticated but that many practitioners have incomplete and limited knowledge of it.

Q: You met many great Okinawan karate masters. How do these masters compare to modern karate practitioners?

A: There is no comparison whatsoever. These great Okinawan karate masters are in a class by themselves because they trained intensively their entire lives — day in and day out — year after year. They were highly motivated to perfect and master their art. For modern practitioners, there are many distractions and less time is spent training.

Q: According to the masters you studied with in Okinawa, under what circumstances should karate be used?

A: They taught that a karateka should use his karate fighting skills only when there is no alternative. In Japan, according to Grandmaster Meitoku Yagi, if someone spit in the face of a samurai, the samurai would bring forth his "Budo" and cut the person's head off with his katana. In Okinawan Budo, he said, there is a saying that deals with this situation much differently. It says, "If someone spits in your face, just wipe it off. That's all." One must use karate, he said, only when one's life is in peril. This is a moral principle of karate that is emphasized in Okinawa. The philosophy at the Meibukan dojo was to avoid any situation that could lead to a physical confrontation. By employing a superior mental attitude, a karate practitioner can find many ways of defusing a confrontation before it becomes a fighting situation. Once, during the late 1930s, Mr. Meitoku Yagi was in a teahouse with his friend Mr. Ryuritsu Arakaki. At that time, Mr. Yagi had a reputation as a prominent karate practitioner. An Okinawan ruffian happened to be there and decided to challenge Mr. Yagi to fight. He dropped into a low stance in front of Mr. Yagi and shouted: "I am going to fight you." Mr. Yagi looked him up and down, and in a very calm, posed manner said: "With that stance?" The ruffian suddenly lost all his confidence and fled the teahouse.

Q: What philosophical and ethical concepts did the masters pass down to Okinawan karate practitioners?

A: The Okinawan masters taught that the karate practitioner should refrain from pettiness and trivialities. Ankoh Itosu, the great Okinawan Shurite grandmaster, said: "The more a karateka practices, the more modest he should be."

The great Okinawan nahate Grandmaster Kanryo Higaonna left an important philosophical saying for future generations: "Those who train in the great Okinawan art of karate should help others. Never seek trouble and refrain from arguments and senseless fights." The founder of gojuryu karate, Grandmaster Chojun Miyagi, taught his students the ethical philosophy of avoiding any serious incidents or confrontations that could lead to a fight. He also said: "Do not hit anybody and do not let anybody hit you." The karateka should strive to have a very calm and unperturbed nature and avoid situations in which it might be necessary to resort to physical confrontation. The greatest form of self-defense is to avoid situations in which self-defense will be necessary. Discretion is the better part of valor.

Q: Could you explain the meaning of the practice of karatedo?

A: Traditionally on Okinawa, gojuryu karate is taught as karatedo or as a "way of life." "Do" is the Japanese pronunciation of the Chinese ideograph tao. Tao, or "the way," is the dominant idea of all Chinese philosophy, the foundation of the ancient Chinese world concept. All things are indissolubly interrelated and influenced by each other. In karatedo, the training will influence the practitioner, and the practitioner will influence the training. The balance between the karateka and his art is influenced by the manner and presentation of the training. Karatedo seeks to attain that most harmonious stage so the karateka will follow the true philosophical concept of karate as a way of life. The practice of karatedo is training with the awareness of jingi (humanity, morality and an ethical code of conduct). It is very dangerous to teach karate without teaching the Do. Do is the true philosophical concept of karate, as it teaches the importance of moderation.

Following is an Okinawan saying, "If the heart is right, then the hand will be right." The karate masters of Okinawa emphasize setting the heart of the student right from the beginning. In the traditional long, slow, patient approach, the true essence of karate is not distorted.

Q: Did you study kobudo under the eminent Grandmaster Shinken Taira?

A: Yes. Grandmaster Meitoku Yagi invited his good friend Grandmaster Shinken Taira to his dojo to instruct the students in kobudo. He was a famous kobudo master, a man of very high reputation. He was in his 60s when I studied with him, but he still moved quickly and adroitly. He was graceful and strong, and his techniques were flawless. He was a great master. We studied mostly the sai, tonfa and bo. Grandmaster Shinken Taira was a traditional Okinawan master, firm and strict, but also a jovial and friendly man. It was enjoyable studying under him. He took a liking to me and was very gracious. He asked me to teach his kobudo kata in the United States when I returned.

Q: Most Okinawan kobudo masters have a background in karate. Was Grandmaster Shinken Taira associated with a particular karate style?

A: Yes. He had studied shorinryu going back to Grandmaster Funakoshi's time. He was a student of Kentsu Yabu, but he didn't elaborate about his karate training. He did mention that he used to work out with Grandmaster Funakoshi in his youth. He taught me some shorin kata on the side. I learned kusanhu kata and chinto kata from him.

Q: Hard and soft are among the most difficult concepts for martial artists to understand. These are frequently discussed in gojuryu karate. What is your interpretation of these terms?

A: When a karateka starts talking about hard and soft, he starts falling into dualistic thinking. The hard and the soft are not separated in true gojuryu karate. The hard and the soft are harmoniously interwoven. It is very difficult to tell when one leaves off and the other takes over. There is hardness in softness and softness in hardness. They complement each other. Many masters in Okinawa spoke to me about the hard and soft aspects of gojuryu karate. The hard external side of karate is easy to understand and practice. The soft side is deceptive and more difficult to develop. When karate students who have developed the soft internal side of their art go through kata, you can notice something different about their performance … something mysterious that is difficult to put a finger on and something unique that denotes a superior mastery. There is a different emotional state in the practitioner. There is something that is not sheer physical strength. Something not based solely on muscular contraction and expansion but based on inner force, the circulation of chi, which has an explosive, devastating power. Hard and soft can only be understood through long practice. In gojuryu, the practice of sanchin and tensho enhance the development of soft internal powers. When I was training in gojuryu karate at the Meibukan dojo, I witnessed Grandmaster Meitoku Yagi's mastery of the hard and soft aspects of gojuryu karate when he taught and demonstrated the various kata. His mastery, especially of the soft inner aspect, was superb. His top student, Master Yushun Tamaki, also showed great inner strength when performing kata and techniques.

Q: Is it true that some techniques do not require power or physical force?

A: No. I do not believe that such a thing exists. I had the honor of meeting the great Tai Chi Chuan master Dr. Cheng Manch'ing. The famous Chinese Grandmaster, Yang Chengfu, who was in Shanghai, taught Dr. Cheng Manch'ing. Dr. Cheng Manch'ing told me that he once asked Yang Cheng Fu to practice pushing hands with him. While they were practicing, he said that Yang Cheng Fu put his hand on Dr. Cheng Manch'ing's throat. He said the hand felt like soft velvet. Suddenly, Dr. Cheng Manch'ing was propelled more than 10 feet backwards against the wall, hitting with so much force that he was knocked out for half an hour. He said that was the first and last time he asked to perform pushing hands with his master. So, there is even strength in soft techniques. There is no such thing as magic. Although the internal energy (ki) looks like magic to the untrained eye, it has great power and physical force when the internal energy is brought forth.

Q: Do you think karate training can increase extrasensory perception?

A: Yes, it might. Master Ryuritsu Arakaki told me that some karate masters do possess extrasensory perception. He said that one day when he and Mr. Meitoku Yagi were training with Grandmaster Chojun Miyagi during the late 1930s in a Naha park, he and Mr. Yagi were walking together. Mr. Meitoku Yagi was a few feet in front of him, so Mr. Arakaki began thinking, "What could Mr. Yagi do if I suddenly hit him from behind? There is nothing he could do because he is walking in front of me." At that precise moment, Mr. Yagi turned around, looked at Mr. Arakaki straight in the eye and said: "What do you have in mind? You want to punch me, don't you?"

Mr. Yagi's younger son, Meitetsu, described to me another incident. He said that when his father was a police officer around 1938, Mr. Yagi arrested an Okinawan for disturbing the peace and causing trouble in a business district in Naha. When he took him to the police station, the man threatened to kill Mr. Yagi. Six months later, Mr. Yagi was walking home late at night on a dirt road. It was pitch dark and the road was lined with heavy bushes on both sides. The Okinawan, whose name was Mr. N, was waiting behind a bush with a knife. When Mr. Yagi was about 20 feet away, he stopped and shouted: "Mr. N. You are hiding there with a knife, and you want to kill me, don't you?" The man ran away because he was so unnerved by the fact that Mr. Yagi could sense the danger without even seeing him. When I was training in Mr. Yagi's dojo, I repeatedly had the feeling that Mr. Yagi could sense my innermost thoughts. He has extrasensory powers developed by his karate training.

Q: In the 1950s, what did the Okinawans think of foreign students?

A: The Okinawans were skeptical and with good reason. The karate masters wanted to know the true intentions and characters of all their students. The masters were very observant, and I felt I was watched very closely at first. Eventually, after I proved that I could handle the physical and mental rigors of the training, I felt accepted. I had to show that I was sincerely and honestly interested in learning the art of goju-ryu karate-do. In 1958, I represented the Meibukan at a large martial arts demonstration in Ginoza, which is in Central Okinawa. There were more than 2,000 people in attendance. I was the only Westerner participating. When I got up to perform shisochin kata, the crowd began booing and whistling. When they saw me performing and recognized that I was a serious student, they calmed down. When I finished, they gave me one of the biggest ovations of the day. After the demonstration, some of the Okinawan karate masters commended me on my performance. Okinawans were very gracious and friendly once they saw that you had a respectful and sincere attitude towards their national art of karate.

Q: What differences do you find in the way Okinawans and Westerners approach karate?

A: In Okinawa, and in Asia in general, one of the goals of karate training is to minimize the ego. In the West, unfortunately, the emphasis in much of martial art training is in building the ego, which is quite the opposite of the training in Okinawa. There's a saying in Okinawa that comes to mind. "When the rice grain is plentiful, the stalk bows. When empty, it stands tall." This saying is analogous to the Westerner saying, "An empty barrel is apt to make the most noise." The Okinawans are generally more disciplined, patient and motivated than Westerners in their approach to karate training. Also, the Okinawans have an initial advantage as karate is their national art. Therefore, the Okinawans have a better awareness of the goals of karate training than Westerners. In the beginning, self-imposed discipline will make the karateka feel uncomfortable and restricted. Okinawans understand and accept this, while most Western karate practitioners are unwilling to endure this initial hardship. After a while, of course, the self-imposed discipline brings the practitioner tremendous inner freedom and harmony.

Q: What were the major styles of karate practiced in Okinawa when you lived there?

A: The major, official styles of Okinawan karate, as recognized by the Zen Okinawa Karate-do Remmei, were goju-ryu, uechi-ryu, matsubayashi shorin-ryu and kobayashi shorin-ryu. These were the four preeminent styles. This is still true today.

GOJU RYU LEGENDS

Q: Were relations between the major styles friendly?

A: Yes. I frequently attended the meetings of the Zen Okinawa Karate-do Remmei in Naha City. This is where the leading masters and their top students would come together and discuss matters of mutual concern, including how best to enhance the development of Okinawan karate, how best to present it, standards of etiquette and standards of promotion. I attended these meetings with my second karate master, Ryuritsu Arakaki, and also occasionally with Grandmaster Meitoku Yagi. These were very polite, dignified gatherings. The masters were courteous to each other and presented their views in a dignified, respectful manner.

Q: Did you meet the leading masters of the other styles?

A: Yes. I met many of them. The head of the kobayashi style of shorin-ryu was the late Grandmaster Chosen Chibana, and I met him several times at the Okinawa Karate-do Remmei meetings. These were held at the dojo of Grandmaster Shoshin Nagamine, who was the head of the matsubayashi style of shorin-ryu. I also visited Grandmaster Kanei Uechi's dojo many times.

Q: How did you happen to visit Grandmaster Nagamine's dojo?

A: Goju-ryu karate Master Ryuritsu Arakaki invited me to attend one of the meetings. At that time, Master Arakaki introduced me to Grandmaster Nagamine, and I also met many of his students.

Q: Did you ever visit his dojo again?

A: Yes, I would visit his dojo periodically, as the meetings of the All-Okinawan Karate-do Association were held there. I was the only Westerner present at these meetings. As time went on, I became friends with many of his karate students. Some of them were brown and black belts who were very impressive and powerful. Grandmaster Nagamine is one of the most respected and skilled grandmasters on Okinawa, and it was a great honor to have met him.

Q: What were the workouts like at his dojo?

A: The practice at his dojo included a lot of weight lifting. They had a full range of barbells, dumbbells and other free weights, and they practiced many different weight-lifting techniques. Grandmaster Nagamine told me that he encouraged his students to engage in strength building as well as karate training. Even though the students were muscular, I noticed they had excellent speed and reflexes. They were powerful karateka. I still remember seeing one of Grandmaster Nagamine's top students, Omine, throwing sequences of punching techniques. I could hear the sound of his punches breaking the air all the way across the dojo.

Q: Did they practice free-fighting?

A: No. Everything was prearranged. The emphasis in the karate training was very traditional … from the kata to the drills to the prearranged kumite.

Q: How was the training at Grandmaster Kanei Uechi's dojo?

A: I visited Grandmaster Kanei Uechi's dojo in Futenma City many times. He is a highly respected and very powerful grandmaster. Uechi-ryu and goju-ryu karate systems have a natural affinity. They both were influenced by the martial arts of Fukien Province in China and have a common geographical background. The uechi-ryu karate training was very intense, and the students were superb karateka. They had a controlled form of free-fighting that featured classical uechi techniques. They exercised enough control that they stopped their techniques short of full contact.

Q: What was your impression of their unusual method of kicking? I'm referring to their toe kicks.

A: Their toe kicks were devastating and very impressive. They toughened their toes by hitting them against baseboards and other hard objects. I saw one student break five wooden boards just with his big toe.

Q: I've seen films of their sanchin testing. Perhaps it was only because of the camera, but it looked extremely hard. Were the students really being tested that hard?

A: Yes, it was hard. I remember seeing 2-inch-by-4-inch boards broken over the students' arms, legs and abdomens. I saw Grandmaster Kanei Uechi, in a horse stance, testing the sanchin by hitting the students in the abdomen with hard punches. The students looked rugged and highly conditioned, and it appeared as if their entire bodies had been hardened through sanchin training and testing.

Q: Did you meet other eminent goju-ryu karate masters?

A: Yes, several. I met the late Grandmaster Seiko Higa many times. He was an excellent teacher and had been Grandmaster Chojun Miyagi's assistant. When I met Grandmaster Higa, he was in his late 50s. When he performed goju-ryu kata, he had great power, speed and control. As a master gets older, the techniques do not depend as much on physical technique as on internal strength.

Q: Grandmaster Kanryo Higaonna's most famous students were Chojun Miyagi and Juhatsu Kiyoda. Did you ever meet Grandmaster Kiyoda?

A: Yes. I had the great honor of meeting him in 1958 at his home in the city of Beppu, Kyushu, in Japan. He was in his early 70s when I met him, and he was an extremely powerful man. His posture was erect. He had a strong voice, and his eyes were very sharp and penetrating. He was a large man. I saw a photograph of him in his younger years, and he was six feet tall or more and perhaps 180 to 190 pounds. He had a very muscular build. Grandmaster Kiyoda told me that the study of kata should be supreme. He said: "The true karate is in the practice of the kata, and the practice of kata is true karate." I will never forget those words. I also met his son, who was more than 6 feet tall and around 200 pounds. They showed me their photo album that went back many years. They had a variety of group photographs with Grandmaster Kanryo

Higaonna that included Juhatsu Kiyoda, Chojun Miyagi, Kenwa Mabuni, Higa Seiko and many other great Okinawan karate masters. There was one particular photograph of Juhatsu Kiyoda wearing the traditional black uniform used in Okinawan festivals. He was holding a thick wooden pole about six feet long. I asked his son what Grandmaster Juhatsu Kiyoda was doing. When practicing karate in Okinawa around 1920, two advanced students would sometimes be paired in a controlled version of free-fighting, he said. This fighting was designed to practice the techniques of a specific style. When the students engaged in kumite, two masters would stand on either side of them. If the action got too fierce and there was the possibility of severe injury or even death, the masters would cross the poles in front of the students and end the fight. He said that this was a very fierce form of kumite that was practiced only by highly trained karateka.

Q: Grandmaster Miyagi's teacher, Grandmaster Higaonna, who trained in China for more than 20 years, laid the foundation of goju-ryu karate. Is there one particular Chinese style to which goju-ryu is related?

A: Yes. Okinawan goju-ryu karate is related to Chinese chuan-fa. Kanryo Higaonna sailed to Foochow in the Fukien Province, China, when he was 15. There he met the famous Chinese chuan-fa Grandmaster, Liu Liu Ko with whom he studied for more than 20 years. Kanryo Higaonna became Grandmaster Liu Liu Ko's top student. Little is known about the actual style that Liu Liu Ko taught. Some karate masters say it was the hung style; others say it was another style that had been indigenous to Fukien Province for more than 1,000 years.

Q: Who was Grandmaster Liu Liu Ko?

A: There isn't much written information on Grandmaster Liu Liu Ko. I was told that he was of the Chinese nobility and had been tested to become the equivalent of a knight three different times. He failed the imperial test at age 37 and again at age 50. On his 73rd birthday he was tested again, before the Emperor of China, after walking hundreds of feet carrying a rock weighing 180 kilos strapped to his back. When Grandmaster Liu Liu Ko arrived in front of the Emperor, he performed sanchin kata and passed the test. The Emperor then knighted him. Grandmaster Liu Liu Ko's training was said to have been very arduous. Anyone who aspires to practice karate must keep in mind the Chinese character "Nin," which means "to endure." There is no easy way of attaining mastery. It was through this long and difficult kind of training that Grandmaster Kanryo Higaonna was able to develop his exceptional skills. In 1890, he returned to Okinawa and began teaching in Naha. His skill, knowledge and dedication soon became legendary.

Q: When he returned to Okinawa from China, did Grandmaster Higaonna make changes to the Chinese martial art that he learned from Grandmaster Liu Liu Ko?

A: Yes. Grandmaster Higaonna did make changes to the Chinese martial art that he learned in the Fukien Province, China. Even though the style that he mastered in China was superb, he felt the need to revise and adapt some of the techniques to make his art suitable to the Okinawan lifestyle and culture. Also, Grandmaster Higaonna, for some unknown reason, changed the name of the highest kata from the Chinese pronunciation yepatlinpa (meaning 108) to suparimpei.

Q: Was Grandmaster Higaonna a strict karate master?

A: Yes, a very strict teacher. He would not allow or teach any student with a violent nature. He was very selective as to whom he accepted. His training was very strenuous. The sanchin kata was practiced for three to four hours during each session. A new student was taught only the sanchin kata and this went on for as long as three to four years before going into another kata. While practicing the sanchin, some of the students would collapse from sheer exhaustion. That's how intense Grandmaster Kanryo Higaonna's training was. The sanchin kata taught at that time by Grandmaster Higaonna was performed open-handed. When Grandmaster Higaonna demonstrated his sanchin breathing kata, he would occasionally allow four Okinawans to try and dislodge him from his standing position. They could not move him. When he finished the sanchin kata, the floor where he stood would be hot from the friction of his toes gripping the floor.

Q: Who were Grandmaster Higaonna's top students?

A: Juhatsu Kiyoda, Chojun Miyagi and Kenwa Mabuni. Miyagi founded goju-ryu karate from Nahate; Kiyoda founded toon-ryu, a karate system named after the first character in Grandmaster Higaonna's name; and Mabuni founded shito-ryu karate.

Q: Did Grandmaster Miyagi make any changes in the naha-te system that he inherited from Grandmaster Higaonna?

A: Yes, Grandmaster Miyagi studied with Grandmaster Kanryo Higaonna for 13 years. Upon his master's death, Miyagi went to China for two years to conduct further research into the martial arts. While he was in China, he met and befriended the Chinese White Crane Master, Go Ken Kin. Miyagi then traveled around with him to several provinces, studying with a number of great Chinese masters. When Chojun Miyagi returned to Okinawa, he decided to take the art of Naha-te and expose it to scientific scrutiny. His approach was very critical, and he discarded the techniques that did not meet strict scientific standards. Chojun Miyagi incorporated many Chinese martial arts techniques that he had learned while in China to the Naha-te system of Okinawan karate. He refined the existing kata and developed his own kata, gekissai I and II and tensho. Chojun Miyagi designed the auxiliary exercises, kata-bunkai-kumite, and other forms of kumite that are performed in traditional goju-ryu karate training dojo. He modernized the training and developed the structures that we still follow. He also changed the practice of open-hand sanchin to closed-hand sanchin.

Q: What is known of Master Go Ken Kin?

A: He was a Chinese white crane master whom Master Miyagi met in Fukien Province, China, in 1915. They traveled together for two years, visiting and training with Chinese masters of various systems of chuan-fa. Master Go Ken Kin introduced Master Miyagi to many great masters. In 1936, Grandmaster Miyagi visited China again and studied Chinese martial arts at the Seibu Dai Iku Kai (Great Gymnastic Association, Pure Martial Arts Spirit) in Shanghai. Years later, Master Go Ken Kin moved to Japan and lived there under the name Yoshikawa. He passed away in 1940 in Japan at the age of 55.

GOJU RYU LEGENDS

Q: There are many versions of the origin of the name goju-ryu. Where did the name come from?

A: From the old Chinese book Wu Pei Chih (Army Account of Military Arts and Science) by Yuan-i Mao. It was published in 1636. Grandmaster Miyagi named the system of karate goju-ryu (hard/soft style) from the term "goju," which appears in the sentence: "The successful method requires both give and take (go-ju)." When Grandmaster Miyagi was asked why he gave this specific name to his style of karate, he replied that goju defines the hard and soft nature of his style. Grandmaster Miyagi named his style of karate goju-ryu around 1932. He was teaching and promoting goju-ryu karate-do up to the time of his death on October 8, 1953 at the age of 65. He was called the last great samurai warrior of Okinawa because of his legendary strength and skill, as well as his intense dedication to the martial arts.

Q: On what principles did Grandmaster Miyagi base the foundation of goju-ryu karate-do?

A: Grandmaster Miyagi subjected the art of naha-te, as received from Grandmaster Kanryo Higaonna, to strict scientific examination. Originally, a martial arts expert was trained for killing an enemy with one blow. Karate, as such, was unsuitable for the contemporary world. Miyagi studied the basic "go" of sanchin and the six rules and formed the ju or tensho form, thus combining soft and hard movements. He also organized the auxiliary movements designed to help develop karate techniques by strengthening the body through calisthenics. He organized these exercises in preparation for practicing the kaishu kata. Thus, he determined the theory for the practice of karate and organized it as a martial arts educational subject, an art of self-defense and as a spiritual exercise. Grandmaster Miyagi spent his entire life contributing to the improvement and proliferation of karate-do. Before his intervention, karate had been considered a very mysterious practice. By using a scientific approach, Miyagi created, through his goju-ryu karate-do, a clearly defined and universal platform for the art, and that gave it a basis for mass acceptance.

Q: Did Grandmaster Chojun Miyagi receive any awards for his contribution to karate?

A: Yes. In 1936 he received a medal for "Excellence in the Martial Arts" from the Ministry of Education in Japan.

Q: Did he hold any official positions?

A: Yes. In 1928, Grandmaster Miyagi traveled to Japan and taught karate at Kyoto Imperial University, Kansai University and Ritsumeikan University, Kyoto. Miyagi is credited as the first master to introduce karate on an international level. In 1930, Grandmaster Chojun Miyagi became chairman of the Okinawan-ken Taiiku Kyokai Karate-do (Okinawa Prefecture Athletic Association Karate Division). In 1934, he became a permanent officer of the Okinawan branch of the Dai Nippon Butokukai (Great Japan Martial Virtues Association). As a result of his great efforts, karate was recognized officially as one of the martial arts of Japan. In May of 1934, Chinei Kinjo, editor of the Okinawan newspaper Yoen Fiho Sha, invited Grandmaster Miyagi to Hawaii. There he gave lectures and taught in order to promote Okinawan goju-ryu karate-do. He returned to Okinawa in February of 1935. In May of 1937, Prince Moriwasa Nashimoto, Commissioner of the Dai Nippon Butokakai, authorized Miyagi, along with the headmaster of shinto shizen-ryu jujutsu and the headmaster of kushin-ryu (also jujutsu), to form the Dai Nippon Butokukai Karate Jukkyoshi (Great Japan Martial Arts Karate Teachers' Association). They inspected and regulated karate throughout Japan until the dissolution of the association. In 1937, Miyagi received the kyoshi degree from the Dai Nippon Butokukai. In 1946, Grandmaster Miyagi was promoted to an official of the Okinawan Minsei Taiiku Kan (Okinawan Democratic Athletic Association). In 1953, Miyagi was instructing at the Ryukyu Police Academy in Naha City, Okinawa.

Q: What is the origin of the term karate?

A: Originally, this Okinawan fighting art was simply called "Te." Then, the Okinawans made a strict distinction between their native art "Te" and "Tode," which meant "Chinese hand" (for the Chinese art of ch'uan Fa or kempo). The Chinese ideogram "To" of "Tode" means "Chinese" or "Tang" (The Tang dynasty ruled China from 618 to 906 AD). A tremendous cultural revival occurred during the Tang Dynasty that was symbolic of the finest Chinese culture and enlightenment. Because Chinese culture was highly respected in Okinawa, anything labeled "Chinese" was regarded as superior. The word "To" is very elegant and raises the value of everything it is applied to. There is a certain snob appeal in calling anything "To." Gradually, the Okinawans came to apply the term "To" to all "te," especially those of Chinese influence. According to Grandmaster Miyagi, karate, written in this way, is the special word used only in the Ryukyu and it came from the Chinese ch'uan-fa (kempo).

Q: When was tode changed officially to karate?

A: On October 25, 1936, a karate symposium sponsored by Mr. Choju Ota, chief editor of the Ryukyu Shimpo newspaper, was held in the Showa Kaikan, at Naha City, Okinawa. Among the Okinawan karate grandmasters present were Kentsu Yabu, Chotoku Kyan, Chomo Hanashiro, Chokei Motobu, Chojun Miyagi, Juhatsu Kiyoda, Chosen Chibana, Mashige Shimma, Asatada Koyoshi and Eijo Shin. At this conference, it was agreed that the Okinawan martial art, which previously was called "Te" or "Tode," be called karate or "empty hands." From 1936 on, the practitioners of this Okinawan martial art began referring to it as karate, using the ideogram meaning empty hands. In this way, the emphasis shifted from technique alone to spiritual values as well.

Q: At what age did Meitoku Yagi start his training with Grandmaster Miyagi?

A: Meitoku Yagi was 13 years old when his paternal grandfather took him to Grandmaster Miyagi, who was 37 at the time. His grandfather told Grandmaster Miyagi that Meitoku Yagi was a descendant of the leading samurai of Okinawa and the first minister of the three ministers of Okinawa … Jana Oyakata. His grandfather also said: "Meitoku Yagi has Okinawan samurai blood in him, and I think he will be able to take over your place some day in the future, so please teach him your karate." That is how Meitoku Yagi was able to start training under Grandmaster Miyagi in 1925.

GOJU RYU LEGENDS

Q: Jana Oyakata was one of his ancestors. Who was he?

A: He was a very important official in Okinawan history. He was so influential that he escorted the king of Okinawa when the king had to go to the peace talks after the Shimazu clan of Satsuma Province, Japan, defeated the Okinawans during the conflict of Keicho in 1609.

Q: Was it Meitoku Yagi's own decision to start training in karate?

A: No, it wasn't. He didn't have any intention of starting to train in karate, but he had to follow the order of his grandfather.

Q: I gather he came from a strict, traditional background?

A: Yes. Grandmaster Meitoku Yagi has been a life-long resident of Kume Village. The Okinawans said they were more afraid of the people from Kume than the military. This was because the religion of the people of Kume was Confucianism. They were very strict and had a discipline exemplified by the saying: "Stay three feet away from the master, but don't step on his shadow."

Q: Did Grandmaster Miyagi have a formal dojo when Meitoku Yagi started practicing karate in 1925?

A: No. According to Grandmaster Yagi, Grandmaster Miyagi did not have a formal dojo; he taught karate in his backyard, and when it rained, he taught inside his home.

Q: You studied with Grandmaster Miyagi's senior student and met many of his other students. How did they describe the Grandmaster as a person and a teacher?

A: Grandmaster Miyagi's nickname in Okinawan dialect was "Busamagunku" or "samurai" Miyagi. He was a very demanding and strict teacher. Meitoku Yagi began studying with him at age 13, after undergoing an eight-month probationary period during which he had to perform chores around Chojun Miyagi's house and backyard. Grandmaster Meitoku Yagi said that Grandmaster Chojun Miyagi had fierce eyes. "When you saw them," he said, "you wouldn't be able to say a word. You would never dream of telling him something that wasn't true." Grandmaster Miyagi was hard on his students. While doing zazen, he would not allow his students to relax as some of the other karate teachers would; instead, he would make the students sit and meditate for one to two hours without moving. Sanchin was taught one step at a time. Sometimes a single movement would be practiced over and over again for several months ... nothing but one movement for hours a day. When Meitoku Yagi would go to the communal bathhouse, people would see the bruises and welts on his shoulders from Sanchin testing and say: "Aha, you have been training with Chojun Miyagi." Grandmaster Chojun Miyagi placed great emphasis on developing the character of his karate students. He only kept those students who had high moral ethics. He was a strict disciplinarian. One day one of the students arrived for karate training with a towel wrapped around his neck, singing a popular song. Grandmaster Miyagi expelled him from the school. The student tried to apologize for his careless behavior but Grandmaster Chojun Miyagi felt that if a student behaved in front of him in such a careless and disrespectful way, then he would do even worse things away from the master's presence. Grandmaster Meitoku Yagi said that an average person could not have tolerated Grandmaster Miyagi's very intense karate training. You had to be highly motivated. Grandmaster Miyagi would often tell his karate students, "Lions push their cubs over a cliff and they raise only the cubs that are able to struggle back up the cliff. That's how I teach here in my dojo." Grandmaster Miyagi taught only those students who could withstand the rigors of the training. If a student dropped out, he made no effort to draw him back.

Q: What were Grandmaster Miyagi's favorite kata and techniques?

A: I was told in Okinawa that Grandmaster Chojun Miyagi's favorite kata was shisochin. He had exceptionally powerful open-hand techniques, especially nuki-te. Open-hand techniques take much longer to master than closed-hand techniques. His other favorite kata were sanchin and tensho. Grandmaster Miyagi had very strong punching and kicking techniques. His punches and kicks had explosive power. He was said to have superhuman strength. Grandmaster Miyagi was renowned for having a vice-like grip. It was said that he could put his hand on a four- or five-pound piece of raw meat and squeeze it into hamburger. When he was in China, I was told that he dropped his wallet in a rickshaw. When he went back to get it, the rickshaw driver refused to hand it over and tried to strike him. Grandmaster Miyagi instantly grabbed the driver's forearm and squeezed so hard that it paralyzed his arm, forcing the driver to give the wallet back.

Q: Did Grandmaster Miyagi teach different versions of the kata to students according to their level of development?

A: Yes. As Grandmaster Chojun Miyagi kept teaching, he kept refining the kata. Also, he taught beginners simplified versions of the kata. Later, as they practiced longer and learned more, they were taught more refined, advanced versions. Therefore, in evaluating the level of any goju-ryu kata, you have to know how long the master studied with Grandmaster Chojun Miyagi. He taught slowly and patiently. Clearly, someone who studied with him for a few years would not have kata and techniques as sophisticated and advanced as someone who studied and practiced with him for decades.

Q: Who was Grandmaster Chojun Miyagi's top student and successor?

A: Grandmaster Meitoku Yagi was the top student and successor to Grandmaster Miyagi. He studied with him from 1925 to 1953. He learned the most advanced and sophisticated versions of goju-ryu kata and techniques. The Meibukan goju-ryu kata of Grandmaster Yagi are unique. They have a flair, elegance and fluidity. Grandmaster Miyagi passed away on October 8, 1953. Ten years later his widow and family gave the Grandmaster's karate uniform and his black belt to Mr. Yagi. According to a speech given on the 25th anniversary of Grandmaster Miyagi's death, his daughter Suruki said that her family had decided to give her father's karate uniform and black belt to Mr. Yagi because he contributed the most and trained the longest with Grandmaster Miyagi. She said: "Mr. Meitoku Yagi was with my father for the longest time practicing karate. I think my father would be glad to see Mr. Yagi getting his uniform."

Q: I understand the Japanese government gave Grandmaster Meitoku Yagi an award.

A: Yes. On April 29, 1986, Grandmaster Yagi received the Imperial Award, a 4th class order from the late Emperor Hirohito in Tokyo. This award was in recognition of his great achievements in the field of karate.

Q: Who promoted you to black belt?

A: Grandmaster Yagi promoted me to black belt. Before I left Okinawa, he promoted me to san-dan [3rd dan]. In 1985 while we were in Okinawa, Grandmaster Yagi promoted me to hachi-dan, kyoshi [8th dan].

Q: What was the occasion for your visit to Okinawa in 1985?

A: Sensei Meitatsu Yagi invited me to participate in a special celebration in honor of his father's (Grandmaster Meitoku Yagi) 73rd birthday. That was on February 10, 1985. As the United States representative of Meibukan Goju-ryu karate-do, I attended this event and gave a congratulatory address and performed the seienchin kata on that day. My wife, Helen, and my daughter, Doreen, presented Grandmaster Yagi with flowers during the ceremony. Representatives from the United States, Japan, Brazil and India were present for this birthday celebration, as well as many prominent Okinawan masters. Grandmasters Kanei Uechi, Shugoro Nakazato, Shoshin Nagamine and Shinho Matayoshi all attended. The son of the late Grandmaster Chojun Miyagi, Ken Miyagi, was there, as was the son of the late Grandmaster Seiko Higa, Seikichi Higa. Hundreds of practitioners demonstrated kata and kumite in front of thousands of spectators. Afterwards a gala reception was held for special guests. This was a major cultural event in Okinawa that featured radio, television and press coverage.

Q: What rank do you hold now?

A: 9th dan black belt (hanshi). Grandmaster Meitoku Yagi promoted me to the very high rank of ku-dan, hanshi in Okinawa on October 21, 1990.

Q: Why did you visit Okinawa in 1990?

A: To attend and participate in the 30th anniversary celebration of the founding of the Okinawan Goju-ryu Karate-do Association. It was held on August 18, 1990, at the Shimin Kaikan in Ginowan, Okinawa. My karate students accompanied me and performed a demonstration at this important event.

Q: Are you the first person to receive the high rank of 9th dan (hanshi) from Grandmaster Yagi?

A: Yes. Outside of Okinawa, I am the first and only one who has received the 9th degree from Grandmaster Yagi, who is the chairman of the Meibukan Goju-ryu Karate-do Association.

Q: Your dojo in Watertown, Massachusetts, is known as the most traditional Okinawan karate school in North America. Have you made many changes over the years in the way you teach karate?

A: No. I haven't made any changes. Basically, I am teaching the same way I was taught at the Meibukan Honbu Dojo in Okinawa. I also keep the same attitude that permeated Grandmaster Yagi's dojo, and that means there is respect, cooperation, discipline and hard work.

Q: Could you describe the benefits of traditional Okinawan goju-ryu karate training?

A: Traditional Okinawan goju-ryu training is very strenuous and disciplined. It develops a very strong foundation of fighting skills in the karate student. Traditional Okinawan goju-ryu karate training emphasizes the repetitious practice of basic karate techniques, kata and sanchin training. Because of these intense and demanding training requirements, it develops and produces the best long-term results in the karate practitioner. Traditional day-to-day, continuous karate training strengthens the body, improves the health, cultivates the mind and develops an indomitable human spirit that can be applied to any activity in life. Grandmaster Chojun Miyagi used to say that winning and losing are part of each other. "Don't be afraid to fail one day," he said, "because the next day you might win." Life is a constant struggle, and traditional Okinawan goju-ryu karate training will prepare a person to face that struggle and deal with life's ups and downs in a very confident way.

TETSUJI NAKAMURA

UNTYING THE KNOTS

SENSEI TETSUJI NAKAMURA, THE MAN ENTRUSTED BY MASTER HIGAONNA TO FULFILL A LIFETIME'S DUTY OF PROTECTING TRADITIONAL GOJU-RYU AND PASSING IT ON THE NEXT GENERATION. IN JULY 2012, SENSEI HIGAONNA ANNOUNCED TO HIS SENIOR STUDENTS AROUND THE WORLD THAT HE WOULD BE PASSING THE FLAME OF GOJU-RYU ONTO SENSEI NAKAMURA – A MAN WHO HAS BEEN ONE OF HIS CLOSEST AND LOYAL STUDENTS. SENSEI NAKAMURA CLAIMS THAT AS HE IS YOUNG AND THAT HE STILL HAS A LOT TO LEARN AS A KARATEKA; DEMONSTRATING THE KIND OF HUMILITY WE HAVE COME TO EXPECT FROM HIS OWN INSTRUCTOR. HE HAS COMMITTED HIMSELF TO SPEND THE REST OF HIS LIFE TO FURTHER PROTECT AND DEVELOP OKINAWAN GOJU-RYU KARATE-DO.

IN 2002, MASTER HIGAONNA APPOINTED SENSEI TETSUJI NAKAMURA AS CHIEF INSTRUCTOR FOR IOGKF CANADA. IOGKF CANADA REALLY BEGAN TO GROW AT SENSEI NAKAMURA'S HAND AND AT THE END OF 2003 HE DECIDED THAT IT WAS TIME FOR HIM TO ESTABLISH HIS OWN DOJO. THIS WAS THE BEGINNING OF SHUDOKAN, NOW ONE OF THE WORLD'S MOST POPULAR GOJU-RYU DOJO. STUDENTS FROM ALL OVER CANADA AND WORLD ASSISTED IN BUILDING THE NEW HOME OF IOGKF CANADA AND SOON THE IOGKF WORLD.

SENSEI NAKAMURA'S EXCELLENT REPORT WITH INSTRUCTORS AND STUDENTS ALL ACROSS THE GLOBE, COUPLED WITH HIS RAPIDLY GROWING INTERNATIONAL FOLLOWING AND HIS UNDERSTANDING AND RESPECT FOR PRESERVING TRADITIONAL GOJU-RYU KARATE-DO.

Q: Sensei, how long have you been practicing karate?

I started karate when I was in high school, so I have been training karate for 40 years.

Q: How many styles have you trained in and who were your teachers?

Only Goju Ryu, but I started Goju Kai under Sensei Shinji Miyoshi two years in high school, and then Koryu Goju Ryu under Sensei Masayoshi Uemura during university for 5 years. Then I went to Okinawa and studied Goju Ryu under Sensei Shuichi Aragaki (student of Goju Ryu founder, Sensei Chojun Miyagi) for the first three years after graduating university and from then I have been training under Sensei Morio Higaonna to this day.

Q: How were your beginnings in the art of karate and your early days in karate?

My first martial arts experience was judo. I started training when I was 13 in junior high school. I also continued judo in the high school judo club. I really enjoyed judo for its physical challenge and competitions. I received the rank of Nidan in judo. One day when I was in the 2nd year of high school, my father told me that his co-worker (Sensei Miyoshi) taught karate near my high school and suggested that I try karate. So, I did. At that time, I was not serious about karate as my focus was on my judo training. I was training in judo 5 days a week at the high school judo club, and I went to train karate twice a week after judo training. I remember that I did not understand their training method of Kihon (basics), Kata (forms) and Kumite (sparring). I could not see the relationship between these three training aspects. After all, I was just a beginner who was not really interested in the art. I was just there because my father told me to do so. The karate classes had point sparring and I felt judo was more practical for street fighting.

Q: Were you a 'natural' at karate – did the movements come easily to you?

I was an athletic kid, so I think it came naturally. But as I was practicing judo, there were certain things to which it took time for me to adjust. But in my opinion, physical talent doesn't help much for traditional karate training as it takes a lifetime. Your continuous commitment to improve yourself, focusing on both technique and your mind is much more important in the long term. I saw many talented karateka that I met when I was young who are not training anymore.

Q: What do you think are the most important characteristics of Goju Ryu?

This is a difficult question. There are several characteristics of Goju Ryu that separate it from other karate styles, such as close distance fighting, Sanchin, circular movements, hard and soft techniques, and so forth. I would choose "Go" and "Ju" as the most significant. In our style, we start training "Go", hard techniques, at the beginning, we learn closed-fist techniques that require physical conditioning to make our strikes and blocks strong and hard. Then later, we would focus on "Ju", soft techniques, such as open-hand techniques and strikes and the ability to keep your whole body or part of your body very soft to absorb your opponent's techniques and allow you to redirect your opponent's power directly against them. Making your whole body or part of your body very relaxed or soft also helps to generate a lot of power and speed. Sanchin kata teaches you how to tighten your whole body; aligning your bone structure and locking the joints in a specific way. On the other hand, there are exercises on how to make your body so relaxed, opening each joint and letting gravity move your body as if water flows from high position to low. We also learn that there are always two opposite sides, and both are equally important. Hard and soft, Yin and Yang, fast and slow, happy and sad, focused and relaxed, calm and upset are some examples of these opposites. There are many times in our life during which we usually focus only on one side. However, the concept of "Go and Ju" (hard and soft) teaches you to realize both sides are very important and you need to understand and learn both sides well and find the balance between them in your life.

Q: Karate is nowadays often referred to as a sport... would you agree with this definition or is a martial art?

I train Goju Ryu as a martial art, but I don't disagree with people who practice karate as a sport. Since karate was spread to the world, there have been so many changes in this culture. I think this happens with anything we do and to any culture that exists in this world. Karate taught me to be open-minded and to respect others. I respect people who practice karate as a sport, and I know there is so much benefit for doing so just like in any other sport activities. After all, it is a personal choice of what you want to learn and how. Even for us traditional karate practitioners, the way we teach now to our students is a lot different than the way our founder Chojun Miyagi Sensei taught his students. However, we are trying to preserve the essential part of the art, to keep it unchanged, and we believe this essential part is greatly beneficial to us and further, to our society. But how we teach this essential part can be changed according to the time we live in, as well as to the society we live in.

Q: Do you think Kobudo training is beneficial for a Karate practitioner?

Yes, karate is a self-defense art, I think it is beneficial to know how to use different weapons especially at the basic levels. In a real self-defense situation, one must use anything around you to survive. Just because you practice empty-hand techniques does not mean you cannot use any weapons. Sensei Shuichi Aragaki told me to learn the basics of weapons. He told me that if you practice karate, you can use these weapons easily using the body movements from karate. So, I learned the basics of Sai, Bo, Tonfa, Tanbo (short sticks) and knife, etc. I am interested in learning how to use weapons at the basic level, not only Kobudo, but any weapon. I have had a chance to learn how to shoot several different types of guns as well. The reason that I say "basic level" is that so I can use these weapons using my karate skills. I know that each weapon requires very deep knowledge to achieve a higher skill level. It would take more than my lifetime to learn them all. For me, learning Okinawa Goju Ryu takes all my time and still it is not enough.

Q: When teaching the art of karate – what is the most important element for you; self-defense or sport?

For me, I focus on the development of my students as human beings both in body and mind. There are many benefits of learning karate such as self-defense, physical exercise, health, character development, learning respect, culture, and so forth. As I do not focus on competition, I never teach my students how to win in a tournament. I am trying to teach a good mixture of the above benefits to my students. So, balance is very important when I teach. If your question is either self-defense or sport, then my answer is definitely self-defense.

Q: Kihon, Kata and Kumite, what's the proper ratio in training?

The ratio of these elements would change according to your age, level of achievement and physical and mental condition. At the beginning, basic techniques are very important and you need to spend most of the training focusing on basics. However, when you reach a certain level, your focus is to practice kata. And training kata is the same as training basics. You practice the same technique of kata again and again just like you train basics. When I was young, I did a lot of kumite training and competition and I enjoyed it. There are benefits in kumite training. Kumite also has many different ways to practice. But for us to be able to use the techniques in a real situation, we need partner training, done in different formats and levels like prearranged kumite to free kumite. At the moment, I spend more time in kata training.

Q: How important is competition in the evolution of a karate practitioner?

For me it is not important. I think for people who compete, it is very important, and they train so hard to become champions. Sometimes I see the videos of competitions and am fascinated by the competitors' skills, speed and power. I respect these people who try to reach their peak performance as athletes. But this is same for any other sports. I respect gymnasts, swimmers, basketball players, and Japanese baseball players like Ichiro. However, this is not something I am trying to achieve. As sports competitors, they try to reach their peak during their twenties or early thirties. But as a traditional martial artist, I am trying to reach my peak throughout my entire life. It will never end and there is no retirement. I am not trying to win against someone else, I am trying to beat myself, to be better today than I was yesterday. I am competing against myself through every day's practice, and this is what I teach to my students.

Q: What really means "Ikken Hissatsu" and how it applies when used in the sport of Karate?

I have no idea as I do not practice sport karate. But in my opinion, I do not think the idea of "Ikken Hissatsu" (one strike to kill) would be needed in sports competition. As athletes, you should focus on winning the match. This means to practice how to win one more point than your opponent, that should be the main object of their daily training. For traditional karate practitioners, "Ikken Hissatsu" is the ideal to follow. I think that we must practice our striking techniques to make them stronger, faster, and more accurate as if it could end the fight with one blow. My sensei, Sensei Morio Higaonna, once told me that you must train your punch as though when your fist hits your opponent's blocking arm, it will break his arm, if you hit your opponent's leg, it will break his leg. Sensei Higaonna's punches are so strong. If you stand there and try to block, you cannot move his arm. It is impossible to block. I saw many times black belt guys twice the size of me who tried to block Sensei Higaonna's punch, and instead their whole body was pushed aside instead of moving Sensei's punching arm. When I sparred with him many years ago. I tried to block his punches. But they were too heavy, so every single punch he threw would hit me. Sensei Higaonna had great control, so he just touched my skin, but if he wanted to, he could knock me out with just one punch. He was going really easy with me, just like a cat playing with a mouse.

Q: How do you see the art of Karate evolve in the future?

Traditional karate teaching methods have been adapted to the time through many generations. At one point, it was taught as fighting skills against enemies, and in modern times, it was taught as self-defense. And now, I believe that the focus is to make our student a better person and to further contribute towards making our society a better place to live. Many karate practi-

tioners never use karate in real life. If you see the number of all practitioners and ask them if they have used their karate skills in self-defense in real life, I think you will find that very few have. However even though the demand of using karate in real life is low, I believe karate training can offer a lot to its practitioners. Martial arts were developed for life or death situations, the former masters spent their lives to develop these arts over many generations. As a result, the culture developed not only skills for how to fight, but also for how to improve its practitioner as a human being in the whole. To become a good fighter, old masters needed to develop their complete being to a higher level. Traditional karate contains the accumulated knowledge of these masters from over many generations, on how to become superior both in mind and body. This is what we can offer to our students along with self-defense skills, and this is the treasure for our society to preserve to pass on to our next generation.

Q: What advice would you do to those who want to focus on becoming a Karate teacher?

My advice will be "don't take your responsibility lightly. Teaching karate is to help your students to become a better person. You must keep improving yourself and keep your students' improvement as a person as a priority all the time. You also have a responsibility to carry and pass on the treasure that was passed down over many generations. So, you must learn it correctly and give it to your students without changing its essence.

Q: What advice would you give to an instructor who is struggling with his or her own development?

My advice is "do not forget the feeling of the day you started karate" In Japanese we say: "Shoshin Wasureru Bekarazu" or "Do not forget the beginner's mind". Everybody started karate for themselves, and some instructors forget the original feeling of why you are doing karate. For me, if I do not continue to improve myself, there is no meaning for what I am doing. The most important thing to me is to improve myself through daily training.

Q: What karate can offer to the individual in these troubled times we are living in?

Learning traditional karate offers a lot of things to practitioners. For example, some of the mental aspects that help me are: I learned to respect other people, to have better control of myself, to stay calm under pressure, to be able to change my mental status instantly to focused, or to relaxed. Many of these mental skills involve breathing techniques.

Q: How important is competition in the evolution of a karate practitioner?

None in the karate I practice. It is just not an essential part even though there are many benefits.

Q: What advice would you give to students on the question of supplementary training?

Supplemental training, which we call "Hojo Undo", is a very important part of Okinawan Goju-Ryu. For practitioners to be able to use the actual techniques, you will need certain strength and movements, and to learn how to use your whole body. Just punching, kicking, and blocking in the air like we do in basics and kata is not enough to make your techniques useful in a real situation. You do not need to use heavy equipment. You need to find the weight that will be beneficial for your own training.

Q: What are the most important points in your teaching methods today?

Balance is the most important aspect for me when I teach. There are many aspects in karate that students need to improve. I have to offer different things in different ways to improve my students to become better in karate as whole. My teaching style always changes as I learn more as well as to whom I teach.

Q: Do you think that Olympics will be positive or negative for Karate?

I think it is positive because people will know more about Karate. But it is not essential. It is okay not to be in Olympics as well. It will not change anything we do essentially.

Q: You are very close to Higaonna Sensei, how would you describe him?

He is the real master that I am fortunate to have met him and to have him in my life. His skills, his personality, and commitment to preserve the art, commitment to improve his own skills are amazing. I do not know anybody like Sensei Higaonna. In the martial arts world, he is one of the most respected masters of karate. Yet he is very humble and always treats everybody with respect. His training sessions are very hard, and he pushes you to the limit. But once training finishes, he treats his students as if they are part of his own family. He always tells me that he is not good enough, so he needs to train more. By watching him closely, I know that there is so much for me to improve, and it gives me the reason to train harder. There is no limit for my improvement.

Q: Goju Ryu has mainly two different branches...Okinawan and Japan... what are the main differences between Okinawa Goju and Japanese Goju?

This is a difficult question for me as I do not know much about Japanese Goju. I learned when I was high school, but I was just too young to judge. But what I can say is that Japanese Goju Ryu originally came from Sensei Gogen Yamaguchi and masters in that time. They studied Goju Ryu before the war and they had only a few occasions to learn from Sensei Chojun Miyagi, the founder of Goju Ryu. So, I do not think they learned deep enough about the art initially. However, since the establishment of their style, there has been many years passed now, and much information has been exchanged, so their knowledge is not the same as when their style started. I consider them as a cousin, a style that branched out at a different time from the same tree and developed their own way, as did we. They must have many good things that we can learn from them.

Q: Finally, what advise would you like to give to all Karate practitioners?

Enjoy your training and enjoy your life. Regardless of whether you chose sport karate or traditional karate, there are so many benefits from your training; stay positive and enjoy your journey. My request to all karate practitioners is that please do not forget "RESPECT". Karate was developed as self-defense techniques in Okinawa. There are many deadly techniques in traditional karate. However, the core teaching of traditional karate is "Respect". It is deeply rooted in Okinawan and Japanese culture. I always say to my students that without respect, martial arts training will become pure violence and only add a negative impact on our society.

LEX OPDAM

A LABOR OF LOVE

SENSEI OPDAM IS THE LIVING EMBODIMENT OF THE CLASSIC KARATE TEACHER. HE IS AN EXCELLENT TECHNICIAN, A SCHOLAR, A QUIET MAN AND ABOVE ALL, A GENTLEMAN. HIS DEEP KNOWLEDGE OF TRADITIONAL GOJU RYU MAKES HIM STAND OUT AS ONE OF THE FEW TRUE ICONS OF THE OKINAWAN KARATE.

THROUGH DECADES OF DEDICATION AND HARD TRAINING, SENSEI OPDAM HAS GATHERED AN IMMENSE AMOUNT OF INFORMATION THAT TRANSCENDS THE PHYSICAL ASPECT OF THE ART AND MANIFESTS IN THE MOST TRADITIONAL KARATE-DO PHILOSOPHY OF LIFE. HIS ULTIMATE GOAL IS PRESERVING THE TRADITION AND ENSURING THAT IT IS AVAILABLE FOR FUTURE GENERATIONS. THIS KARATE INSTRUCTOR DISPLAYS THE QUALITIES OF EVERY STUDENT'S DREAM TEACHER, NOT ONLY IN A PHYSICAL AND TECHNICAL SENSE BUT ALSO IN AN EDUCATIONAL APPROACH TO THE DEEP KARATE TRADITIONS AND PHILOSOPHIES.

Q: How long have you been practicing karate?

After a period of intensive training and high level of competition as a junior in athletics between the age of seven and twelve, which positively influenced martial arts training in later life, I encountered my first training in the martial arts in 1980 at the age of thirteen. At that time I quite athletics because of the strong competitive elements which I did not like anymore and in combination with my fascination of the martial arts, I was inspired and started searching for a martial arts teacher. This brought me to my first physical encounter with the martial arts in the form of the Indonesian martial art Pentjak Silat. My teacher George de Groot was of Indonesian origin and taught the TRI-Bhakti style, one of the many styles of this gracious art.

In 1984 I was working out with a friend in a gym and during the training we got into a conversation with a man who gave karate lessons. He invited us to come over and watch his lessons. Having only experienced Pentjak Silat, I was impressed of what I saw. Before long, we

decided to join his karate school. Described as a Kempo school, the school was in the process of switching over to Goju-ryu, a hard-soft style of Okinawan karate. Here, after my initial introduction into the Indonesian martial arts, my karate practice started. So, until this day I have been practicing karate for 31 years.

Q: How many styles have you trained in and who were your teachers?

I have trained in many different martial arts styles and systems other then karate. Next to karate the Russian Systema (Combat Sambo) has had the greatest influence upon my current martial arts practise. The foundation of my karateroots come from the Okinawan karate-style of Goju-ryu..

As I mentioned before, in 1984 I started practising karate. This was under my first karate teacher, Sensei Harry de Spa in Nijmegen. Sensei de Spa was the Dutch Chief-instructor for the International Okinawan Goju-ryu Karate-do Federation (IOGKF) at that time. I have trained under and with Sensei de Spa untill the beginning of 1993. I trained very diligently and intensively and tried to get familiar with other karate-styles, training methods and teachers from all over the world. This search for education and knowledge I continued for many years.

Within the IOGKF I periodically received instruction from the founder of the organisation Master Morio Higaonna, who promoted me a Nidan in 1990, and met and received instruction from several foreign Chief-instructors from England, Germany, Israel, France and other mainly European contries.

Together with additional training like weight training, I put a lot of effort in developing my martial art, from which karate was and is a part of my martial way. Martial arts like kobudo, aikido, kung fu, tai chi, fighting sports like kickboxing and other more police and military orientated martial systems formed my additional martial training. My effort in the service of my martial way went also as far to investigate the human body and it's bodymechanics resulting in being a certified fitness instructor and having acquaintance with some yoga, qi gong and shiatsu to broaden my understanding of the human body in training and different Eastern en Western cultures and practices.

At the beginning of 1993 I quite the IOGKF because of personal differences with my teacher and overal views of the organisation which no longer alligned with the way I see and choose to engage martial arts. After participating at a Meibukan Goju-ryu trainingcamp in June of 1993 in Israel under Master Meitatsu Yagi, son of Grandmaster Meitoku Yagi, I joined the International Meibukan Goju-ryu Karate-do Association in august 1993. In december 1993, during my intensive visit to the Headquarters of the Meibukan in Okinawa, Japan, I was appointed by Master Meitatsu Yagi as the Dutch Representative of the International Meibukan Goju-ryu Karate-do Association. My dojo became the Dutch Headquarters of the organisation.

In 1995 I visited karate pioneer Master Anthony Mirakian, the Overseas General Manager for the Okinawan Meibukan Goju-ryu Karate-do Association. Master Mirakian was appointed with this honourable position by Grandmaster Meitoku Yagi in 1972 whereafter Master Mirakian formed his branch of Zen Bei Okinawa Goju Ryu Meibukan (All American Okinawa Goju Ryu Meibukan Association). In his role Master Mirakian was given the responsibility by Meitoku Yagi in overseeing Meibukan Goju-ryu outside Japan. From my position as respresentative, but also personally because it came to my knowledge what an unique karate-pioneer and master he was, I had to meet this master. In that time I also became aware of the politics within the Meibukan organisation and decided to join Master Mirakians branche. After two very intensive training periods in 1995, I was accepted as his student and in 1996 became his Personal Representative for The Netherlands for Okinawan Meibukan Goju-ryu Karate-do. At the same time my direct college, Sensei Hing-Poon Chan became the Personal Representative for Canada. Unique for the both of us since Master Mirakian never oppointed anyone else in the world with this honour. I represented his Overseas Branche in the Netherlands officially untill juli 2013. Sensei Mirakian honoured me with the title Renshi and promoted me throughout the years from Sandan, 3th degree black belt untill Rokudan, 6th Degree Black belt in 2006. Two years ago, on my request and in compliance with Master Mirakian, one of my students, Sensei Pascal de Haan, succeeded me. Sensei Pascal de Haan was promoted by me untill Sandan, third degree black belt and was promoted by Master Mirakian after my succesion to Yondan, 4th degree black belt.

From the time I have studied actively under Master Mirakian since 1995, I kept on studying and training under and with all kinds of martial arts teachers in Europe and North America. In North America Master Mirakian introduced me to many of them. Also often Master Mirakian invited other masters and teachers of different martial arts and systems to his dojo to teach. Throughout the years Sensei Fred Lohse was one of those who taught kobudo (Matayoshi-style) on a regular base at Master Mirakian's dojo and I was also fortunate to receive instruction from him in this armed art. I have received Sensei Lohse also in my dojo in the Netherlands to instruct my students and myself in kobudo and some White Crane Kung fu. Sometimes there were also closed meetings in de dojo of Master Mirakian with only one or two students and Sensei Mirakian himself. I remember in 2002 that he told me that he had invited some Russian Systema practitioners in his dojo. Unfortunatly I was not present at that time, but Sensei was impressed of the system's natural body mechanics and showed me some filmfootage of this martial system. Triggered, this lead me to visit seminars in Europa of Systema by Mikhail Ryabko, Vladimir Vasiliev and others and engage even more in this martial system after experiencing it first hand from the masters.

So, from the point of karate styles, Okinawan Goju-ryu gave me my base from which I received instruction within two different international Goju-ryu organisations with two mains teachers being Sensei Harry de Spa in the Netherlands and Master Anthony Mirakian in the United States of Amerika. Over the years I have trained in a more and more eclectic way, to broaden my horizon developing myself both in skill and knowledge, but more important spiritually. Many other teachers, but also a lot of students and other people have crossed my path and all have influenced my live, one way or the other. For me personally, a visual artist by the late Klaus van de Locht, who studied theology and philosophy and was not engaged in martial arts, has influenced my martial art and way of live in a profound way. My personal contact with him in the nineties was intense talking about daily life, but mostly about art and what it meant for us as human beings. He was a true guide to me.

Q: How were your beginnings in the art of karate and your early days in karate?

In the beginning I had a realtively tough learning school. Full blown punches at the solaris plexus and black-and-blue testikels to learn why some techniques worked and some not ..., weekly bruises on the underarms and legs doing bodyconditioning and sparring and occasionally a broken rib and a cracked finger or toe. But all together no Spartian school, but a regular dojo where you would find serious and dedicated students, where the concept of blood, sweat and tears was put into practice in the right way.

The first few years until receiving my Shodan, 1e Dan black belt, was physically hard work. This continued, but I did get used to it and my body and mind liked the challenge, although injuries were never fun. Repetitions of techniques over and over again, a lot of body conditioning and body work like push-ups, sit-ups, squats, jumping jacks etc.. I remember being a white belt doing 10 regular push-ups. Within three years during a regular training I would do 100 full extended two knuckle push-ups after each other. The spirit in de dojo was very good. In these first years there was a strong bound between my fellow karatedoka's and with a select few we would train outside the dojo in parks, homegardens or nearby forests where we kicked trees and doing other fysical stuff, not always taking care of our bodies being the temple of our mind. At the time I was a brown belt, I trained 5-6 times a week for 4-6 hours a day karate training, weighttraining and other additional training. This tight training regime I continued for several years.

My teacher Sensei de Spa was keen on both the physical, pedagogical and philosophical aspects of the martial arts which triggered my own quest. He was also a bouncher at a dancing a few days a week during his time as an pedagogy student in his thirties. In my young eyes at the age of 20, he managed to guide this practical experience into additional elements incooperated into the self-defence methodes he taught and that were techniqually in line with Okinawan karate.

At that time it also triggerd me to see what fear and stress related to danger and exitement did to me. This lead me to competition in both kata and kumite and becoming a bouncher at some dancings for a period of time. This experience had it's positieve and negative moments, but taught me something about myself. It taught me that from a self-defence point of view, everything is very relativly. Confronting fear on different levels has been and still is helpfull for me to understand my own drives and motivations of acting better. Karate competition was a game, a sport and in my eyes had little to do with martial arts. Being a bouncher was dangerous, and also did not ad any value to my martial art, except both gave me first hand experience and were a part of my journey. So my first few years were very experimental in a range of different mental and physical challenges. But it was a valuable time, fully in live and strongly focused upon my art.

Q: Were you a 'natural' at karate – did the movements come easily to you?

I was gifted with a little talent, not much, but still. Together with my determination and experience at a young age with intensive training, it helped me to adopt movements, handling general karate training, center my focus and develop patience. I was very eager to learn and I always tried to engage every technique or movement as somethings new, although I might already have done it a thousand times. I was especially keen on taking every opportunity to see how masters or skilled people demonstrate their abilities. I am typically visually orientated, have a strong visual memory of body movements. Once I have seen it, is resides in my mind. By analyzing body mechanics, adopting movements myself by copying, repeating and giving

instant bio feedback to transform it into my own 'body feeling', the process of 'perfecting the technique/movement' starts. At the beginning and throughout this never ending process, the questions rises in me how does it suite me, why does or doesn't it suite me, can I adjust, should I adjust, what do I feel both mentally and physically when I interact these movements with others doing kumite forms, learn from the outcome and implement it. This interactive process, combined with the theoretical information and my required knowledge and experience, I use to fine-tune techniques/movements until I reach a certain free feeling and therefore, had made it my own. The most interesting part is the moment when you are physically trained enough to shift your focus more and more upon the mental part. First you learn what tools (your body) you have and how you can use it, than transform that into a natural way of create something with your mind, giving it spirit. A process that is never so black and white and already active from the start but differentiates during your development.

Q: What do you think are the most important characteristics of Meibukan Goju Ryu?

Nowadays I teach and train eclectically, I am independent of any organization and not involved into politics, commercialization, cultural bloodlines or other enhancements nor distractions. I teach and train in what I believe in and dare to question myself and let others question me. As a teacher I have only very few answers for my students, but a lot of questions and challenges both physically and spiritually. I am just a guide with the intention to let us grow as human beings and use martial arts as an instrument. I don't present any style or teacher (anymore). Having said that, I have learned a lot of investigating the history of martial arts and have encountered firsthand the style of Goju-ryu karate and the teachings of the Meibukan in particular. Some answers I give are straight forward, others point towards subjectivity.

As far as I can compare the teachings of several masters and Grandmasters of different Goju-ryu karate schools like Jundokan, Shoreikan, Seibukan and organizations like the IOGKF and the Japanse Goju-kai, I would say that the Meibukan school founded by Meitoku Yagi has some body movements that are more Chinese like than most other Goju-ryu schools. But compared to another Okinawan style of karate called Shorin-ryu, with its swift and dynamic tai sabaki (body shifting), this distinction is not worth mentioning. All Okinawan karate styles have fragmented ways of moving with a lot of focus upon power and linear directions as seen in their kata and often also certain kumite forms, which you could translate in the famous words 'One blow, one kill', typical for karate. This is in contrast to Chinese Kung fu, which is softer and has more fluid, more circular in movements, but for Chinese standards general Kung fu is still an external, and hard martial art. All is relative.

Most Goju-ryu schools have the same basic curriculum as formalized by its founder Chojun Miyagi being specific kata together with other forms of kumite, hojo undo etc. The Meibukan school has on top of this also unique Meibuken kata, with more Chinese like postures and movements developed by Meitoku Yagi and included into the Meibukan curriculum. They are typical for the Meibukan school and you will not see those anywhere else. (For those who are interested, in a book I wrote titled 'Karate Goju Ryu Meibukan', characteristics of Goju-ryu and the Meibukan school are explained in detail. In there you will find a treasury of information about the style and Okinawan karate history and masters.) Also ude tanren (body conditioning of the arms) was introduced in the Meibukan curriculum after a visit of Meitoku Yagi to Taiwan in de 1960's. Nowadays ude tanren is introduced in many Goju-ryu schools together with drills from other arts like Uechi-ryu, another Okinawan karate style which is known for its hard body conditioning.

You can compare things like Okinawan karate with Japanese karate in all its elements, the different karate styles with each other and Okinawan karate prior to World War 2, the 1950's till its present day and look at many other comparisons. However, for me it is more interesting to look at the principles behind the curriculum and the methods that are used to achieve certain goals. What lies behind it?

Within the Meibukan organization, there are many different branches, schools and teachers. Some are very sport orientated and others are more spiritual. This is the case with most karate-schools, be it this style or another, be it in the West or in Okinawa and Japan itself.

Every teacher influences the methods, techniques or other elements resulting in different teachings and schools. I think it is good to ask oneself what a style, a ryu is, which position does it take in this or another culture. How does tradition fit in, what goal has it? How is it interlinked between something so changeable like humans, like our society, our environment? In my eyes it all depends on who is teaching with what intention, in what way and why. Without these questions, foremost interactive questions towards our own practices, karate is dead. It should be alive, organic and although foundations are important, ultimately, you should transcend above all. I have seen unique footages and films of the Meibukan and other styles throughout the '50 until the beginning of this century from the private collection of Master Mirakian, which he often himself filmed. You see that things grow, change, being adjusted in curriculum, but also the way body dynamics changed over the years. For those who are interested in the history of Okinawan Goju-ryu, I would recommend reading the articles of Mathieu Ravignat, a Canadian federal politician, Goju-ryu karate teacher and practitioner, who I have met in the USA and Canada and who has visited my dojo in the Netherlands. He wrote for the Meibukan Magazine about Goju-ryu history. You can still find the old editions of the Meibukan Magazine (which in name is not related to the Meibukan of founder Meitoku Yagi)) on my personal webpage www.krijgskunst.org .

Q: Karate is nowadays often referred to as a sport... would you agree with this definition or is a martial art?

If you talk about sport (karate) or the art of karate, you talk about two different things. For me, one of the most interesting questions is what the meaning of art and sport is. Even great institutions differ on what is one and what is the other. So in the framework of this interview, my words fall short already, but I will try to explain how I see it.

Self-defense is the vehicle of a martial art, but secondary. We use self-defense in martial arts, being techniques, movements, exercises, confrontations, body awareness etc., in a matter that has a higher purpose. A purpose to develop ourselves as a human being. This is a process that is internal orientated.

Within a martial system, self-defense is primary. Clinically seen, without ritualization and mainly focused upon survival. Survival can mean attacking before attacked; it also can mean defending when being attacked. Using al there is, without limitation, just one goal: to survive.

Sport has to do with competition, about winning (over the other) as a primary goal within the framework of fixed rules. Like a martial system, the enemy, the opponent is outside. It is someone that should be concurred, overcome. This is a process that is orientated outside ourselves. I don't rule out that within sports there is a place, there is room for self-reflection, but our culture, our superficial needs, commercial and political interests have a strong influence on sport. So for me, the purpose of martial art is focus internally, to grow as a person, to overcome myself.

The purpose of sport is more in line with that of the martial system: external focus to overcome the other.

Q: Do you think Kobudo training is beneficial for a Karate practitioner?

From a point of self-defense, I certainly think that it is beneficial for a karate practitioner. Personally I did not practice jumping kicks much myself, nor do I spend much time teaching jumping kicks to my students. It is useful to learn the technique, to know by experience what an opponent can do with that technique and how to deal with such an attack when implemented upon you. This also goes for using weapons. So, from that point of view it is good to know how it works, to practice how to deal with armed opponents and get familiar with all kinds of weapons or objects that can be used as weapons. Although the battle between an armed and unarmed person is an unbalanced one.

From the point of body dynamics, I also see beneficial ways to teach the body to move and get familiar with something outside the body (the weapon as a tool) and become one with it.

Do you need Kobudo for the development of karate used as an art form? No, don't think so. You don't need all the kata, the entire curriculum of a style or system to practice martial arts and therefore you also don't need another martial art like Kobudo. A simple technique as a punch or a body shift could be enough to practice your martial art. But on a self-defense level, it can make you more universal, more developed, enhancing your abilities and possibilities.

Don't forget, karate is the Way of the Empty Hand, although originally the word "karate" was a way of expressing "martial art from China." On the surface, it deals with the physical component of emptiness, without weapons, with our bare hands. More interesting is that it also refers to empty our mind, our spirit to look at things as they are.

Q: When teaching the art of karate – what is the most important element for you; self-defense or sport?

When teaching the art of karate or any martial art, you commit yourself to the other, your student. As a guide, you try to form formulate the questions the student has, but of which he is not (sufficiently) aware. Being a guide you also give direction to your student's journey of self-cultivation. This is only possible when the student opens up himself to you.

I use self-defense to reflect upon the students own conflicts. This is the core of my teachings. Practicing self-defense can be very useful and is confrontational both physical and mentally. In my opinion self-defense, clinically seen, can also be very useful to confront the enemies inside. Is it the martial art which directs it into something meaningful. Sport has no additional value for me in this context.

Q: Kihon, Kata and Kumite, what's the proper ratio in training?

It's all depends on what your goals are, what is needed to reach those goals and what time you have at your disposal to train and under what circumstances. So, to my opinion, there is no fixed ratio that can be applied for everyone.

With this in mind, one should first investigate the curriculum's content. Not such much what it contains, but what it means. For example what kata means. Where did it come from and why? For what purpose was it created? How was it perceived throughout its history? What purpose does it have now? What purpose has my teacher given it and what do I want with it. The same is applicable to kihon and kumite.

I personally believe that what is the closest to us humans, from a physical point of view, should be the departure of self-defense. A martial system should in my opinion support the primal instincts reactions and reflexes. Beyond these we try to gain control over body and mind to support our chances of survival in self-defense. Training and practicing supports our body and mind reaching that goal. Within this context of self-defense you can create a martial system with room for individual competences. This is something that can be trained. Within the context of an art, we add, adjust, exclude to form the conditions for a higher goal than only self-defense. This is something that requires practicing.

Q: How important is competition in the evolution of a karate practitioner?

Having been a competitor myself in both kumite and kata for a few years in the late eighties and early nineties, looking back I personally see no importance for a karate practitioner in the light of martial arts practice to engage into competition. Don't get me wrong, everyone has to choose his or her own path, and a path in life is never straight forward. One of the reasons I have chosen to use the symbol of a labyrinth to present my martial arts school.

Maybe one sees competition being beneficial and for someone else it has no meaning. It all depends on your own goals. I think competition can teach you something, but is has also contradictions towards the goal of karate as a martial art and can work against you. Again, you should ask yourself with what purpose you want to do something. Investigate what competition in all is aspects and ask yourself why you should participate in it.

Q: What really means "Ikken Hissatsu" and how it applies when used in sport Karate?

Ikken Hissatsu means to annihilate or solve resistance with one single technique of blow. As I mentioned before referring to the power of karate translated into 'one blow, one kill', technically the focus or kime (total movement of the muscles chains bringing it to a maximum energy outcome) in delivering a devastating technique to finish of the opponent, is typical for karate. Karate is known for its powerful techniques, especially its straight punches. The strong input from the legs and the hips attached to a strong conditioned body, a body that is used to resistance training like makiwara practice, can deliver such a powerful punch. Don't get me wrong, in self-defense, finishing of an opponent with one technique is not an easy thing to do and tactical and more realistically there are numerous technical combinations possible and trained for the purpose to annihilate a physical threat. With most of the regular sport karate, powerful techniques are not always permitted or hardly can be performed. Often the body and fists have too much body protection and one needs to focus upon speed and retracting power to score points and therefore will not take the risk of losing points doing otherwise. This is somewhat different with full contact karate, but again, you may fully punch at chudan levels, often not on the face. But this is still superficially. Ikken Hissatsu goes beyond that. It is also a question of finishing of an attacker who wants to kill you. If this is the case, you want to defend yourself and want to stop a physical threat immediately, annihilate the threat at any cost since your life is in danger and nothing else has more priority than preserving your life. So no half decisions, only one decision right now, right here and so effective as possible with every technique possible at any location on the opponents body. No rules like in sports. Here you find its deeper meaning. Originating from you basic instincts, it is the will that has chosen to act, without hesitation, without holding back giving orders to the body to focus all its energy into one single action. There is a mindset to take one's life in order to preserve your own. This intention has no place in sports. There is concentration, there is focus en determination in sports, but not with such a mindset. It's life or dead. From a technical point of few, this is also the case in martial systems like for example the Israeli all-round self-defense system of Krav Maga.

So in my opinion in sport karate related to kumite it has no place. Demonstrating Ikken Hissatsu in kata could be. Then it should be demonstrating Ikken Hissatsu in its pure form, with the proper mindset and body movements / outcome. No distractions, no additional goals.

Unfortunately, in demonstrating kata in sport events, there are so many other goals and therefore adjustments made that there is nothing left of the concept.

Practicing kata, or even no ritualized kata but just shadow fighting on an imaginary opponent, you yourself form your own process by visualizing. You could bring yourself to such a mindset, the question is if the body can deal with punching in the air without damaging your body. But again, it is possible to initiate the thought through the correct mindset starting to perform the technique, but withholding it at the last moment, to come back often before overstretching yourself since there is now real body contact and therefore no body resistance where the released energy can go into. I have seen many kata champions performing for points, not for a demonstration of their mindset being in Ikken Hissatsu. Controlling balance, exact embusen (patterns), decently and fully aligned artificial postures are focused and trained upon by many. Demonstrating Ikken Hissatsu with visualization of fighting applications (bunkai), creates to much risks of not winning the contest. There are exceptions, but I personally hardly saw them in sports competition on any level at all.

Q: How do you see the art of Karate evolve in the future?

I am not sure how karate will involve. For my own practice and teaching I have an idea of the direction I would like to take for the near future. I think it is important to express and illustrate the spirit of martial arts since it is meaningful for life itself and I believe it can be of value for others as well.

I have seen all kinds of martial sports and shows pass by. It is ok that these forms of 'karate' exist, but they unfortunately overshadow the true spirit of the martial arts. At the moment I have noticed that karate is back on the agenda to be nominated as a sport for the Olympics. If karate becomes an Olympic sport, I really hope that out of respect for karate deeper meaning, they change the name karate for this purpose in something else that defines it as sport karate, being nothing else than an offshoot of an Okinawan martial art used fragmented for sport purposes.

Q: What advice would you do to those who want to focus on becoming a Karate teacher?

First of all you should be aware of the task before you. It is a great responcibility to teach something like karate to others. Karate is not meant to entertain someone. Karate techniques can be very brutal, when not guided properly by respect for others and values related to society and us as social human beings. Karate practise can be physical harmfull when not carrefully approached. Know why, in which way and to whom you teach. So, be aware of your intention and be clear and honest in what you can offer people. Be also clear in what you expect from each other, teacher to student and student to teacher. Karate is a long term proces, not a take away product.

Q: What advice would you give to an instructor who is struggling with his or her own development?

Development can come from the interaction with many things. Karate in its deeper meaning is not contained to techniques, form, etiquette and rituals alone. It is intertwined with life. I found myself often too much focused on what was told, what was demonstrated, what was framed by so called authorities, be it a teacher, organization, culture, or subculture like a certain martial environment I was in instead of seeing what really matters. My advice would be to actively search contact with those people who are looking for answers, not those who think they possess or know the truth. If an organization (or a person) promotes itself by saying that this is the only way, this is the true way, the most traditional one, be aware... Try to form a strong basis, but also try to look behind your own horizon, behind your organization and style. Don't withhold yourself, empty your cup more often. Dare to ask yourself fundamental questions and, above all, try to listen to your inner voice and act accordingly. In this context Sensei Mirakian often said that you should not wear someone else's suit. The chances are it might not fit. To me, this is very true.

On different levels, I felt the need to find out myself what was suitable for me and what was not. I couldn't find one system, style, way or teacher that had it all. Not only for the self-defense part but also for my personal growth and self-education. And I don't believe that it is possible to find all the answers in one location / with one style or teacher. I believe everything is already there, all the answers are available within oneself, but you have to find your own way, push the right buttons, dare to leave something behind, embrace something unknown, listen to your inner voice and find your way by yourself. What do you have to lose? You can only gain if you want to develop from within. Struggle is something natural. I struggle every day. I can only see a direction, no final answer.

Q: What karate can offer to the individual in these troubled times we are living in?

To my opinion the art of karate or any other martial or non-martial art, can give a person direction. For me, martial art has everything to do with mindfulness, everything else is secondary. Especially in this troubled times, we need to find a place for ourselves but also for sharing with others, were we can meet not only physically and socially, but connect also on a spiritual level. We should be more aware of the masks we wear and feel confident to take them off, reaching out to each other in love on a journey that leads us to who we are, to our true self. With all our strengths and weaknesses searching for connection with ourselves and others.

I am aware of the connection between our body and mind that we as human beings have and believe martial practice can confront us, putting a mirror in front of us, openly exposing ourselves and help us develop as a human being.

Q: Tell us about your relationship with the late Sensei Anthony Mirakian.

I have never met a more charismatic person than Sensei Anthony Mirakian. He was one of a kind. Before I first set foot in his dojo, he asked me more than once what my intentions with karate were, what my history was. By letter, by telephone and again upon arrival when he first welcomed me in his house and dojo in 1995. He was keen on all the details. This continued for quit a long time. Like a sort of never ending trial period.

GOJU RYU LEGENDS

I heard from his students, of which a dozen or more trained under him at that time for more than 20-25 years, that Sensei Mirakian taught 4 times a week in his dojo for 2,5 hours a day. Three times a week for the adults in the evening and on Saturday a class for children followed by a class for adults.

In the periods I visited his dojo in Watertown, Boston MA, USA, he would open up his dojo earlier, and often stayed until midnight, sometimes even gave an extra opportunity so I could workout. In the first few years I would spend more than 5 hours a day training in his dojo under him or with his students. I was therefore very honored and fortunate. Not only because he gave me the opportunity to practice and receive instruction so much, but also in giving personal attention to me when we sat down after training or welcomed me in his house, discussing karate for long periods of time, watching old movies. The same warm hospitality I received from his students.

Sensei was, like he would call it, the 'Rock of Gibraltar'. He was always present in the dojo, since the day he started his dojo in Watertown back in the sixties. He sometimes joked about this and mentioned that his wife Hellen, with whom he had a good relationship, called herself a karate widow since he was away from home so many hours a day, teaching karate besides his job and when he retired sometimes even more. He was someone who you could build on, who not compromised his way teaching karate and did not commercialize it. Sensei often spoke with me about karate history, his own experiences with the masters he had met and trained under, but also about the political circus of the many martial arts organizations, be it Okinawan or otherwise. He disapproved what was happening in the world with karate. He felt that karate should not be about politics and sport, but had to focus on self-realization. He also often spoke about the fact that there were distortions in karate history by consciously manipulated egoistic motivations. Sensei Mirakian never expressed his thoughts in public out of respect for others, especially to honor his master Meitoku Yagi, but even within the Meibukan organization from the moment Meitoku Yagi stepped back from his active role within the Meibukan, he had his thoughts and doubts about the succession and direction of the organization and continuation of the late Grandmaster Meitoku Yagi's heritage.

Never the less, he continued acting in accordance with what he believed in and tried to stay out of the politics as much as possible. "People call me a dinosaur", he told me once. "But I rather be a dinosaur that is about to become extinct, than selling my principles for money or power. I would rather die". His voice, his eyes were fierce on those moments, like the mindset when he demonstrated techniques in de dojo. For some things there was no in-between for him.

Sensei was very strict during the workouts. Workouts that were as rigorous as the ones he received in Okinawa in the 1950's. He did not gave much compliments or was coddling during his classes. The only time when he said something about my personal physical abilities, was after the first two weeks I was in his dojo, where I trained every day for more than 10 hours nearly until exhaustion. "Your well trained" were his words. For me the message was, 'you are serious, let's move on'. Years later, when I taught some lessons to his students in de dojo, he said; "You are a good instructor". That was all, during all these years. And it was good. I wasn't looking for compliments, I was there to learn, to practice.

When we as his students were not moving around, stood still, you could hear a pin drop. His eyes saw right through you when you were working out. He saw the flinches when your concentration would lack for a moment and pull you back on track with his exceptional penetrating voice. After the training session ended, he would transform and become milder and was very approachable. He was laughing, getting food and drinks for all those who were present and telling stories. And stories he had, with his photographic memory and colorful way of telling things!

Sensei Mirakian had strong personal relationships with his students. He helped them in finding a job or gave them advise in personal issues and brought students and family together also outside the dojo. Many of his students started doing karate since childhood under the watchful eye of Sensei Mirakian and therefore had become like a father figure to them.

When I came to Sensei Mirakian, I was already formed in my way of karate in Goju-ryu, but was fortunately to have meet this exceptional master, receive his instructions, advise and insight, but above all, his kindness in taking care of others. There is so much to tell about the legend Master Mirakian, that I want to refer to the interview with him that was originally published in the famous Fighting Arts magazine. If you read that intensive and long interview, with its unique pictures, you will grasp something of old school Okinawan karate and the unique position of this Western karate-pioneer at The Golden Age of Okinawan karate.

Although I am very grateful for what Sensei Mirakian has done for me, and the great honor he has given me, I had to follow my own path. This was not an instant decision, but a longer progress. I had to listen to my inner voice and wear the suit that suits me best, my own suit. I am dedicated to the higher goals of martial arts which I shared with Sensei Mirakian, but still, I needed the freedom to form my own structure without framing it into somebody else's style, form, organization or otherwise.

Sensei Mirakian will be in my memory as a great teacher, a gifted master, a unique karate pioneer and above all, a human being who cares about others and offered his guidance with the intention of making the world a better place.

Q: Finally, what advice would you like to give to all Karate practitioners?

Ask yourself the question every single day if it feels good what you do for yourself and for others and I don't mean fulfilling materialistic or short term satisfactory goals. What does really matter? How can you be part of society developing yourself and helping others in doing so? As human beings, social as we are, we share goals with each other and when we accept who we are, we will accomplish a lot, inside and outside the dojo.

AKIRA SAITO

BEING PRESENT

Sensei Akira Saito initiated karate with Wagner Piconez Angeloni for Shotokan style. Later, he traveled to Japan and started his training on the Goju-ryu style with Hanshi Konomoto Takashi – 9th Dan, at the Shizuoka Goju-ryu Honbu Dojo (Japan Karate-do Goju-kai Association), in the city of Sagara, Province of Shizuoka. He received the authorization to use the name "Shizuoka Goju-kan" in Brasil as a subsidiary. Back in Brazil, he continued his training with Hanshi 8th Dan Watanabe Ryuzo, representative of IKGA (International Karate-do Goju-kai Association) in South America until his death. Sensei Saito affiliated with the WKF (World Karate Federation) in Japan, when I lived there, by the JKF (Japan Karate Federation) and in Brazil by CBK (Brazilian Karate Confederation).

Based on tradition, but open to new forms and training ideas, Sensei Saito has evolved to the highest levels of skill and understanding. The way he explains the philosophy and technical foundation of karate, using common sense and keen logic, is refreshing and soothing in these days when martial arts in general are leading us to more combative and violent approaches. Sensei Akira Saito is a living example of how the past and the future can work together.

Q: How many styles - karate or other Martial Arts methods - have you trained in and who were your teachers?

I've trained judo when I was a child for five years with Paulo Takahashi Sensei, nowadays I also practice Kendo and Iaido from the Shinto-ryu style with Marcelo Haafeld Sensei, where I am Shodan and Bojutsu Ryozen Chikubushima-ryu with Luis Kobayashi Sensei. In parallel I practice Shibu-do and Kenbujutsu, Shoko-ryu style with Kato Shoetsu Sensei, being graduated 4th Dan. I train all these arts at the Fukushima Kenjin Association in Brazil, province from where my grandparents come from.

Q: Would you tell us some interesting stories of your early days in karate?

The stories from the beginning of my training are familiar to all apprentices, difficulties with motor coordination, enjoyed training more due to the physical practice, rather than the philosophic side and liked to fight (laughs). But an interesting fact happened when I was living in Japan and in order to start my training at my Master's Dojo, since I was the first Brazilian to practice there, I needed to find a "Hoshonin", a kind of surety whom would be responsible for my acts, in case I did not use the karate according to the standards of that Dojo and with the Karate philosophy. I think I left a good impression and gained my Sensei's trust, because after my graduation, no other Brazilian needed a "Hoshonin" in order to practice in the Dojo.

Q: Were you a 'natural' at karate – did the movements come easily to you?

Truthfully, I always liked martial arts, especially when a child, enjoyed the movies. Seeing the kicks, made me want to try to copy them. I take myself as an endeveavoured person, not skilled, the hits are not easy for me, especially if studied deeply. I believe I still need to practice a lot in order to have my movements and strikes close to what I judge perfect.

Q: Please, explain for us the main points of Goju Ryu and its differences with other styles like Shotokan or Shito Ryu?

I believe that the differences between the styles are in the characteristics of its origins. The techniques are similar, but its concepts are sometimes different. I see an important point in Goju-ryu the effort on strength concentration, stiffen the muscles to support and absorb impact from the hits applied when practicing the kata Sanchin, the flexibility of the circular movements applied in the kata Tensho and the Ibuki, the correct respiration, performing the "Tanden" and the energy flow, characteristics of the Naha-Te, that are worked differently than the styles that come from the Shuri, like the Shotokan-ryu, as an example. The "maai" is also different, in the Goju-ryu style, the strikes are closer, emphasizing the short distance, while the Shotokan-ryu the emphasis are in long distances and its movements lean to be more straight and less circular. The Shito-ryu style, aggregate a bit of the techniques from each school, adopting the circular movement techniques from the Goju-ryu and the straight moves from Shotokan-ryu. In the Goju-ryu style techniques, the circular movement causes the end of the each defense, the forearm to remain "glued" to the attack, permitting to grab the opponent to hit, kick or knock him down for the finisher.

Q: Tell us a little about Gogen Yamaguchi.

Master Yamaguchi Gogen was born in January 20th, 1909, in the province of Miyazaki. Master Yamaguchi Gogen studied in the Ritsumeikan University, where he met and initiated his training with Master Miyagi Chojun. In 1937 received the name "Gogen" from Master Miyagi and the authorization of promoting the karate-do Goju-ryu all around Japan. In 1950 founded

JKGA (Japan Karate-do Goju-kai Association) and by 1951 received from Master Miyagi the 10º Dan graduation, being considered one of the biggest Masters of Karate-do in all Japan. In 1964 managed to reunite the Masters of the present styles in Japan, initiating the creation and foundation of what is known today as Japanese Karate-do Federation. In 1969 Master Yamaguchi Gogen creates the IKGA (International Karate-do Goju-kai Association), entity that regulates the Goju-ryu style from the Yamaguchi family all around the world, nominating in each country and continent a representative. Master Yamaguchi Gogen died in May 20th, 1989, at eighty years old, leaving his legacy to his son Yamaguchi Goshi – Hanshi 8º Dan.

Q: What do you think are the most important characteristics of the Goju style?

I believe that the most important facts in the Goju-ryu style is the Ibuki, the correct breathing, the energy concentration applied and the connection between Heaven, Earth and Man (Tenchijin), concept used for example, when we do the kata Sanchin. Also, as a characteristic, being a style that comes from Naha, its members callous training, fingers and joint are very present. In the philosophical part, I think that an important point is the application of the rigid GO concept and flexible JU, in the day to day life, human character preparation. It is like the steel of the Japanese katana, if it is only rigid, it will break with the impact, on the other hand, if it is only flexible, it will not stand the hits, the same happens with our day to day like, we need always to seek the balance.

Q: Karate is nowadays often referred to as a sport... would you agree with this definition or is a martial art?

The Karate-do is a martial art, cannot be simplified to only a Sport, even though the sports have its benefits. The sportsmanship and competition part of the karate have its value, because it is through the sports competition that it is motivated the practice among the children, for example. I see no harm in competition. I do not see with good eyes teachers that instruct their students to only practice for competition. That would be wrong. The Karate-do is a noble martial art, for personal and moral aggrandizement, of a search of spiritual elevation, the competition, in this case, is only a small fraction of the real meaning of the karate. At our Dojo, we teach Karate-do Goju-ryu at the traditional form and we have various champions in the competitions. In the competitions, there are rules, which need to be understood, respected and also an strategy to win with those rules. Specific training, physical, techniques and strategy is also needed, but nothing changes the concept of martial arts. Sport limits you to a range of age, while karate, as Martial Art, thinks that we can practice it until our last breath.

Q: What are the most important qualities for a student to become proficient in karate?

It is necessary that the student be perseverant, a lot of willpower, discipline, humbleness and above all determination to win. Not only winning his adversaries, but winning oneself. Winning your problems, your weakness, your fears. The person that wins oneself each day, will achieve, for sure, your goals.

Q: When teaching the art of karate – what is the most important element; self-defense or sport?

I learned with my Sensei that everything within the karate has to have the "Imi", in other words, meaning. Sports could have its meaning, but it is not the reality of all practitioners.

Now, on the personal defense, the essential, since all the movements of the art are based on defend and counter-attack, if the practitioner does not learn the real meaning of the movements he is doing, will only be doing physical exercise, just a movement.

Q: Kihon, Kata and Kumite, what's the proper ratio in training?

In my opinion, it is essential to practice a lot of Kihon and Kata, before accomplishing properly the strikes in the Kumite. In the Kumite, the kit being performed without the correct technique and application, could lead to a risk of lesion to the trainee and his partner. I don't know if there is a way to measure the exact training proportion, but I believe it would be about 50% dedicated to the physical invigoration exercises and techniques refining through the Kihon, 40% dedicated to the study of the techniques, some of them secret, within the Katas and 10% dedicated to the specific practice of the Kumites. Of course, all of this, being trained in the traditional Karate. If it is directed to the competition, it would be necessary a bigger percentage in the specific area.

Q: How has your personal expression karate has developed over the years and what is it that keeps you motivated after all these years?

I believe that the changes happened mainly in my point of view. Fact that has influence due to the age and maturity. When we are young, we practice karate in a more physical manner, much more emotional than rational. When we get older and more mature, we begin to understand the techniques and that all the training was developed not only to build a strong body, but also the spirit, mind and energy. This brings harmony and balance and capabilities to train till the end of life. What motivates me every day is the fact that when we practice, we seek perfection, not only a perfect technique, but also the perfection of the spirit.

Q: How important is competition in the evolution of a karate practitioner?

I believe that not all practitioner needs to dedicate to competition. But in the competition, there are positive facts that can be used by the practitioner, mainly in children cases. In the competition it is possible to teach to win, going through obstacles which are needed for the human being development. Winning the fear before the competition, the physiological fact, the fear of losing to the opponent. Learn the value of competition, learn to win and lose, learn with the failure and convert it into motivation to reach your success.

Q: What really means Ikken Hissatsu and how it applies when used in Karate?

The term "Kill with a strike or fist" arouse, in my opinion, due to the fact that in an unarmed combat versus an armed opponent, were your life is at risk, the training must be so intense that in this situation, you can kill the opponent, with only a hit. In the Japanese martial arts there is a concept of Ichi Geki Hisatsu, "kill with one attack", which is normally used in the Kendo and Iaido, and I believe the concept is the same. Nowadays the concept could not only be used in the technique itself, but in our day to day life. If we think that everything we do, we have only one chance of making it right, do it well done and not postponing.

Q: How do you see the art of Karate evolve in the future?

I see the evolution of the karate, mainly in the scientific field. Lots of the traditional exercises, today, not used exclusively in karate, has scientific answers, in the physiological and biomechanics sphere, seeking a better performance and efficiency. I believe that new discoveries and

also the evolution of technology will bring a lot of benefits to the karate training. Of course that all of this should be added, never substituted. The karate-do is the evolution of human beings, the more we evolve in science and physics, more we evolve and learn with Karate-do. I see karate-do as an art of infinite evolution, because, we are the tools.

Q: Do you feel that you still have further to go in your studies?

Yes, I believe I'm only in the beginning of my journey. Karate-do is an art very rich and we can learn something new. It is necessary to be training intensively and vigorously, to maintain your mind always humble and open to new discoveries.

Q: What advice would you give to students on the question of supplementary training?

I always motivate my students to seek for supplementary training. The accumulation of knowledge enables you to a better understanding of the techniques and concepts. I do believe that all knowledge should be added and not substituted.

Q: What advice would you give to an instructor who is struggling with his or her won development?

The recommendation I also tell them is that to maintain yourself humble, it is necessary an intense and vigorous practice, your personal limits will always tell you who you really are. The instructor needs to know that the only thing is has above the other practitioners is the responsibility and nothing more. We are in a constant progress, the experience of life and maturity will always give us a different point of view. There is a long path and we should always learn with it.

Q: Have been times when you felt fear in your training?

Yes, I have felt fear lots of times. We should not banish fear from our feelings, but yet, should learn to control it, not being ashamed of feeling it, but facing it courageously.

Q: Do you think that Olympics will be positive for the art of karate-do?

I think there are lots of motives and reasons to think that Karate in the Olympics will bring benefits. One of them, for sure, will be the mass media exposure and a bigger publicizing of the sport. But I also think that this could lead a certain number of practitioners to dedicate themselves only and exclusively to competition, and that is bad. Mainly now with the present rules which they want to establish a sport karate, with no distinguish from the styles. The styles are the origins and its concepts, the traditional and martial part of the karate-do and it cannot be turned into just a sport.

Q: What are your views on kata bunkai?

I see bunkai kata as a way, not the only one, to apply the techniques comprehended in the kata (lots of times hidden – "kakushi"). It is important for the traditional techniques of the karate-do within the kata be learned and

transmitted in its original structure. Differently from the Bunkais shown in the competitions from WKF by the kata team manner, where lots of times we see the techniques (lots of them not even from the karate) being used with more emphasis in the esthetics, like a tv show. This has a value, only in the sports sphere, a way to please the audience.

Q: Goju Ryu doesn't have a large number of kata, does this make a difference compared to other styles whose number of kata are higher?

Reaching the perfection and understanding of the katas, is the main point. In the competition point of view, yes, is does make a difference due to the used system of simple elimination, where, in an official competition, the athlete usually needs at least seven katas, being two of them mandatory. Demanding in some cases, that the athlete use katas from other styles in order to compensate the requirements in a competition.

Q: How do you like to train yourself? Has this changed over the years?

When I was younger I liked to train the combat part of the karate. Today I see the karate-do in a more complete form/angle and all the training is important. I always liked the physical exercise, the fortification of the body. The human body needs to be exercised every day, for that reason, today, besides the karate-do, I also practice kendo, Iaido, Bojutsu, Shibu, Kenbujutsu and long distance race. When we are young we mainly think in the physical sphere and conquests, principally in the competitions case. More mature, we begin to comprehend better the values of the Japanese Martial Arts and with that, we change our goals.

Q: Shotokan, Shito Ryu, Goju, Ryu etc...How do you think the different branches/styles affect the art of Karate?

I think that the styles are different from one another on their techniques and origin concepts, not from its philosophy. The Budo, if practiced in the correct form, shows exactly that the martial arts assist to a spiritual evolution of the human being, above all.

Q: Do you think Kobudo training is beneficial for a Karate practitioner?

If the intention of the practitioner is the deep study of the traditional techniques of the karate-do, yes. Like the Goju-ryu, for example, which is originated in Naha, where they had lots of arts of combat with weapons (some of them existing till today). Lots of techniques were originated from these arts and some other techniques founded to combat them. I imagine that it is hard for a karate practitioner that does not have knowledge of the Kobudo, to understand and apply these defense techniques in its essence, as the name itself suggests, "karate-do" (way of the empty hands) was the art that in those days, did not use weapons against your armed opponent.

Q: What is your opinion about the "Shobu Ippon" division in Karate competition?

I noticed that today, the karate competitions have become more dynamics and more alike the sports. A price paid to get an "Olympics Status" and have support from the mass media and tv. I do not see today, in this context, the same space for the "Shobu Ippon" as a competition sports.

Q: What are the most important points in your teaching methods today?

I believe that the most important point to teach today is the importance of the moral values, citizenship, of how reaching your goals with your own sacrifice and maintain the culture and traditions. Another important is the good understanding between the traditional education and all the evolution of an Era. All the scientific evolution comes to benefit us and with that, add a lot of new possibilities of exercising. The competition cannot be considered the Art of the Karate-do, but part of it, and yet, nowadays its practice is very important, mainly for kids, since it is a way of stimulating the practice, in a playful way of experimenting the combat and a way to learn to loose and win.

Q: What karate can offer to the individual in these troubled times we are living in?

The karate-do can offer more than just the physical benefits, a way of relieving the stress, a way of helping to succeed obstacles and daily problems, a way of self-understanding, cultural enrichment, a way of learning and spiritual evolution, besides being a way to rescue moral values, today forgotten by a big portion of the society. Not mentioning also the preparation of the individual for a probable self-defense, if needed.

Q: After so many years of training, what is it for you that is so appealing in this style of karate and why?

As much as I practice, more I feel attracted to the art. I face the practice of the Karate-do Goju-ryu, or any other art that I practice, as a new daily discovery. This motivates me a lot, since I always see new possibilities of growing and new targets to be reached. I always think of seeking perfection of the techniques and not only in learning new ones.

Q: Finally, what advise would you like to give to all Karate practitioners?

My advice is to always practice, with emphasis, will force, with no excuses. Instead of giving various justifications for not training it's better to have just one good reason to train.

GENE TIBON

STILL WATERS RUN DEEP

SENSEI TIBON IS A MAN OF OUTSTANDING ACCOMPLISHMENTS AND A LEADING INSTRUCTOR IN THE ART OF GOJU RYU UCHIAGE-KAI KARATE. HE HAS DEVOTED HIMSELF TO THE TRAINING AND STUDY OF MARTIAL ARTS SINCE AN EARLY AGE WHEN HE BEGAN PRACTICING UNDER THE TUTELAGE OF HIS FATHER. SENSEI TIBON'S INSIGHTS INTO THE ART ARE NO LESS EXCITING THAN THE MAN HIMSELF.

BESIDES BEING PROFICIENT IN THE TECHNIQUES OF KARATE, SENSEI TIBON HAS THE TRUE PRINCIPLES OF THE PHILOSOPHY OF BUDO INGRAINED WITHIN HIM. THIS IS APPARENT IN THE FOLLOWING INTERVIEW, IN WHICH WE LEARN NOT JUST ABOUT KARATE BUT LIFE ITSELF FROM THE KNOWLEDGE GARNERED BY THIS EXCEPTIONAL KARATE MASTER.

Q: How long have you been practicing the martial arts?

I was introduced to martial arts when I was about 11 years old by my father, Gene D. Tibon Sr., who also is a martial artist in Goju Ryu, Escrima, Boxing, and good old-fashioned street fighting. Along with my brother Darren, sisters Leslie, Regina, and Jackie, and cousins, I learned from my father. So, you can say I have had 42 years of exposure and training in the martial arts, including the years with my father. My grandfather and great-grandfather also were involved in the martial arts. My great-grandfather was a highly experienced Escrimador who actually had to use his art for self-protection. He caused serious injury to seven men who attacked his family. The injuries his attackers sustained were so bad, he had to leave the country for 12 years. What is known of great-grandfather Marcos Tibon, I'm sure his father, grandfather, and his great-great grandfather also were involved or had some knowledge of martial arts. We just have no records that far back. Based on our current knowledge, it has been in my family for at least four generations with me, five generations for my sons, and six generations for my three grandsons, Dylan (6 years old), Miles (4 years old), and Gavin (nearly 3 years old); each now training at Tibon's Goju Ryu Fighting Arts, their "Papa's" dojo in Stockton, California.

Q: How many styles (karate or other methods) have you trained in?

I have been involved mostly with the Goju Kai Yamaguchi system during my childhood and teen years with my father, the Goju Ryu Uchiage-Kai System, then the Yamani Ryu Kobudo system, a little AAU boxing for about two years, and a little bit of Serrada Escrima Filipino stick fighting techniques. I am currently a 6th Dan Goju Ryu Uchiage Kai and 6th Dan USA National Karate Federation Dan Certified. For the past 12 years, I have been on the USANKF Technical Committee and a "Class A" examiner for the National Federation, as well as also one of three examiners on the USANKF Coaches Selection Committee the past eight years.

Q: Who were/are your teachers? (Please mention specific characteristics of teachers you have trained under).

As I mentioned earlier, my father Gene D. Tibon Sr. was my first teacher. He also was a young Olympic Boxing hopeful and very versed in street fighting, with a mix of karate from his many years of training in the Goju Kai Yamaguchi system. He was very strong and very strict in his push for strong combinations, and even a stronger attitude about not showing any pain. We grew up hearing, "to show pain is a sign of weakness." To this day, my dad has that look, that warrior eye, that will make you feel uneasy with his strong, piercing glare. I have to say even now, when I compare my father's speed and combinations along with his warrior attitude, I've still not seen many that could match him in his younger, prime days.

I trained in the Goju Kai Yamaguchi System under then a 3rd Dan, Sensei Rodney Hu. He was on the first United States Karate Team, attending the first World Championships in Japan. The newspapers in Japan nicked named him "Roundhouse Rodney," as he put many away with the devastating power of his roundhouse kicks. Sensei Hu was a very strong and technical

Sensei, whom I respect very much for his detail to small things and his keen eye to perfection in Kata. Our Kihon Kata was explosive, and when done with our whole group, you could hear the cracking of the gis and popping from the punches and kicks. To this day, I still run my classes the same way.

It was during these years that I decided to follow in my father's footsteps and took up AAU boxing for about 18 months with Frank Dobales of the Stockton Police Boxing program. Coach Dobales was a very nice and hard-working man, who worked with many young kids to give them boxing as an alternative to gangs and getting into trouble. Next, I moved over for more training with 6th Dan Sensei Akio Takahashi, an All-Japan Champion. A good friend, Sensei Malcolm Equinoa, now deceased, introduced us. Sensei Takahashi was an explosive and powerful technician. Unfortunately, it was hard to bring him in from Japan for training, and the cost was very expensive to go to Japan and train.

Eventually, I asked some good friends for their advice of whom I should train with; I asked them whom they considered the best in Goju Ryu Karate. With the recommendation of Sensei Fumio Demura, Sensei Yoshiyaki Ajari, Sensei Kyoshi Yamazaki, and Dr. Julius Thiry, I was referred to Grandmaster JKF 9th Dan, Kenzo Uchiage of Osaka, Japan. He was the JKF past president, and his son JKF 7th Dan, Takeshi Uchiage, the Pan-American Goju Kai chairman in Canada, as appointed by Grandmaster Shozo Ujita, the JKF president at the time. I then contacted Sensei Takeshi Uchiage and was introduced to him through Sensei Kyoshi Yamazaki.

I'm still currently teaching and training in Goju Kai Uchiage-Kai System under the International Chairman of Goju Ryu Uchiage-Kai, 7th Dan Sensei Takeshi Uchiage. Sensei Takeshi Uchiage has a wealth of knowledge handed down to him by his father, and I consider him my mentor and friend. Also, Yamani Ryu Kobudo with 7th Dan Sensei Toshihiro Oshiro. I would say Sensei Oshiro is one of the most powerful men I ever have witnessed swinging a bo staff. I've personally seen him snap a hardwood bo in midair with solid snapping strikes while doing a Kata. His power and speed is unequalled among those I've seen. I trained a little bit in Serrada Escrima with my brother Master Darren Tibon, who also is one of the nation's foremost Escrimador instructors, and is one of my first black belts.

Q: Would you tell us some interesting stories of your early days in karate?

I read a lot about the old days of training in Japan and Okinawa, and I was very intrigued by the stories of the old masters who would train in the forest. They wouldn't consider themselves as having true strength in their punches and kicks until they were able to kill a tree. Well, in the front yard of my first apartment, where I lived with my wife and young son Gino, there was a very large tree in the front of my residence. I worked out every day against it, just to develop my strength in my punches and kicks. Being poor in those days, as a young man, and wanting to train hard, we used whatever we could find. One day, my landlord came knocking on the door with a major complaint, because the huge tree in my front yard was dead. All of the leaves had fallen off and it dried up. My father heard about it, laughed, and said, "Well I guess you have some power in your punches and kicks now, but you probably looked like a nut out there beating up a tree." Most people today wouldn't understand my motive.

The other story I have is the first time I broke a brick with my head. It was a six-inch thick, piece of concrete. Again, I would always revert to remember the old stories of karate: empty hand, and your whole body being a weapon. I had to test my strength in my neck and head to smash that slab of concrete, which would confirm what I could do to somebody's face with a head butt. This is even more of a test, because you are putting your life on the line with this type of psychological and physical test. You have to step over a psychological barrier with total devotion and commitment in completing this test. You have to be at your maximum level to know that you have this strength in being able to step over this line and accomplish this feat. I concentrated and put my mind into total commitment in smashing this brick with no hesitation. I knew I would suffer more with the issue of self-defeat by hesitating, or not giving my all, coupled with the injury that could result if I failed to break the brick. After smashing through the concrete slab, I almost felt as if I had discovered something more than just being able to smash this piece of concrete with my head. I felt there is nothing I cannot accomplish if I totally dedicate my whole being to it. If I believe and fully commit myself, then I will succeed in my attempt. For some reason, these two stories stand out in my mind the most but, believe me, I have other stories of different training test in my early days.

Q: How can the influence of training in Martial Arts help the young (kids/teenagers) generation in becoming successful as individuals in the future?

Karate has a huge influence on young kids, if they are in a program that strives for the student to look at leadership, self-challenge, determination, honesty, integrity, discipline, and the competitive spirit of winning at life. Everyday life is a true comparative to their karate training. Life is a conflict; everything we do, including waking up in the morning, is conflict. You always want to hit that alarm clock to ring again in five minutes, just to get that little extra sleep. Once you learn that karate is life, all aspects of the work and determination in trying to perfect a movement or technique are no different than working and preparing to win at a spelling bee contest, earn that new position at work, being a great role model for others, or by attracting a new customer in business.

Our young students are engaged in their schools and challenge themselves as class officers, or high academic achievers, just as they do on the dojo floor, working on their techniques. That same pride and hard work go hand and hand with each other. The life skills that we teach in our dojos are a direct influence of the hard work and the intangibles that come with karate-do, the empty hand way. This attitude will follow the practitioner his or her whole life, if one practices long enough to understand one is the same as the other.

Q: Were you a "natural" at karate; did the movements come easily to you?

I was a natural in all sports. I was a very fast runner and ran track in junior high school and on the high school varsity team, and played high school varsity soccer. I also played on the varsity football team during my senior year. Everything I did in sports, I did pretty well. If I saw something, I was able to pick it up easily. Growing up with martial arts training at a young age, we had footwork drills in boxing training, we ran a lot, and started lifting weights just going into junior high school at age 14. That continued through my senior year in high school, when I bench pressed 450 pounds to lead the school in the 450 bench press club. There were different category clubs from 200 to 450 pound club at that time. I continued weight training until I started boxing and wanted to increase my speed.

The basic Kihon development I received from Sensei Hu was my formal concrete development in stance foundation in Goju Ryu Karate. I found this training to be what made me fall in love with Goju Ryu Karate, because of how difficult it was to achieve the stances without thinking, and to make them a natural application of the movement during kata and sparring. All of my early training with my father and sports really flourished when I started the traditional training under the Goju Kai Yamaguchi system.

Q: How has your personal expression of karate changed/developed over the years?

It has changed a lot as far as development. I think a person starts at the beginning of anything with a certain idea of karate. Once you really study and search to understand what the first masters were thinking, or what their interpretations may have been, then your personal creativity kicks in. In regard to the application, you are taught a basic understanding. Your own creativity and attitude begin to understand more of what you are doing. I teach very differently today, compared to my first "garage dojo" some thirty years ago.

Now, I have leadership training for my instructors to set out the direction of a particular type development I want taught in our programs. When I first started training under Sensei Takeshi Uchiage, he told me that I was too hard in my expectation of my students, and the majority would not be able to do what I was asking. So I started searching into myself, to see how I could modify my program to teach the quality I expect from my students, and not compromise my thinking of what my black belts should look like. After all, I still was passing on my family's tradition of attitude to my students, and did not want to lose that psychological aspect. I want my students to be physical, technical, and psychological. I want them to have strength and flexibility, along with a winning determination. I didn't care too much about the competition aspect at this time; I was more into developing an organization of quality karate that I could be proud of. I wanted my students to be breathtaking in their demonstrations or competition. They say there is no better sound than to hear somebody other than yourself saying something complimentary about your students. I believe this, and within a Federation competition, where everybody wears the same patch and it is not apparent which dojo a student is part of, it is gratifying to hear the wonderful comments from people you respect, and their positive comments about your students. I don't think I ever will get tired of hearing that.

Q: What do you think are the most important qualities for a student to become proficient in any art of Budo (not only in karate)?

Especially when looking at the most important qualities in any art of Budo from the perspective of a USANKF Technical Committee member, I absolutely feel the qualities of humility, character, respect, manners, spirit, self-control, and being proper are very important. I think that our duty as the National Federation is to protect the Budo in our art, especially at the sport level.

One of the most important ways to do this is to not allow athletes to celebrate their own technique, rejoice at the misfortune of others, berate, or talk trash to another competing athlete during a match.

This absolutely drives me crazy, when I see some elite athletes running around the ring cheering for himself for scoring a technique, when it has not even been awarded yet. It is even worse when a referee or judge watches this sort of action with no response, allowing it to happen. In

my estimation, to keep the Budo in karate, the sport aspect has to make clear not to allow any type of celebration during the match, until it is over and a winner is declared. A penalty should be given automatically for this type of behavior. Zanshin should be a large part of this, continuous mind from the beginning to the end of the match. In my estimation, it is a direct violation of the most important code of Budo in any martial arts a when there is a breakdown in humility and character for the purpose of entertainment.

Q: With all the technical changes during the last years, do you think there are still "pure" styles of karate?

I think many want to think there are special pockets of "pure" styles of karate. But after so many different generations of instructors, with creative and ingenious minds, they actually take their art sometimes further from their predecessors. Many will break off from the first generation masters, after they have passed away, to create their own legacy of style or organization. Many have ideas that while locked into an organization style are held fast to that one way, until they break away and create their own version of interpretation or style, which has been happening for centuries in China and Japan. All we can hope to do is try to maintain the traditional structure of the old ways that have been handed down from previous generations to the next. I know I personally have trained with many great Goju Ryu – Goju Kai masters who all have had their own creative genius and all influenced me to the understanding I have now. I respect all of the old masters for their contributions to the art as we know it today, especially those who work to keep the essence of the traditional katas solid in movement and applications. I don't know how many "pure" styles are out there due to evolution of man's thinking and technology. Just look at the Olympics of old, in comparison to now. I would venture to say there are more styles of creative traditional interpretations of highly skilled and confident generations of masters, which styles still try to represent the original "pure" style they originated from. But who is to determine what is pure and what is not?

Take for instance the first car built by Henry Ford, the Model A. Even though you still have the same gas combustion engine idea with four wheels and a steering wheel to control the vehicle, you can't compare it to today's Porsche, BMW, Mercedes, Cadillac, Toyota, Honda, etc. They all have the same standard structural idea, but look what creativity, technology, and an open mind have allowed.

Q: Do you think different "styles" truly are important in the art of karate? Why?

I think styles are important, because the traditional essence of the kata still is defined by that group of practioners. I look at one of history's most brilliant Okinawan pioneers, Grandmaster Kenwa Mabuni, whose magnitude of research included most of all major katas of the time. Grandmaster Mabuni tried to create a "Karate" that represented all styles by combining all the katas under one name. At the time, there was a very important reason for this. Yet, when I see a Goju Ryu Kata performed today by a different stylist outside of Goju Ryu, some very important ingredients, very specific to the style, are missing. Some of these practitioners did not research, as did their grandmaster, which could have helped preserve the essence of a kata's original style. The strength and power in some katas is enhanced by a particular stance, which in some cases may have been changed from the original style. I personally feel that the styles do work to maintain the original essence of their system, and I feel they are important to maintain. I've dedicated my life to Goju Ryu and still feel like I learn something new every day.

Q: What is your opinion of fighting events such as the UFC and Mixed Martial Arts events?

I think everything has its place; there are those who wish to train in hard contact martial arts and others who want to mix the kicking with the boxing concept under specific rules. You have others who wish to help preserve the traditional arts as best as we have been taught, to pass on to their students who one day hopefully will wish to pass it on to the next generation. A lot of times you can't get a major sponsor to underwrite a television show, or a documentary, so the marketing aspect for the major traditional systems often is not seen. Since the airing of the current television shows on the Discovery Channel, showing traditional martial arts in the homelands of their origins, the public has become more aware of the different types of martial arts throughout the world. There just is not enough exposure of traditional karate in comparison to the current national television coverage of Mixed Martial Arts.

The fight entertainment world looks to events like the UFC, especially when you have Mike Tyson-types talk about getting involved in it, as a multimillion dollars promotional event. It is as close to full all-out fighting with very limited rules as you're going to see in a sport. Yet, to compare the history and beauty of a two-thousand-year-old kata against power kicking to the legs of an opponent, or a fighter brutally stomping the face of an opponent stuck against the base of the cage in a televised match is very difficult. The extreme brutality of these matches has mesmerized the common public, which is intrigued by the violence but does not wish to participate in it. Sort of like the old days with the gladiators: lots of people cheering, but not very interested in getting down on the floor of that venue. With millions of dollars spent on promoting a nationally or closed circuit television show for millions across the world, the music and the Hollywood sensationalized hype has really made it hard for the old style traditional karate stylist to compete.

Q: Karate nowadays often is referred to as a sport. Would you agree with this definition or is "only" Martial Art?

I think any martial art is a sport, if it is in the competition arena with rules, a referee, scoring, or a doctor who is ready to stop the match because of injuries. This is just a small part of kumite, although the test of physical control, techniques, and the attitude still has some of the vital ingredients of budo. To have all the competitive rules-based ingredients missing, and the only award for winning between two combatants is the one who survives, that is pure martial arts. The only exception is during a time of war when you are on the battlefield, or you and your family find yourself in a life-threatening situation. If you find yourself in a position of personal risk and have to protect others or yourself, you really are experiencing the true essence of the martial arts. Training for these types of situations could happen on any given day. It is when Karate is not being a sport, but again is empty hand, is a means to survive a life-threatening attack. Again, the evolution of time and laws of the land has had a great affect on the martial arts of old to the present.

Q: Do you feel that you still have further to go in your studies?

Absolutely; as my old Sensei used to say, "You learn until you die." It also is said that "By learning, you will teach; by teaching, you will learn." I try to read and research all aspects of our art and how they relate to each other from China, Okinawa, Japan, to Kung Fu, Okinawa-te, to my style, Japanese Karate. The market is full of many different types of investigative books on history, such as the translations of ancient master pieces of strategies, like the books recently written of Sun Tsu to Musashi Miyamoto, the Book of Five Rings, and the different strategies of war, along with the how to apply those concepts to business and community. The true test of an effective art is how you apply it to everyday life. This is why the search for understanding and knowledge is constant until you die.

Q: How do you see karate in the U.S. and around the world at the present time?

I see karate in the United States as very fragmented, and in some cases confused. Many are asking why we should support karate in the Olympics. Others are saying we need to be in the Olympics for worldwide exposure of the art. There are some who say should we stay isolated in our own world? Others say let's create our own way. Some want to get as close to full blown combat as they can get; others just want to try to preserve what they have been taught, and not change or express any more than what they were taught.

Here in the United States, "the land of milk and honey," creative expression is expected. Of course that is the American way. Really, what is that? I think it means the right to choose what makes you happy. There is so much diversity in the United States, a melting pot of ideas, culture, and creativity that makes us unique in the martial arts world. As for around the world, I see in South America that the styles almost all are Japanese Okinawa Karate and Korean Karate. The same strong influences exist in Europe and Africa. Canada is close to the way the United States has been influenced, by diversity. There you will find many different styles and ideas of martial arts. Due to differences in ideas and styles, I don't know that we ever can have everybody on the same page regarding martial arts. Today, especially with martial arts being run commercially, some dojos have become specialized in modified day care programs, specializing in young kids. Some dojos only teach games interjected with some martial arts drills. People are paying big money for this and some instructors are making six figures and more, teaching these kinds of programs.

Because there is a market for this type of program, and there seemingly is a strong customer base, Traditional Karate is having a tough time. The old style hard-core dojo never can grow larger than 30–50 students, and many traditional Senseis struggle to make a simple living, let alone support a retirement investment plan. The state of the economy also has a direct bearing on the martial arts business. To survive in the New Age, Senseis have to think outside of the box for business strategies to make their programs work, be profitable, and not compromise their teaching values.

Q: You are involved with the organization of Disney Martial Arts. Tell us why and how this was developed?

Many years ago, I created a non-profit organization call "Martial Arts for a Better World Promotions," where I raised more than $52,000 for children's charities in my city. The tournament I hosted back in the early '90s was one of the first of its kind. I had Kung Fu people judge the Kung Fu divisions; and Traditional Karate, Escrima, Tae Kwan Do, and Open Style Karate, each judged within their own divisions. It was the first venue to offer a "Five-Discipline Tournament" with 12 rings; at our first tournament, we had 1,300 competitors.

During this time, I met and worked with Tiger Claw's owner Thomas Oh, who brought in some movie stars like James Hong and Professor Toru Tanaka to highlight the tournament. In 2006, Tiger Claw started working with Disneyland Martial Arts Festival directors and proposed the same concept that I had introduced in the early '90s. The first tournament ended up so small it almost was cancelled the following year. Sensei Kyoshi Yamazaki was the coordinator for Classical Karate that year and, because of his international travelling schedule, mentioned to the Disneyland Martial Arts Festival directors that I might be better suited to promote Classical

Karate. It also was at this time that Thomas Oh, mentioned the past tournaments I had hosted, and he also recommended me. I then spoke with Rob Hartman, one of the Disneyland directors and he asked if I would be interested in being the Classical Japanese Okinawa Karate coordinator. I agreed, as long as I was able to promote my way of karate to the public, and that I was able to keep Sensei Kyoshi Yamazaki on as my international coordinator. Rob agreed and we have now implanted our way of Classical Japanese Okinawa Karate into Disney's Martial Arts Festivals.

I'm now the senior coordinator for Classical Japanese Okinawa Karate & Kobudo, and Martial Arts, which also oversee Iaido with coordinator Sensei Roger Jarrett, Chanbara with Coordinator Sensei Dana Abbott, and my Disneyland Classical Karate coordinator Sensei David Crockett. Sensei Crockett also is my Disney Martial Arts Classical Karate Chief Referee. We have great talents like the international referees Chuck Sweigart, Gary Tsutsui, Michael Shimabukaru, Douglas Smerek, Miguel Serano, Julius Parniczky, Jo Pledge, Michelle Lewis, Mary Crawford, ☐Tomohiro Arashiro, Mike Musto, Tony Wright, Raymond Toy, Ronny Guzman, Adam Tibon, Bernard Dougherty, and many more great friends to create this extra ordinary team of referees and judges. This team works to give the public a true look at our way of Karate while being judged by some outstanding talents.

My wife, Yvonne Tibon, is my registration coordinator and also the registration auditor for the Federation. With Darrell Goodyear, Frenchi Charmaine, Robert and Pam Gonzales as logistical staff support, and Roger Moore as my legal counsel, I have to say this is the best, most trusted, and dynamic teams in the country. I have them all working with me and many different high level Senseis around the country as Classical Karate promoters hosting qualifiers for a Classical Japanese Okinawa Karate finals at the Disney Martial Arts Festival at Disney's Wide World of Sports Complex in Orlando, Florida. This has helped me elevate our exposure around the world.

Just look at young 2007 Disney Martial Arts Festival Grand Champion Alejandro Cepero, who as an intermediate challenged the young black belts and was able to make his dreams come true and win a custom made crystal by Disney Martial Arts Festivals. He since has been featured in two major national and international magazines, a special on Univision Television around the world, and his local Television Station Channel 7 sports special in front of millions of people promoting the classical Karate and the Disney Martial Arts Festival. I was able to introduce Glen Norman, CEO of Omega 360 Television to the Disney Martial Arts Festival, where they unveiled for the first time the new state of the art technology of 48 cameras with separate motors over our center ring televising our International Karate matches. This can be seen currently at the website at www.360replays.com. This introduction and the work to promote Classical Japanese Okinawa Karate and Kobudo won me the 2007 Disney Martial Arts Festival Coordinator of the Year Award, competing with the coordinators of all 15 different disciplines. It was a great year for promoting our way of karate to the public.

Q: What is the final goal of the Disney Martial Arts Festival?

My goal is to have Classical Japanese Okinawa Karate, Kobudo, and Martial Arts presented to the world through the Disney media opportunities. The goal is to reintroduce our way of Classical Karate to the public, while introducing some of the top talents through our National and International Qualifiers. Holding these events through the Disney Martial Arts Festivals allows families to create memories and at the same time participate in our way of karate, at a world-class resort.

Q: When teaching the art of karate, what is the most important element: self-defense or sport?

I think the most important part of the art of karate starts with respect. The important element in self-defense understands the bunkai and depth of its meanings and true applications in kata. I'm passionate about the self-defense aspect of karate. I teach my adult students the practical applications, especially ones that work in law enforcement or a department of corrections.

The sport aspect is developed in special classes. I want to give our athletes true understanding of Karate-do, and also have a good understanding of sport karate and do well in it if they desire to compete in that game. Bottom line, I like preparing my students in both aspects to their highest level, so they are prepared to defend their life if need be, and to have the speed and technical know-how to take down their opponent for a 3-point follow to finish the match in competition. The sport side is a testing ground of battle, under the condition of rules.

Q: Forms and sparring, what's the proper ratio in training?

I like almost 70 percent kihon, kata, and bunkai applications, and 30 percent ippon kumite, ju kumite, footwork drills, hooks, slants, and combination development.

Q: Do you have any general advice to pass on to practitioners?

Yes, become passionate about your art. Learn all you can about it, understand the roots so you can appreciate the fruit.

Q: What do you consider to be the major changes in the art since you began training?

I see the cost to be a legitimate dojo as the major change—cost of a building, cost of insurance, cost of utilities, cost of supplies, cost of equipment, cost of learning to run a business, and the cost of marketing just to be competitive. You have to be trained to understand safe traditional development of athletes. The last thing you want to do is have your students doing something that is outdated and become injured from it. Suddenly, you have a lawsuit filed against you for negligence. The laws have changed a lot regarding how classes are taught now from my earlier days. You have to be more sensitive to special needs of people who have many different reasons why they are training in karate.

Q: Who would you like to have trained with that you have not (dead or alive)?

I would have loved to train with Miyagi Chojin Sensei, the founder of Goju Ryu. He was from a wealthy family that afforded him the ability to really research and find the best in Goju Ryu, and to work to develop it to its fullest potential in his students. I would imagine he was totally passionate about his art to dedicate his whole life to it.

Q: What would you say to someone who is interested in starting to learn karate?

Take a trip to all of the dojos in your town and watch the beginning class, and then the advanced class. If you don't see much difference in the quality, move on. Talk to the Sensei and see if he truly has enough time to talk to you about the history or the art he teaches. See how knowledgeable he is. If he does not want to take time to talk to you as a prospective student or customer, then you may experience the same kind of treatment when you are a student of the program. The instructor is everything in guiding you to truly understand the system you are going to learn from him. Find one with a consistent record of developing his students in quality of technique and life.

Q: What is it that keeps you motivated after all these years?

My motivation is love for what karate has given me. It has introduced me not only to scientific physical strategy, but also life strategies. I'm able to handle all types of conflict with an attitude of total confidence. I have met some of the finest people on this earth through karate, and I would venture to say I'm not done meeting more wonderful Karate-ka's around the world. The life skills I have learned from karate I continue to pass on to my family members and my students. I truly feel I have influenced people in making their lives better through karate.

Q: What is your philosophical basis for your karate training?

Try to teach my students to love it as I do. It is so much a part of my life that I have been able to test myself with the idea that both my wife Yvonne and I share, that we are in a "Race for Life." How much can we accomplish before it is our time? The test in Kata "Sanchin" reminds me of my life. It means mind, body, and spirit. The test is the focus on breathing, tensing of the muscles, and focusing on the power of total concentration while your partner strikes your muscle groups to make sure your muscles are tight and strong, and that you are rooted and grounded in your stance. Every day, I work with a constant bombardment of issues, circumstances, conflicts, emotions, chaos, but yet I feel I'm just floating along handling all of those issues without a blink of distraction. I love that I can handle conflict management in such an easy manner, and I give all of the credit to Karate and Sanchin Kata. As an investigator for the last 17 years, at the company I work for, I find myself in very unpredictable circumstances every day. You are in a constant training mind of Karate-do. Technique is only real if you can use it in life applications.

Q: Do you have a particularly memorable karate experience that has remained as an inspiration for your training?

I have a memorable experience from JKF 9th Dan Grandmaster Kenzo Uchiage, who was one of the Class-A Examiners from Japan testing me for my 5th Dan, many years ago. As I finished Kata Sesan, Grandmaster Kenzo Uchiage walked up to me with his son, JKF 7th Dan Goju Ryu Uchiage Kai Chairman Takeshi Uchiage, and said to me in Japanese, "Your hands are better than Japan Technical Committee." First, I was shocked, then I was honored, and then I smiled and asked, "Sensei, does that mean I passed?" Sensei Takeshi Uchiage said, "Sensei Tibon, Sensei Tibon," shaking his head, as my question was inappropriate. I smiled and bowed with respect to Grandmaster Kenzo Uchiage. I will never forget that moment as long as I live. I trained for almost three months in my swimming pool, doing kata so I could develop the fluid hands I wanted for my katas. When I did kata, I wanted my hands to look like floating seaweed in the ocean. Grandmaster Kenzo Uchiage confirmed that my training was correct. I still practice doing kata in the swimming pool to maintain the fluid hand techniques. At the end of that testing seminar, Grandmaster Kenzo Uchiage and the Class A Examiners presented me with a large poster photo of all of us together. Each examiner signed his name over his individual photo. I look at it everyday hanging on the wall in my dojo.

Q: After all these years of training and experience, could you explain the meaning of the practice of karate?

When you are young, you have that "I can do anything" attitude. You do all of the crazy breaking of bricks, wood, tiles, punching, and kicking trees. Your body become tempered and fast. As you get older, your body moves slower, but you are able to make strong power with less effort. As you get even older, your mind becomes more understanding and more conscious of movements, and those applications can mean so much more. I know I teach a lot more technical things now at the age of 53 than when I was 23 years old. I think the meaning of practice is two levels, first the body and the spirit, and then with age, the mind's knowledge ultimately becomes the strongest part of the overall training experience.

Q: How do you think a practitioner can increase his/her understanding of the spiritual aspect of the art?

The spiritual aspect of the art comes to me in kata. The movements are so intricate and complicated. It is my thinking that the ancients were amazing people to develop such a technically

physical spiritual set of movements that encapsulates a variety of defenses of a lost era. Yet, today, we study the same movement, as done so many hundreds or thousands of years ago in the honor of those who created this wonderful art of humanity. At one of my first tests with Grandmaster Kenzo Uchiage, we had some 40 plus black belts from around the world. The masters drilled us for three days, for about 22 hours of physical training. When you barely are able to walk or hold a bar of soap in your hands, you then get tested to be your best level for your next Dan certification. It was a true stripping of our physical self, and a test of our will to put all of our aches and pains aside, to perform at our best to pass our test. I was lucky to be one of nine who passed the test. Many went home not so happy, but understood the test and its reason. I think this was a true test of the spiritual aspect of the art for me. My suggestion is to read all you can on everything pertaining to Budo, Bushido, Karate-do, Kung Fu, Tae Kwon Do, Wu Shu, Book of Five Rings, and Sun Tsu's Art of War. Books of martial arts strategies will help you better understand why they say, "Karate is life."

Q: Is there anything lacking in the way martial arts are taught today compared to how they were in your beginnings?

I have to say some of the great teachers are gone; our generation is responsible to carry on their legacy. If we don't carry on and do our job to promote karate the way the old Masters did, then our way of karate will be lost within the next two generations. We must work together to help preserve and instill in our future Senseis that they must pass on the old ways—the old secrets handed down to us, pass on the stories that make you think about how really deep that technique or that spiritual attitude really goes. A lot has changed since my beginnings, and my charge is to do my part to help pass on and promote our way of karate so those in the public may find us and hopefully help continue its legacy.

Gene Tibon

Q: Could I ask you what you consider to be the most important qualities of a successful karate practitioner?

The most important qualities of a successful karate practitioner are honesty, integrity, and true character of a human being. I know some men who truly have these qualities, and are people I'm proud to call my friends. These people understand "DO," the Way. I also have met many who lack all of these qualities; they are willing to cheat, to lie, to speak ill of others to make themselves look good. They have hidden agendas to promote themselves any way they can, by manipulating people or the political system for their own personal benefit. Believe it or not, we have these kinds in karate, also. These people are still lost.

Q: What advice would you give to students on the question of supplementary training (running, weights, et cetera)?

Supplementary training always is good, especially if you want to be at your best level to execute a technique or a series of combinations. I tell my students: your body is like a perfect gun, but if the bullet is only partially filled with gun powder, the bullet does not fly so far, and therefore not effective when it makes contact with its target. Your body may have strength, but without the wind or endurance to maintain the strength to effectively hit or kick your target, you will be vulnerable to expose yourself to a counter by somebody who has all of his weapons intact. The supplementary training will help that bullet be potent and effective when you fire it.

Q: Why do you think that preserving the cultural values of Budo is important in our modern society?

I read this quote from the book "Budo Secrets" by John Stevens, "For a realization to be authentic, one must be able to apply it in the actual world. True understanding is reflected in one's technique and also in one's daily life. This is the real battlefield where one's enlightenment is constantly tested." In the book "The Way to Black Belt" by Lawrence Kane and Kris Wilder, they quote, "Etiquette and manners is an integral part of budo, for without it we would be practicing nothing more than basic violence." These statements say it all. If people really understood these quotes in our modern society and lived by them, we would have a very different world.

I'm currently the President of the USANKF of Northern California, Inc., the Regional Sports Organization for the development of traditional Karate in Northern California. It's a nonprofit 501(c)3 public charitable organization. My idea in our RSO is to support, nurture, develop, certify, and acknowledge our athletes, coaches, referees in the Northern California RSO. This group will make its contribution to traditional karate by giving motivation and energy in developing our future athletes.

Q: Have there been times when you felt fear in your training?

Yes, many years ago, while working for my present employer, I was loading some very large equipment. I stepped in a hole and snapped my ligaments in left ankle, where they attach to my foot. They were severed so badly they had me on the operating table for two hours, reconnecting all three of them. The doctor said: give up karate, boxing, and all I was doing in the martial arts, and that I would be a cripple the rest of my life. Well, when the cast came off my leg six months later, my left leg was two inches smaller in diameter than my right leg. I remember the doctor telling me to tiptoe to develop my strength. I thought to myself, "tiptoe" –

you've got be kidding me. At that time, prior to the accident, I was bench-pressing right at 410 pounds and I was leg pressing 750–850 pounds. I tried to tiptoe on my left foot and nothing was there. I was scared for the first time in my life that I really might be done with what I loved most, Martial Arts. Well, the next day I started running – better yet, let's call it "hop-jogging" – until finally I regained my strength in my leg. So, when I went back to the doctor four months later, he measured my left leg and it was 1/8-inch bigger than my right, so I felt good and continued with my training. This also become the point where teaching became a larger part of my life. My oldest son, Gino, then 10, brought over six of his friends and asked if I would teach them karate in our garage. That's when and where our first dojo started.

Q: Do you think that Olympics will be positive for the art of karate-do in case that happens one day?

I think the WKF is working hard to get our sport into the Olympics. It is keeping with the JKF Shite Kata for standardized mandatory forms, so the world is seeing specific kata the way Japan deemed it to fit each system. The katas will have a standard compulsory requirement. This is much like gymnastics with compulsory floor exercises, required to be performed in front of the judges. Now, the only problem is to insure we have referees and judges who know and understand the essence of each of the standardized katas of the four major systems. This is the most difficult, because we have many referees and judges who really don't understand the systems they are judging. It's up to the Technical Committees around the world to teach or insure that the referee corps understands specific traits of the four major systems. This way, the true winner can be selected, and not the person portraying a kata that is so animated for entertainment, for that actually will be recognized as being incorrect.

Kumite is starting to transition to face shields, mostly for more of a safety aspect, and for the perception of our sport. The world will be watching. Many will not like the face shield, and it will be hard for many to get used to. I think if you look at the other contact sports, like boxing, you have mandatory head, hand, and groin protection. Tae Kwon Do has chest gear, headgear, hand, and groin protection required. Yet Kumite has only a mouthpiece, hand, shin gear, booties, and groin cup. Due to the amount of contact in our sport, many who will make the decisions may want to see more protection for this contact sport. I think it may help with the broken noses and the shattered cheekbones, so it may prove an important piece of safety equipment. The foot protection has helped with broken feet and toes, but because of the foot protection and shin protection, the kicks are coming in with full impact, and hands and arms now are suffering the injuries. I feel that as Karate goes into the Olympics, it will be good for the promotion of our art, and with the right type of marketing will help grow our art in the world.

Q: What are your thoughts on the future of karate?

As far as the future of karate, it is a little frightening to me when I see how many non-traditional schools are out there versus the traditional schools. The new non-traditional schools are totally commercial and look at every way to get the student in with different marketing tools so that many in the traditional schools are used to the old idea of, "if you want the traditional dojo, you need to search for me." That has changed a lot; the attitude for karate is not the same it was back in the '50s, '60s, and '70s. There was a special mystical perception of those who were in karate and attained the black belt. Karate seldom was seen; then it became such an entertainment value in the movies that soon everybody wanted it. Unfortunately, many of the non-traditional who are very smart and know how to make money from the marketing craze on television turned karate into a jazzercise mixture

of kicking and boxing, full contact, and holds barred matches that took away the mystical perception from karate. Too much of something, and pretty soon you take it for granted, and many in a world of wanting everything fast want their black belts in less than two years. Some commercial dojos promise this type of program, with kids as young as 6 to 8 years old receiving a black belt. I've even seen them on talk shows demonstrating to the masses with the quality of karate moves one would expect of a beginner in a traditional dojo.

I'm hoping that all Traditional Japanese Okinawa Karate can come together and support each other in having karate represented at the Olympics, representing the United States as a united group of traditionalists working together to preserve the Budo in Karate, and at the same time helping us develop a United States Karate team to represent us in the Olympics.

TAKESHI UCHIAGE

UNVEILING THE MASTER

Sensei Takeshi Uchiage was born in 1948 in Osaka, Japan, and made his first steps in Goju Ryu Karate-Do in his father's dojo at the age of 6. When he studied Physical Education at the Tenri University in Nara, he also practiced Kenyu Ryu under the direction of Master Tadao Nakano. After his graduation in 1971, he became trainer of the Tenri University Karate-Do team in Nara, Japan, and a technical advisor for the Taiiku-kai Karate-Do team of the Osaka Keizai University.

In 1972, the first typical Martial Arts building outside Japan was inaugurated in the Steveston district of the city of Richmond, Canada. Because of the amity between Richmond and Wakayama-city, Shozo Ujita, who was mayor of Wakayama-city, also was present. He was astounded by the fact that Karate-Do would not be practiced in this new Martial Arts dojo. Therefore, being president of J.K.F. Goju-Kai and vice president of J.K.F., he requested one of his top students to leave for Richmond, Canada, as a goodwill ambassador for Karate-Do. Sensei Uchiage left for Canada in June 1973.

He is chairman of Goju Ryu Karate-Do Uchiage-Kai, which is a member of J.K.F. Goju-Kai, Chief of the Technical Committee of Osaka Keizai University since 1980, and former W.U.K.O. (WKF) Kumite referee and Kata judge. This is Sensei Uchiage, a true gem of Goju Ryu Karate.

Q: How long have you been practicing the martial arts and who were your teachers?

I have been practicing martial arts for more than 55 years. In Karate, I have trained in two different styles, Goju Ryu and Kenyu Ryu. I also have a Sho-Dan in Sumo. My first teacher was my father, Grand Master Kenzo Uchiage. He was a very humble person and never showed off his skills to others. He had the ability to see and to improve the student's strengths. He also taught with the rules and teachings from his teacher, Sensei Miyagi, and hewas the person who received the highest Dan from Sensei Miyagi. Also,

Shozo Ujita for Goju. He was a student one year higher than my father at the Ritsumeikan University. He was a very gentle man, and a very strong person.

Kenyu Ryu is under Grand Master Tadao Nakano at Tenri University, Nara, Japan. He always took on challenges head-on with a pure heart, and this is also the way he taught Karate.

Q: Would you tell us some interesting stories of your early days in karate?

During the summer, my mother prepared ice water for after my trainings. The ice water was something I looked forward to, to get through some of the hard trainings. Also, during the summers in Japan it gets really hot, and running barefooted hurt the bottom of my feet. I was your average student to begin with. It took many hours and many repetitions to get to where I am today. When I was a white belt, in the All Japan championships for my style, I still was able to finish fourth against other black belts. I figured out that it's not the colour of your belt, but how much you know and attained through training.

Q: Do you think training in Martial Arts and Budo can help the young generation in becoming successful as individuals in the future?

Yes. It teaches individuals to respect their seniors (senpais). I believe it is important no matter what profession that you respect the people who were there before you, along with the people you work with.

Q: What do you think are the most important qualities for a student become proficient in any art of Budo?

To always strive to become better. Not only to improve your techniques but also to improve as a person. One's techniques reflect his or her characteristics and personality, so it also is important to strive to become a better person, not just a better martial artist. Karate is a deep martial art, and when a question arises, it takes a long time to come up with the answer. It is like a bottomless pit; the knowledge and meanings or techniques are endless.

Q: With all the technical changes during the last years, do you think there still are "pure" styles of karate?

I believe that the Dojo techniques have not changed much in the last years. However, techniques used and geared toward competition and tournaments have changed. The techniques have changed in order to provide judges and referees with what they're looking for to be successful in competition. I still believe that there are "pure" styles of Karate left; it's just that we don't see them as much, as they don't show in competitions.

Styles are important because each one of them has its good characteristics and its own special techniques, which no other style has. Also the different styles have developed because of where their Karate was formed and it's important to keep the history and tradition intact.

Q: What is your opinion of fighting events such as the UFC and Mixed Martial Arts events?

If many people support these kinds of martial arts, then I think it's a good thing rather than a bad thing. I have not personally trained in these Martial arts so I cannot comment regarding if its good or not.

Q: Karate nowadays often is referred to as a sport... would you agree with this definition or is "only" Martial Art?

You train it as a martial art in the Dojo, but when you think of it as a sport looking to make it into the Olympics, it has to be as a sport. If you want to keep the "pure" karate, then it's still a martial art. I think that many people refer to it as a sport because people only see Karate during competitions or sports events.

Q: How do you see karate in North America and around the world at the present time?

I don't know if it is lack of advertisement, but in Europe a lot of people who don't even train Karate come to watch the competitions; on the other hand, in North America, very few people who have nothing to do with Karate come to watch the competitions. I think it would be fair to say that Karate is more popular in other parts of the world.

Q: Do you think that the amount of Kata of the style is relevant in the mastery of the art of Karate?

The number of Katas that each style has doesn't have anything to do with mastering the art of Karate to that style. Kata Bunkai is extremely important because otherwise you will not understand the techniques needed to be used in certain situations, and during Kata it must look like

you are fighting opponents who are not there. By understanding the Bunkai, you can perform a Kata that has meaning.

Q: When teaching the art of karate, what is the most important element: self-defense or sport?

It depends on what your student is there to attain through Karate. If students are there to learn self-defense, then I will teach self-defense. If students are there to train for sport and competition, then I will teach accordingly.

Q: Forms and sparring: what's the proper ratio in training?

If it is someone who competes mostly in Kata, then a majority of the time should be spent training Kata. But they also must train Kumite, and vice versa. If it's someone who does not compete, then they should train both equally in order to understand all aspects of Karate.

Q: Do you have any general advice to pass on to practitioners?

The results will not come right away. It is not like in movies where things can be attained at a fast rate. Take your time and be patient, and things will come with time. Karate must be studied for a lifetime as new things come up almost daily. The most important thing is to train slow and steady. You will get as much back as you put into it.

Q: What do you consider to be the major changes in the art since you began training?

The techniques. Currently in competition, speed is more important than power. Also, you see that there is a reduced amount of kicks compared to many years ago.

Q: Who would you like to have trained with that you have not (dead or alive)?

Master Chojun Miyagi.

Q: What that keeps you motivated after all these years?

The closer you think you get to the answer, the further away you're getting.

Q: How do you think a practitioner can increase his/her understanding of the spiritual aspect of the art?

To not forget the roots, and keep the history in mind, but also to imagine your opponent standing in front of you and always putting forth your best. Always concentrate and do things at your best. You don't need to train long, but you must train efficiently, and concentrate.

Q: Is anything lacking in the way martial arts are taught today compared to how they were in your beginnings?

There is a lack of emphasis on defense. People now think that offense is the best defense, and because the punches people do now are fast and have speed but lack power, there is less fear of being hurt.

Q: What do you consider the most important qualities of a successful karate practitioner?

They have strong will and a strong spirit. In modern society, it's easier to attain things, so there is less patience and effort in order to get what one wants. It's important to always strive to improve, and always test your limit in order to grow as an individual and become a more well-rounded individual. The meaning of practicing Karate is to help those weaker or in need, and to head straight on with 100 percent of what you have to those who're stronger than you.

Q: What advice would you give to students on the question of supplementary training (running, weights, et cetera)?

It's there to enhance your karate. If you weight train, you must weight train to help your karate. Building too much hard muscles will slow you down. But it is different for each individual, so it may be best to ask a personal trainer to train for your own body and strengthen your weaknesses along with growing your strengths.

Q: Have there been times when you felt fear in your training?

When I saw someone's arm being broken when they were blocking a kick.

Q: Do you think that Olympics will be positive for the art of karate-do in case that happens one day?

I stayed at Sensei Jim Kojima's house for six months when I came to Canada in 1973. Sensei Kojima was the chief Referee for the International Judo Federation. I think Karate rules will change if it's in the Olympics, but I think this will give an opportunity for many athletes to receive funding from their respective National Olympics Committee's. However, I am not sure if you really can call it "Karate" if there is only a Kumite division in the Olympic Games. Even now in the Pan American Games, Kata is not being included. If it's truly "Karate" I think both disciplines should be included.

Q: What are your thoughts on the future of karate?

We should try to maintain our different styles of Karate and its characteristics. I fear that if and when it becomes an Olympic sport, everything will become "sport karate" and we no longer will have different styles of Karate and the styles will lose its identity.

RAMON VERAS

GOJU WITHOUT FRONTIERS

RELATIVELY LITTLE HAS BEEN WRITTEN ABOUT SENSEI VERAS BUT ANYONE WHO SPENDS ANY AMOUNT OF TIME RESEARCHING THE WORLD OF KARATE KNOWS THAT HE IS ONE OF THE TOP GOJU RYU INSTRUCTORS IN THE UNITED STATES. SENSEI VERAS EXPERTISE AND KNOWLEDGE OF THE TECHNICAL ASPECTS OF GOJU RYU ARE SECOND TO NONE. MANY YEARS OF HARD TRAINING AND HAVE PROVIDED HIM WITH AN IMMENSE UNDERSTANDING OF THE ART. WHEN HE MOVES, IT IS WITH PRECISION AND DIRECTION; ALL HIS ENERGY FOCUSED TOWARD THE END RESULT. BUT GOJU RYU KARATE TO SENSEI VERAS ISN'T ALL ABOUT PHYSICAL TECHNIQUES, IT IS ABOUT RELATIONSHIPS, FRIENDSHIPS AND STRONG BONDS WITH HIS STUDENTS. HE IS ONE OF THE MOST REVERED AND RESPECTED BY THOSE HE TEACHES. HOLDING NOTHING BACK—WHEN A STUDENT IS READY TO LEARN, HE SHARES. AND THIS TEACHING EXTENDS TO LIFE AS WELL AS TO THE DEVASTATING ART OF GOJU RYU.

SENSEI VERAS TEACHES HIS STUDENTS WITH THE SAME PATIENCE AND DEDICATION THAT HE USED TO BECOME A MASTER OF THE ART "THE KEY," HE SAYS, "IS TO BALANCE EVERY SINGLE ELEMENT IN YOUR TRAINING SO THAT ONE ASPECT WILL HELP THE OTHERS. YOU DON'T WANT TO BE UNBALANCED IN MARTIAL ARTS. REMEMBER THAT THE SECRET IS BALANCE, NOT ONLY IN MARTIAL ARTS BUT IN LIFE AS WELL. TO BE SUCCESSFUL YOU HAVE TO HAVE GOALS AND WORK IN THAT DIRECTION.

YOU HAVE TO TRAIN HARD AND SMART—OTHERWISE EVERYTHING YOU WANT WILL JUST BE A DREAM. A GOAL IS AN IMPOSSIBLE DREAM IF YOU DON'T TAKE THE NECESSARY STEPS TO MAKE IT HAPPEN."

Q: How many styles have you trained in and who were your teachers? Do you practice any other art in conjunction with karate?

I basically have only studied Goju-Ryu deeply, and I am still learning. Every time my sensei comes from Japan, he makes feel like a beginner all over again.

However I have attended many seminars and workshops in Shoto-Kan and Shito-Ryu. I have attended seminars with Takayuki Mikami of JKA Shotokan, and with Kanazawa Sensei, Also of JKA Shotokan, and n Shito Kai with Choko Sato from Venezuela. Shito Kai is the father of Karate in Venezuela. Also, I have studied Kobudo with Sensei Anthony Marquez and Master Shinpoh Matayoshi in Okinawa. About 15 years ago I began to study Chen Style Tai Chi with Master Xu Zhong Xin; this martial art really interests me as much as Goju-Ryu.

Q: Would you tell us some interesting stories of your early days in karate?

I really don't have too many stories. But one event sticks in my mind. When I started karate, I trained with three friends. One of them was Sensei Domingo Llanos who went on to become Vice World Champion in WUKO . We were really dedicated to our training. We would train at the dojo three times per week. The dojo was about ½ hour by car and two hours walking. We would usually get a ride to the dojo, but sometimes we had to walk back home. After at least two hours of vigorous training! On our days off from the dojo we would train on our own in the basement of my sister's house. Training in those days was full contact fighting with no protection. We'd go at it practically non-stop for 1.5 to 2 hours. During one of these sessions I got round kicked in the left eye by my friend Domingo Llanos, and for about 8 hours I could not see out of my left eye. A very scary moment in my life. And facing my parents was even scarier. But next day I was back at dojo, but only to watch the class. When I told Sensei Merriman my story, he just smiled and said, "why didn't you block like this?"

Q: Were you a 'natural' at karate – did the movements come easily to you?

I was not a natural and had to work hard, and I still train to keep my level up. But, honestly, karate is not a natural thing for anybody. You must work and repeat the technique to look good. I don't feel natural for karate, but karate feels natural for me. I can train in karate, or read about karate, or watch karate videos, and I am still training with passion after 40 plus years in karate.

Q: Please, explain for us the main points of Goju Ryu and its differences with other styles like Shotokan, Wado Ryu or Shito Ryu?

When you contrast Goju-Ryu with Shoto Kan and Wado, the differences are obvious. The kata names are totally different; Goju-Ryu use more circular blocks as opposed to the linear movement in Shoto Kan and Wado, and the stances are normally longer and the movements are bigger in Shoto Kan. As for Shito and Goju, well, here you will find more similarities. The same katas in Goju-ryu exist in Shito, but in Shito Ryu they are done with linear movements. Goju-Ryu is a close-range fighting system. It places a lot of emphasis deep abdominal breathing to generate power at close distance. All defense incorporates circular movement, the kicks are always below the belt and they use a lot of joint attacks when applying the katas and when using controlling techniques.

Q: Goju Ryu has a low number of kata compared to other styles like Shotokan or Shito Ryu, do you think that the number of kata within the style affects the mastery of the art of karate or not?

This is a good question and it has been asked many times.

In my opinion, it's not the number of techniques or how many katas you know that defines mastery. Quality, not quantity defines a mastery. For instance look at golf. How many ways can someone swing the club? Not many. But some golfers become masters and other do not. It is the time one spends working on each technique that produces mastery – for that technique. You can become a master of one kata or just one technique. And it is very difficult to stay at that high level unless you keep practicing.

If you have logged over 10,000 hours of training in one kata or one technique over the years, you can be said to have reached a mastery level for that one kata or that one technique, but you have not mastered the ones you practice a few times every other month. Technical skills, or katas – that is, a set of fixed techniques – are learned in three stages: the learning stage, the practice stage, and the mastery stage. No matter what level you are, you will be in these stage when you learn a new skill.

Bruce Lee said it well: "I fear not the man who has practiced 10,000 kicks once, but I fear the man who has practiced one kick 10,000 times."

Q: How do you see the different "branches" of the Goju Ryu style...Goju Kai, Okinawan, etc...?

Many different groups and organization promote Goju-Ryu with different names. Every group has a different mission and goals. As long they teach in good faith and are fair to their members, I don't see a problem. The group out there teaching good karate and good Goju-Ryu is good for society. The communities we live in need more dojos teaching proper karate. I respect all the different groups, but I do think that they should at least do the same 12 katas, and follow the principles of Goju-ryu as closely as possible to the way Chojun Miyagi left it. The katas are models for training and mastering the techniques and don't need to change much. Nor do I feel we need to add more katas or unnecessary movements to the katas.

Q: Karate is nowadays often referred to as a sport... would you agree with this definition or is a martial art?

Yes and no. Karate can be practiced as a sport, as a life-long personal improvement tool, as a physical fitness program to improve ones health, as a self-defense martial art, or just as recreational activity for joy of learning. It all depends on your goal. At different stages in one's life, one can practice karate with different purposes. The young people can just practice for the sport aspect, for fun, and for personal improvement. A woman living in the city can learn it for self-defense. As we get older, it can be the perfect fitness program to stay functional as we age. However, we become good at what we practice: if you train for sport, your skill does not really transfer to self-defense, and if you train for just self-defense you may not be prepared to enter a tournament. As a karate instructor, I personally like the totality of training, from the physical preparation, nutrition, technical tactical, and self-defense, teaching, and participating in tournaments. I have been a competitor, a coach, a referee, a teacher, and, first and foremost, a student for life.

Q: What are the most important qualities for a student to become proficient in the Goju Ryu style of karate?

The most important quality for a student to become proficient in Goju Ryu or any other martial art style is persistence – that is, to show up on a regular basis for classes and dedicate time to practice what they learn in in class. Class time is not enough.

Q: As a teacher of the art of karate – what is the most important element of your teachings?

As a karate instructor, I try very hard to keep up my own training and stay up to date with any new sport science methods of training in strength and conditioning. I personally work to stay physically fit and pass whatever I learn on to my students. Sometimes I bring experts in sport science to my dojo for lectures to educate me and my students. I try to connect with my students to find out what their goals are and try to give them what they want from the training. Everyone wants something different out of his or her training.

Q: Kihon, Kata and Kumite, what's the proper ratio in training?

This a very complicated question because it depends on the individual student's goal. If students train for recreation, a balanced approach with a good variety of training is adequate. If the students just want karate for fitness, a different training plan is required. If the students are focused on competition, the training should be very carefully planned, using periodization; the percentage of physical, Kihon, kata and Kumite will vary depending on how close they are to the competition and when they need to peak. In these days the competition at the Elite level is more specialized, focusing on either Kata or Kumite. Very few people do both these days. For a one-hour, general training class, I divide my training 25 percent physical preparation, 25 percent kihon specific for kata or kumite, and 40 percent either kata or Kumite, and 10 percent cool down and stretching. I teach kata and Kumite in different classes.

Q: How has your personal expression of karate developed over the years and what is it that keeps you motivated after all these years?

My perspective has changed a lot over the years. When I started to train in the early 70s, karate training was very different. The training was a lot more serious; the students came to the dojo to seriously train. We didn't focus so much on belts. We would get promoted when the sensei surprised you. He would call out and say you were ready to move up in rank. It was a 'wow' moment.

Now the kids and the parents want to know how soon can my son or daughter get the new belt. It's very different now in that respect. The tournaments were a lot different with multiple

disciplines participating: karate, tae kwan do, and kung fucompeted together. However, now the tournaments are much better organized and specialized by style and discipline. Karate, tae kwan do and and Kung fu have their own Tournaments. The instructors now are more safety conscious than when I started. There are fewer injuries in training,

Q: How important is competition in the evolution of a karate practitioner?

Competition has played a big role in the evolution of karate. Competition is a big part of a modern society and has made karate better known all over the world. The competition is a part of karate and it has a played a big role in my karate life. I really enjoyed competing when I was growing up, and it has kept me in karate all these years. I really enjoyed trips to competitions around the East Coast: New York, New Jersey, Connecticut and the Boston area. But competition is not the only reason and should not be the main reason to do karate.

Q: What really means "Ikken Hissatsu" and how it applies when used in Goju ryu Karate?

Ikken Issatsu is a concept used in Japanese Martial arts. The meaning is to train your fist and foot and body to become a killing weapon and kill or knock down your opponent in one blow. I haven't had the opportunity to put this theory in practice yet, so for me it is just a theory. It more practical for Kendo and Iado because an expert with the Katana could chop someone's head and kill with one cut. In Karate you know how difficult it is to just score a point. In the UFC, which is the more realistic fighting system today, the competitors hit the opponent at full power with multiple rapid punches and the opponents get up and walk it off. So for karate it is better to train for multiple blows in combination.

Q: How do you see the art of Goju Ryu evolve in the future?

Goju Ryu and all karate can keep evolving and at same time maintain the traditional culture of karate. It is very important to know about the history and tradition of Goju-Ryu. I try to stay connected with my past teachers and pay them the respect they deserve. These things should not change about karate. The instructors are the ones that need to evolve and make the training more scientific, safer and interesting and effective. There are lots of resources these days online on sport science that can help us make our training more interesting. I think getting more education about the science and methodology and periodization of training can make our training better and more interesting for future generations.

Q: Do you feel that you still have further to go in your studies?

Yes, of course. I have a long way to go in my study of Goju-Ryu and in learning about the how and why of training and how to teach better. This objective for me will never come to an end.

Q: What advice would you give to students on the question of supplementary training?

Supplementary training is an important part of Goju-Ryu training but it should done in conjunction with technical training. It should enhance your technical training. It should be done with small progression over time. We should never over-do it so we can train again the next day. If you train hard one day, go light to medium the next day. Never train hard too many consecutive days.

Q: What advice would you give to an instructor who is struggling with his or her won development?

I've been there and I have seen many people plateau in their training.

When this happens we need to change our training. Training the same way for the same numbers hours with the same intensity day in and day out will lead to saturation after six weeks. No matter what type of training you do. Variation of training is necessary to avoid stagnation. Vary the volume, the intensity, and duration of training and how you train, at least every four to six weeks. In karate we have so many choices in techniques, Katas, and physical training, that we should always have a new, interesting training plan.

Q: Have there been times when you felt fear in your training?

No not really, I have always enjoyed my training. I enjoy teaching karate as much as practicing Goju-ryu karate. That's why I've kept at it so long . I simply enjoy my Goju-Ryu training and talking to people about all aspects of karate.

Q: Do you think that Olympics will be positive for the art of karate-do?

I really don't think karate will be an Olympic sport in my lifetime. For one the Olympics don't have room for another sport in the their agenda. At present they allow 28 official sports in the program. That means an existing Olympic sport would have to be taken out, and that's not very easy to do.

As for whether it would be a positive event, certainly the publicity Karate would get as an Olympic sport would be positive. But if Karate becomes an Olympic Sports, Karate will become more and more a pure sport, and maybe that's not a good idea. Not too many people really join karate because they want to be in the Olympics, and that would likely change.

Eventually the sensei would become just a Coach and the traditional sensei would disappear; you would get fewer karate dojos serving the community.

I don't see too many judo schools, and the Tae Kwan Do Schools that teach Olympic style are disappearing in my Area.

More people these days are interested in Okinawa Karate because it is not so focused on Sports. Traditional Karate has more value to offer the community than just as a sport.

Q: What are your views on kata bunkai? Is it bunkai really important?

In Goju-Ryu the Kata Bunkai has a lot of value, so it is very important. The kata without Bunkai is just a physical exercise, which is fine, because we need this part of karate as physical conditioning. The bunkai gives the kata meaning; it gives you a reason to practice the kata. Goju-Ryu Karate is a practical self defense art. You will find the self defense part of Karate in the Bunkais. When people understand the bunkai in the kata, it is easier to for them to practice the katas. When we practice kata, we should be mindful of the bunkai in the technique being practiced in the kata and make the practice as real as possible. In Goju- ryu, kata practice is visualization of self-defense techniques.

Q: How important is for a Goju Ryu practitioner to know all the Kata of the style?

The kata are a big part of Goju-ryu, but in Goju-ryu we don't have so many katas as in other styles. You can practice other characteristics of Goju-ryu, such as basics and application of the basics, pre arranged kumite, kumite drills, supplementary training for body conditioning. I emphasize kata depending on the age and maturity of the students. Kata is very hard for young kids so I teach them basic for kata and a lot kumite drills early on. Eventually they will be ready for kata. The adults enjoy the kata and bunkai practice more than kumite. But you don't need to learn all the katas unless you want to become an instructor, you can just focus on a few katas. I once met Master Sakiyama, one of Chojun Miyagi's students in Okinawa. He was a Master of Zen and a master of Sanchin. Although he know all the Goju Katas, he said Sanchin was enough. His Sanchin kata was amazing.

Q: How do you like to train yourself?

My personal training these days is very straightforward and very general.

My main goal in training is to stay fit and healthy and maintain my karate level good enough to teach. Three times per week in the morning I train some basic and the basic katas and a follow it with strength training. My weight training is a mixture of Hojo Undo and modern weight training, not too intense but very specific to karate movements.

The other days of the week I practice Sanchin kata and one advanced kata; I end the kata practices with Tensho and stretching. I repeat this over the week so I cover all the Goju-ryu katas. Twice a week I find some time and I do ten rounds on the bags with different techniques to get some cardiovascular training. I do the traditional Okinawa Goju-Ryu articulation warmups and stretching every day.

Q: Shotokan, Shito Ryu, Goju, Ryu etc…How do you think the different branches/styles affect the complete art of Karate?

These styles are all karate.Each style is a model for training and to polish and perfect self-defense and fighting techniques. Each style has some unique training methods. They are all equally effective for self-defense, and they are all part of karate history. They should all be preserved for future generations.

Q: Do you think Kobudo training is beneficial for a Karate practitioner in general?

I have done Kobudo training before; it is a very good martial art.

I trained in Kobudo first with Sensei Kimo Wall, Sensei Anthony Marquez, and Master Shipoh Matayoshi. Kobudo is very interesting but I don't think it will help your karate. If you want to be good in Karate you need to focus on Karate, and if want to be good in Kobudo you should focus on kobudo. However if you want to just learn kobudo for the sake of learning, by all means learn it. Learning is never a waste of time.

Q: What is your opinion about the "Shobu Ippon" division in Karate competition?

I been in the tournament environment from the mid 70s and I have competed with all of

them: Shobu Ipoon, Shobu San Bon, and now the current rules WKF rules. It's just another form of competition. Competition is just that – competition. You learn the rules and train to compete within the parameters for the rules. In the old days with Shobu Ippon , the match was just one point, but it was not that easy to get an Ippon and the match was boring. Everybody played it safe and there was not much variety to the techniques. Now there more opportunities to get points, and the matches last longer. In the new WKF style of competition, the competitors need to be in better physical shape, the match is more exciting to watch.

Q: What are the most important points in your personal training these days?

In these days technical training is still very important, but it's more important to enjoy the training. And it's much more important to have balance in your training between physical and technical; balance is essential to staying fit and healthy.

Q: What karate can offer to the individual in these troubled times we are living in?

Yes, modern life can be very stressful these days. We spend most of our time driving to work and at work. Most people have sedentary jobs, they lose mobility and flexibility just sitting at work. Karate training can be an escape from the daily stress. From the fitness point of view, karate keeps people functional so they can stay healthier and more productive in society.

Q: After so many years of training, what is it for you that is so appealing in Goju Ryu and why?

I love everything about Goju-Ryu: I enjoy the physical training, the katas are very interesting and very well balanced and practical. I have a great Sensei Muramatsu who visits my dojo every year to share with us his special training methods. When I visit Okinawa, I train with many great seniors in the Okinawa Goju-Ryu Karate Kyo Kai. My sensei is 68 years old and still looks great physically – and technically super great. He does things like one-arm pull ups, push ups with one arm in one knuckle. I want to look close to him when I get up in my 60s and 70s and beyond. He is my inspiration for training.

Q: Finally, what advise would you like to give to all Karate practitioners?

I want to tell all karate practitioners to continue their training no matter what, to have multiple goals in training; to keep improving in karate and in all areas of their lives, and to contribute to the sport of karate if they do it as sport. If karate is not done as a sport, contribute in your dojo and keep the tradition moving forward for the next generation.

GOSHI YAMAGUCHI

PROTECTING THE LEGACY

While his small stature and gentle demeanor might belie his martial skill, there is no doubt that Goshi Yamaguchi's mastery of Goju – the art of hard and soft – passed to him by his father, the great Gogen "The Cat" Yamaguchi, is excellent.

Despite his many interests and goals, Goshi's first love is karate. He considers it an art and attributes all his success in life to what he calls the great "experience of karate practice." Unlike some instructors who profess to be experts, Yamaguchi Sensei minimizes the sensational and melodramatic aspects of karate. "Karate is a skill that requires time and thought," he says. "One who intends to use it aggressively is only disillusioning himself. Humility and self-restraint are very important in true karate-do."

When in action, his movements are relaxed, yet one can sense the unbelievable speed and force at the termination of each technique. The apparent destructive power of each action is overshadow by the beauty of the continuous flowing movement that is typical of the Goju-kai school.

This calmly forceful karate sensei recognizes the difficulty of describing the art in a clear-cut format for everybody to understand. "It is extremely hard to tell people what karate is because it is something that must be experienced to be understood — not just discussed. What you learn in the art of karate can always be used in your daily life."

Q: Shihan, how old were you when you started karate training, and what are some of your memories of that time?

A: I started karate at eight years old. At that time, we had no class for the children, so we trained with the adults, and the classes started late at night. What I remember most is that I could not eat supper if I didn't take class. So, every night I had to train or my parents wouldn't give me food! When I was in high school, I thought about how to commit to the art and study karate better. It was very stressful growing up as the son of one of the most famous Japanese karateka, Grandmaster Gogen Yamaguchi, because everybody said, "You are the son of Gogen Yamaguchi." So, I couldn't choose my own life. At that time, I was under a lot of self-imposed pressure all the time. I'd think things like, "I have to do my training; I have to be strong."

Actually, this was very good for me, because my brother kept reminding me or menacing me about what things would be like when I was grown up.

Q: As the son of Gogen Yamaguchi, was the training tougher for you?

A: Yes, of course. When I was a child, I couldn't say "daddy" all the time. I had to say "sensei" or "hanshi." It was always something like that. It was not like father and son; it was always teacher and student. It was difficult.

Q: Have you ever studied any other martial art?

A: Yes, I have. I did Chinese kung-fu. When I was a child, my brother also taught me judo, and I did kendo, too.

Q: In regards to karate, are you going to bring up your son like your father brought up you?

A: No, it will be quite different. That type of relationship is very difficult, so I have changed it. When I grew up, however, it was OK because I had older brothers, and everyone had it the same way.

Q: How about outside the dojo. What was life like with your father and mother?

A: My mother loved me and always took care of me. I believe my father loved me very much, but he didn't show it. So, I have no memories about playing with my father. I always had to say, "Good morning, teacher." When we walked together, I had to step back from him. That is what it was like. It was not like daddy and children.

Q: Your father went to Manchuria (a mountainous region of northeastern China) during World War II. What do you know about his experience and why he went there?

A: At that time, I was not born, so I know what my father told me. One of the reasons he went there was to see General Ishihara, a very famous general and shogun. He wanted my father go with him to Manshu (Manchuria). His group was a special organization — not the military — and it was throughout the Manchuria country. He had a very special position. You could say that it was underground, and he got news or intelligence in this manner. Of course, he taught karate, so he had good connections for Manchurian Chinese kung-fu and different martial artists he had taken to Japan. Everyone was able to communicate with each other, so they used to demonstrate the respective arts. As a result, on two occasions, the general took members from China to Japan.

Q: When you started your karate training, who was your first instructor?

A: My brother taught me very well at the outset. When I started in class, of course, my father taught, but my brother had already taught me well.

Q: Was your father a Shinto priest, and what did that mean?

A: Yes, he was. A high position, too. He liked to meditate, and he did this every morning. He also liked to pray, because Shinto is, as most Japanese people know it, like a culture. He also liked to use Shinto ideas in his karate.

Q: How did his Shinto spirituality and practice influence you and the goju-kai today?

A: A lot, of course, but these are different ideas. He liked to use Shinto in all aspects of his training, but he didn't say that everybody must do that, because this [Shinto] is a religion. He believed everyone had a right to his own religion, so he never told anyone he had to do it. Some people liked to follow him. I studied with him, but the influence of Shinto is not the same as training in goju-kai. Shinto reflected his personal ideas.

Q: How and when was he introduced to yoga?

A: He knew a very famous yogi, but I don't remember the name. I do know that he was from India. In Japan, there was a big organization that studied yoga, and my father had good connections through that group. So, he studied with the instructor from India and one from Japan for a long time.

Q: Did the yoga influence goju-kai? If so, where were the influences?

A: Yes, of course, he liked to put it all together. The yoga and the Shinto, too. This was his idea. We believe yoga is good for your breathing, and this comes in handy when you are working on your breathing. In the goju classes, my father taught the students how to do breathe properly ... as they would learn in yoga. If there's good breathing in yoga, there's good breathing in karate.

Q: Is that where ibuki breathing comes from?

A: No, goju breathing comes originally from Okinawa and there might be some Chinese influence, too. My father called it ibuki because the Okinawans and yoga heavily influenced him. We didn't say ibuki.

Q: How would you describe the state of goju-kai around the world?

A: Let me start by saying that I'm the president of the All-Japan Karatedo Goju-kai and of the International Karate-do Goju-kai. We have blocks in Oceania, Europe, South America, Africa and North America. Goju-kai also has many members. Outside of Japan, the Australian block has the oldest history.

Q: In the martial arts, we see many styles split and instructors break away from their masters. Why does this happen?

A: Some people say that this natural, and it follows from the concept of shu-ha-rei. "Shu" means that you study well continuously and "ha" means ideas. Finally, "rei" means to leave. As you know, we have many different styles of martial arts. Some martial arts start within one group. Then people have different ideas so they make many groups. This is the truth. If you teach well and maintain a good responsibility over your school, you can keep it attractive for all the members, even for some who are considering starting different groups. My father had many students and some formed new groups, some of which are now gone. But my father agreed that they could start or go their own way. Mas Oyama Sensei of Kyuokushin is an example of one who broke away. He was a member of goju-kai a long time ago. He and my father discussed many things and expressed many ideas. Of course, Oyama Sensei studied goju-ryu extensively, but one of his ideas was to start his own group, which my father approved. As a result, he started kyokushin. Even now there is still a very good friendship between the groups.

Q: What is the most important job of an instructor?

A: Well, of course, he has to teach well technically, but he also has to teach about life, such as how people can do well for their country and how they can contribute or work toward world peace. Every instructor must develop his own, good personal style.

Q: Some instructors who break away to create their own style don't have a complete understanding of "do" or neglect it in their teaching. To a student who isn't being fed the philosophy of the martial arts, what would be your advice?

A: If an instructor focuses only on the technical and doesn't think about this side [philosophy] anymore, a student might have to think about moving to another instructor. In karate, however, you can learn many things from technical training. Not only can you learn technique, because karate is selfdefense, you can also mature, grow up and learn to become your own person without copying someone else. In goju-kai, many instructors stress technical training, but there aren't enough who focus on proper spirit for self-development. If there were, there would be more harmony in the teaching. Somebody mean by how good the teacher, the suggestions from the teacher.

Q: What does karatedo mean to you?

A: Karatedo, in my personal view and in my own way, means you should study the art from a more technical perspective. If you do this, it enables you to find out who is stronger. Whether I am stronger than you is irrelevant. What is important is whether I am stronger. This happens all the time. Sometimes I may want to escape, and I may want to look after just myself, but that is not correct. If I do karate, I have to be big, all the time. So karate is good for friendship and personality. It's also good for communication between countries and groups ... in a sports way. So I believe karate-do is good for training and for self-defense.

Q: Is the emphasis of your teaching on sport karate or the traditional art?

A: We don't need to separate sport and the traditional element. Many young people like to have a chance to participate in sport karate competition, and it is very good for them. In the process, they make friends and grow up. But people cannot neglect the mental aspect of training. It's just as important as the technical aspect. It's important to note that being a champion does not mean that the individual is the best [all-around] competitor. Of course, in sport, the champion is on top of the mountain. When you talk about traditional karate, however, the objective [top of the mountain] is not that at all. This confuses people. Karatedo is more than just how well you can do for yourself personally. It is also how well you interact with the public.

Q: Do you ever see karate becoming an Olympic sport?

A: The idea is good, but if it becomes an Olympic sport, I'm concerned that something [traditional ideals] will be lost. Ideally, we'd find a way to get it into the Olympics and maintain the

ideals. The instructors and organizers have to look at both ways. In Olympic competition, people think of one thing and one thing only, and that is how they can get a medal. Of course, the Olympic games are very good for contributing to world peace, but we need much more respect for the other things. The art is much more than training, competing, winning a medal and setting a record. Some practitioners who win medals are very good, but if they only think only about competition, they are not thinking about their attitude and manners.

Q: Do you encourage your students to compete?

A: Of course, because I was an international referee. I also think it would be good for the art to become an Olympic sport. When I teach, I teach both the way of sport and the traditional martial art.

Q: Did you compete yourself in your younger days?

A: Yes I did. When I was young, I participated in kata and kumite. I wanted to try more, but my father said, "One day you have to change. If you participate in tournaments, it's likely that you are always thinking about how you lost or how you can win." So my father told me to stop competing. My last tournament was a goju-kai tournament.

Q: Was your father in favor of sport karate?

A: I don't think so. He didn't like it because when he started training for kumite or real sparring, my brother started jiyu kumite. At that time, my father didn't think about competition like we are doing now. I think he would have accepted the idea of training in traditional karate first and then competition later. If you do competition karate, you are not using real karate. In competition, you are only seeing who is faster and who scores the point.

Q: Have events like K1, Pride and the UFC affected the martial arts?

A: Any martial art sport must have rules. In K1, people fight to see who is the strongest. I don't mean to say that this is bad. In fact, it is OK for some different groups. But goju-kai is nothing like these events. We must throw controlled punches. Of course, in training, we study how to throw a hard punch with the intent of killing. But of course, we do not actually do that. Now there is peace in the world, and I don't believe we need to show how strong we can kick and punch in the ring. We won't stop anyone else from doing that, but that is a different philosophy than what we have.

Q: For the last decade, there has been a growing trend among students to cross-train in different arts. How do you feel about this?

A: This is a good thing. Of course, some people say you should stick with only one art ... whether that is karate or some other martial art. But my father told me that it is not good to concentrate on just one art. In the Budo, a long time ago, every samurai could study many different ways. My father felt the same way.

Q: In terms of self-defense, does goju-kai have any particular strengths or weaknesses?

A: Although goju is very dangerous, my brother taught me the art is not for fighting in the street. Nevertheless, we have some other techniques ... not just punching and kicking. I think goju has many techniques that make it good for selfdefense. As you advance in your studies, you learn the more advanced bunkai from the kata.

Q: How have the martial arts and karate training changed?

A: Some have maintained the traditional way, but karate came from China and then it went to Okinawa, where it was changed. Then it went to Japan, where it became modern. Now we can learn many different martial arts. As the training used to be, we do not only follow the traditional way. So goju has the old way in it, but then tournaments came along. Because tournaments have high kicks, we now have to teach high kicks for competition training. Without the competition influence, goju does not have high kicks ... only low kicks. So I think we've changed most for the sports angle.

Q: Do you feel kata is still necessary in training?

A: Kata is of the utmost importance. When people study freely — everything, including kata — gets changed. Kata is like the culture for this school. Goju has goju ideas, and these are in the kata. That is why we must study one standard. Afterwards, we can do more development. If there were no kata, there would be no standards. We would have fighting in the street. Practitioners must train in kata every day. Sparring is about somebody having strong muscles; a strong body can be good, but kata is different. You need to train [to improve]. Kata is about the battle within yourself. This is why everybody can start karate and study little by little. Sometimes people think, "I'm a good fighter." Well, that's not enough. In kata, nobody attacks. It's just about yourself. When I show myself, this is fighting myself. When a beginner's kata is not so good, it's like his opponent is not so strong. When they advance to green or brown belt, of course, they are much better than before. Now they have to show that their kata is much better than before.

Q: Has bunkai, the practical application of kata, always been a part of the goju system?

A: Okinawa has always had bunkai ideas, but at that time there were only some kata techniques. In goju-kai, we used to do all the movements in the application. Of course, this is not the only way; some people have different ideas. Now in goju-kai we decided to standardize it in a format. Of course, when grading for instructors, we ask, "Show your application for some kata."

Q: Like a "textbook" of the system, are all the techniques of goju contained within the kata?

A: Yes, and some goju instructors came up with this idea. They studied many things and put them in the kata. So kata, as you said, is like a technical training textbook.

Q: What are your plans for the future of goju-kai?

A: It's not only important to make many branches and grow, but it's important that Gogen Yamaguchi was the founder of these. Of course, I hope in the future there are many members and many branches, and I hope people will study the ideas from Gogen Yamaguchi and myself. We have the WKF, which is like a sports organization that members from all the various countries can enter. Thus, they can grow up all together. But goju-kai is like a private organization, so everyone has a different reason for putting on tournaments and winning is not always the main thing. It's not so important if you take a medal, but it's how we keep going.

Q: What is the biggest problem currently facing the martial arts?

A: People think that the martial arts are only for fighting or selfdefense. If you only study how to fight and become strong, this is not the true way. The most important things, in the study of any martial art, are how to personally develop and keep your life good. When something happens, some people use punches, a sword or something else. The next thing you know

they are in jail. Karate is about how you can have a good life, but I'm not talking about money. I mean how you can be at peace with yourself. When my father was alive, he told me, "You must die when you die." He first mentioned this to me when I was a small child, but I didn't understand. When I graduated from a university, I asked him what he meant. He explained by telling me that some Russian soldiers took him while he was in Manchuria and said, "We will kill you, because you are good at martial arts. You are dangerous." My father was extremely nervous. He could not move because they said they would kill him. But then he changed his outlook; he said, "If I must die, I must die. OK, it's no problem." So he stood up and followed them. Soon, they stopped somewhere to kill him. He said, "If I believe I'll die, I cannot get life again, so it doesn't matter." If you study the martial arts, you must understand how to die. Everybody must die, right? But nobody thinks about it. Nobody knows when he will die. My father said in the martial arts that bushido is thinking about this.

Q: Many instructors have no idea about the code of bushido in martial arts. How important is it to you?

A: In bushido, it's not how much you think about yourself. That's the most important point. At the same time, there is a king or a lord in bushido, and everybody must follow somebody. Thus, the rule in bushido is that members devote their lives to the leader. When the leader in the group is killed, the members have to do something. They cannot say that it is not their problem. In bushido, you don't think about yourself. You think about your boss and your country. That is the main idea. My father said that I must go higher than him. He said, "I'm getting old. You're young. When you study in the future, you'll have more than me, because I have taught you. It's not enough for you to study from me. You must study on your own. Then you will grow further than me." This is one idea he expressed to me. He also said that I trained on my own, so we could both grow together. Many people think, "I study from some teacher, so now I am better than my teacher. [Now it's time that] I study some other teachers." I am not saying that this is wrong, but it's only looking one way.

Q: Loyalty is lacking in many dojo nowadays. Hence, there are many breakaways. What's your opinion on this?

A: In Japan, bushido must be a way of a loyalty. The Japanese have the concept of giri, which is an obligation to loyalty. Thus, for yourself, if you believe there's someone better — with more knowledge, stronger or whatever — this is better for your humility. Many people who break away from their teachers believe they are best … even better than the teacher. They've lost the plot because suddenly they believe they are the best. Of course, they don't have any loyalty.

Q: When grandmasters die, organizations often break. When your father died, however, goju-kai was reasonably intact. There were not too many problems. Why?

A: After my father died, many students asked me the same question. I told them, "You already respect my father very much. Now my position has changed. I will be the president. My brother's position will also change. You can choose. If you would like to go, you can." Everybody wanted to stay with me, so I'm very happy. They had good memories of my father. [Despite his death], they could study happily to keep a harmonious life. I was not going to pull at people. Because they support me, goju-kai is still strong, I believe.

Q: How do you think goju-kai will be practiced in 50 years?

A: It probably won't be the same, but the main ideas won't change. Things will stay like they were under Gogen Yamaguchi. There might be some new training methods, and instructors will have to teach separately for sport and the traditional way. I do believe that goju-kai is developing, growing up. In many ways, it's like koBudo, which is something that cannot change. It will always be the same. The philosophy must be the same, but there could be some minor adjustments in some areas.

GOGEN YAMAGUCHI

SIMPLY "THE CAT"

A KARATE LEGEND WHOSE FAME TRANSCENDED THE ART, GOGEN YAMAGUCHI WAS BORN ON JANUARY 20, 1909, IN THE CITY OF KAGOSHIMA IN SOUTHERN KYUSHU, THE THIRD SON OF TOKUTARO YAMAGUCHI. REGARDED AS ONE OF THE FOUR MAJOR KARATE MASTERS OF ALL TIME, HIS CHARISMATIC AND POWERFUL PERSONALITY, COMBINED WITH HIS CAT-LIKE MOVEMENTS, GAVE HIM BOTH HIS NICKNAME AND A RECOGNITION THAT FEW MEN OF BUDO EVER ACHIEVE. DEVOTED TO PERPETUATING THE SPIRITUAL TRADITIONS OF SHINTO AND YOGA, IN CONJUNCTION WITH THE ART OF KARATE, YAMAGUCHI SENSEI ESTABLISHED A REMARKABLE REPUTATION, NOT ONLY FOR HIS EXCELLENT TECHNICAL KARATE-DO SKILLS BUT ALSO FOR HIS UNSURPASSED ABILITY TO APPLY THE PHILOSOPHICAL ASPECTS OF BUDO TO DAILY LIFE. DURING HIS MANY YEARS OF TEACHING AND INSTRUCTING, STUDENTS ALL OVER THE WORLD COULD FEEL HIS PROFOUND LOVE AND RESPECT FOR HIS TEACHERS — A LEGACY THAT HE DILIGENTLY UPHELD UNTIL THE LAST DAY OF HIS LIFE ON MARCH 20, 1989. SELDOM HAS A SINGLE MAN HAD SUCH A PROFOUND EFFECT ON THE DEVELOPMENT AND PROPAGATION OF KARATE-DO. IN RECOGNITION OF HIS DEDICATION TO THE JAPANESE MARTIAL ARTS, HE WAS HONORED IN 1969 BY EMPEROR HIROHITO OF JAPAN WITH RANJU-HOSHO, THE BLUE RIBBON MEDAL.

Q: Master Yamaguchi, it is said that your nickname "The Cat" comes from a ferocious fight you had with a tiger, is that true?

A: Let me ask you something; what does karate have to do with fighting a tiger?

Q: I believe, nothing.

A: So whoever said that is either a fool himself or is trying to fool others. Karate-do has nothing to do with fighting animals, breaking boards, walking on fire or similar things. You are not a better karate-ka for breaking 10 boards or fighting a bull or a tiger. You are a better karate-ka for practicing good karate. Do you understand my point?

Q: Completely, Sensei.

A: The nickname of "The Cat" came when someone said that my physical movements doing karate were similar to those used by a cat. I have always used short and fast hand actions and my favorite posture is neko-ashi dachi, or "cat-stance." That was the reason.

GOJU RYU LEGENDS

Q: When did you first start martial arts?

A: I was 13 when I started to study goju-ryu karate kenpo with a man named Takeo Maruta, who was a carpenter from Okinawa. He taught me everything he knew and helped me to truly understand the real art of karate. My physical condition really changed after starting karate training under him. Before that, I had trained in other arts like iaido and kendo. I studied Law at Kansei University in 1928 and Ritsumeikan University in Kyoto from 1929 to 1932 and received my law degree. To this day, I am still qualified as an attorney. While studying

at the university, I initiated a karate club for training and to develop the free sparring that I consider very important. I did that based on the fact the ancient training consisted mainly of kihon and kata. By this time, all karate schools in Okinawa and Japan practiced kata and pre-arranged application exercises, and they never attempted to practice any free-form sparring. I decided that it was a positive thing and started to introduce it in my classes. At that time, the art of karate-do was not considered a part of budo by the Butoku-kai. I was one of the karate masters who really worked hard for karate to be accepted as a true Japanese martial art form. This happened thanks to Mr. Seizaburo Fukishima, who at that time was in the Judo Department of the Butoku-kai and also was the leader of the Giho-kai.

Q: When did you meet Miyagi Chojun?

A: In 1931, when I was 22 years of age. Meeting Choyun Miyagi was the best thing that could have happened to me. Under his guidance I realized that I wanted to practice this art for the rest of my life. He not only influenced my physical training but also the philosophical and spiritual aspects of my life as well. His personality had a profound influence on me. I remember he told me I had already mastered the hard part of goju, but that I needed to concentrate on the soft side of the style. Master Miyagi gave me the name of Gogen, which means "rough," due to the way I was doing karate then. Years later, he appointed me as his successor and the leader of the goju-ryu school in Japan.

Q: Is it true that you went into isolation for long periods of time in order to train and mediate?

A: Yes, it is. I often spent long periods of time staying at Mount Kurama where I subjected myself to ascetic exercises and hard physical training, especially training sanchin kata, meditating and enduring intense fasting.

Q: How was your experience during the Japanese-Russian war?

A: Not very good. Between 1938 to 1945 I was sent to Manchuria on government and military assignments. On several occasions, my skills in karate and my mental training kept me alive. I was taken prisoner of war and sent to a prison camp in Mongolia. For over two years I was there under very bad conditions.

Q: Did you keep training?

A: Yes, I did. I believe that was what gave me the strength, both physical and mental, to survive.

Q: What is your opinion on how the art of karate is evolving these days and its future direction?

A: The art of karate is gaining international recognition now – but this has nothing to do with how I was taught in the past by my teachers. Things change and we all have to understand this. Unfortunately, I see practitioners emphasizing only the sport aspect of karate. They focus only on trophies and prizes and not on the true spirit and essence of what the art is all about. They are becoming like baseball players. When you put your mind only in winning you are making a big mistake. Karate-do is mainly about learning to overcome defeat. When you lose is when you are facing your fears and your limitations. It is then when the true values and spiritual foundations of karate-do come to your life. You have to use them in order to move on. That's the value of karate-do and not simply winning trophies.

My wishes for the future are few and very specific. Some day, the leaders of karate-do, the ones who learned the art directly from the first masters, we won't be here anymore, and it is important that the new generation knows how to preserve the art and philosophy of this beautiful art. I would like to see practitioners all around the world study yoga and some kind of religious philosophy such as Shinto to balance their lives. In sports there are losers and winners – but in true karate-do everybody is a winner because everybody has a chance to become a better individual. Through sport you simply can't understand budo, because budo is about life and death, it is about to kill or be killed. My goal is to teach students to understand karate-do in the spiritual way.

Q: Do you think change to a sport emphasis is happening only in the West or also in Japan?

A: Sadly, it is happening in Japan, too. The lack of spirituality in the practice of karate-do is not something that you only see in the Western world, whom are not the ones to blame since their cultural background is totally different than Japan. Too many people think the power of karate-do is only physical, but it is not. Karate relies on inner strength and power, an invisible power that is not recognizable by the human eye. That's why the spiritual aspects are so important.

Q: Why did you found the International Karate-do Goju-kai Association?

A: I simply founded IKGA in order to regulate and maintain uniformity among my students all over the world. It was never meant to be a controlling nucleus or a dictatorial organization. It is true that I am the Chairman of the Board, so to speak, and things are done my way. In every boat there is only one captain, and I know what I want for the art of goju-ryu within the Goju-kai.

Q: How have you seen your karate change with the passing of the years?

A: When I was younger my training was very hard and demanding. I have tried almost everything possible. But with the passing of the years I have realized that karate-do is a very simple art if you have the right attitude. Don't misunderstand me, I am not saying it is easy, I am saying it is simple. After years if training your karate becomes more natural, more supple and more straightforward. You become one with the art. You don't practice karate; you are karate. You find the right ways of practicing and training the techniques and it eventually saves you time and unnecessary injuries. When you practice right, you save a lot of pain and suffering to your body. It is true, though, that hard training will bring you to a higher level of consciousness – but it is also true that your body will pay for it. My advise for practitioners is to focus on individual aspects of the art so you can prioritize your goals. Undertake the practice of karate-do as a lifetime journey so you can improve little things here and there without being overwhelmed by the idea of being an expert at everything. Don't fool yourself, you'll never be an expert at everything karate has to offer. And some karate styles that I see can't be practiced when a person gets older. Proper karate is "natural" for the human body. It is a difficult point to understand but it is true.

Q: How important is it for students to copy their teachers?

A: It depends on who the teacher is and what the student is trying to accomplish. To begin with, some teachers perform the techniques in a very specific way, and by this I mean that they have already adopted the main principles of the physical technique to their own characteristics, to their own bodies. If a student tries to simply copy his teacher's movements without analyzing and studying the principles behind the technique, then he is going to have some problems later on. Problems begin when a student with insufficient technical knowledge and understanding tries to make the techniques fit their body and starts to change and modify things. The understanding of one's own body is crucial to the correct execution of the techniques, but today we have lost understanding of how our bodies work because of our daily chores and responsibilities. We have too many devices to do physical work for us.

Q: What qualities do you like to see in your students?

A: To me, the most important quality a student can have is good character. Without good character, everything else is irrelevant. He must respect others and be a good person, otherwise I'll never teach him the essence of the art. If my student's character is good, then I'll do my best to teach him everything and make him as good as he is able. A good teacher is like a parent who wants his child to do better than him. That's my philosophy and that is the most important thing a student should have. I'm not really interested in physical ability since this is something that usually creates problems in the student's mind. When they see they are capable of doing things better than other students, they get a big head and humbleness goes by the window. I want a student with good character and humble attitude.

Q: How effective is karate as a self-defense method?

A: The art of karate is a self-defense method. What you are trying to ask me is how good karate is compared to other arts. All I can say is that karate-do is a martial art and as such it is as effective as any other martial arts style – but the important point here is the level and skill of the practitioner. If a karate-ka loses a fight, we can't say that karate is not good but rather only that the practitioner has not achieved real karate skills.

Q: And what is "real" karate skill?

A: Being able to use karate not only for health and sport but to protect yourself. This is a very advanced aspect of the art since it requires understanding techniques that are not used in sport competition. These are techniques that can seriously hurt another person such as groin kicks, finger jabs to the eyes, blows to the throat, kicks to the knees, et cetera. This kind of karate has to be trained for specifically, and kata bunkai is the main tool for this. This is a kind of karate that you don't usually see at most of the dojos around the world. The style of goju-ryu is very useful for this since it involves close and tight hands movements for attack and defense, uses postures covering the groin, and employs many empty-hand attacks combined with low-line kicking. Goju-ryu can be described as a close-quarter style of karate. If you know where to look and how to look, you'll find very interesting elements for effective self-defense in the goju-ryu method.

Q: Do you teach women karate?

A: Yes, I have female students and I have to say they are very conscious of the little details, especially in kata training. They don't have the hard-headed mentality a man has, therefore their approach focuses more on the details that make the kata beautiful and graceful. My own daughter Gogyoku (Wakako) trains diligently under my guidance and she has achieved a high level of skill.

Q: So kata training must focus on the details?

A: Yes, but not only that. Kata training can be divided in two simple aspects – the actual performance of the form and the application and use of the techniques found in the form. If you are good at performing the kata but you don't have a deep understanding of how to use the techniques of the form, then your training is meaningless. It becomes simply like a ballet. That's good if you are practicing ballet, but if you are training in budo then you need to know more about kata that simply the movements. I practice karate-do as a discipline, the budo way. In the early days, we practiced a lot of basics and kata. Kata was broken down into segments that we trained repetitively. Nowadays the emphasis is on the overall physical performance of the form, not in the self-defense principles hidden in the kata and their combative value as fighting tools. If the student wants to develop a good understanding of kata, then he needs to develop good basics of bunkai and kumite, because every single part is interrelated with the others. The basic requirement for good karate is good kata.

Q: What is your opinion about the different styles of the art of karate?

A: In Japan we have many different styles of karate. This is good and bad. It is good because it makes the art richer by keeping different traditions. On the other hand, it creates differences and make practitioners think their system is better than the one practiced by other karate-ka. To combat this, we organized the Japan Karate-do Federation. We are trying to organize the art of karate-do for future generations.

Q: Goju is said to exemplify both soft and hard karate aspects. How can it do both?

A: Both ends are complementary. Please don't look at them as opposites because they are not. Both principles are exemplified by the katas sanchin and tensho. Sanchin shows the hard side of goju-ryu karate and tensho teaches the soft principles of defense and attack. These two are the basic kata that teach the student the fundamental principles used in any other form in the style. The training of both forms balances the body and is very healthy for the practitioner. Don't forget goju-ryu is a close-quarter art which is calm and relaxed. From this calm and relaxation comes great speed.

Q: How do the breathing methods you teach apply to the practice of these two katas?

A: We have two different breathing methods. One is ibuki which concentrates on keeping tension in the body. The other form is called yin and is softer. You have to learn to combine these two breathing methods to get the most out of it. Properly combined, these two breathing methods will develop what is called "kyoku" power, which is a kind of power that comes from the internal organs. It is not based on muscle but on internal energy. This type of power can only be achieved by using proper breathing methods.

Q: Yoga strongly focuses on breathing. Did this influence you to adapt it to karate?

A: I never adapted yoga breathing methods to karate. There are similarities and, of course, masters of karate and masters of yoga came to the same conclusions as far as the right breathing methods are concerned. Both practices complement each other perfectly. I obtained the rank of Swami in yoga and I tried to adapt some things to make the breathing in karate much better and healthier. But, for instance, the ibuki method of breathing is called kumbaka in yoga terms. To me, goju-ryu karate and yoga are complementary to each other. By practicing karate, you improve your yoga breathing and by practicing yoga you help your karate technique. They complement each other perfectly.

Q: Shinto has been a big influence in your style of karate and your life. What can you tell us about it?

A: First of all, I must say that Shinto has its roots in the cultural heritage of Japan and therefore is common to all budo students. It is used for the spiritual aspect of the training. Karate-do requires a spiritual aspect to balance the physical techniques, and that's when Shinto comes into play. Only through practice, meditation and spirituality can you achieve the invisible power that I mentioned previously. Shintoism is practiced for yourself – I do it for myself, you do it for yourself. It is a very individual and private thing. With a better understanding of Shinto, your karate practice will improve.

Q: How do you combine these three elements of karate, Shinto and yoga?

A: The main idea of karate is to hit someone hard. This is only physical. Using Shinto you can defeat an opponent without fighting. That's the highest level of Shintoism and karate. I like to think of it like a pyramid – one dimension is the physical side of karate, the next dimension is the Shintoism aspect, and the third is the yoga training. Maybe this is difficult to understand but this is the way it is.

Q: Is any style better than the rest?

A: You always hear people saying that this or that style is the best. There is no "best" style, it is simply a matter of personal preference. I've yet to see an art that I don't rate. But I have seen many individuals I don't rate – but that's is due to their personal weaknesses and does not reflect on their art or style. The main objective of karate is to bring enlightenment, which includes humility and self-respect. It is not right to go out and look for trouble or to get into fights to get experience. Not only does this go against the code of karate-do but it's also against Shinto teachings. It is important for young men to have a purpose in life which they can direct themselves toward. This purpose will give them direction and will be a tool to experience things and know themselves better. I would recommend that instructors teach not only the physical art of karate but also the spiritual aspect of life, too. Although I have been very busy all my life, I have never neglected my spiritual side. A true man, a true karate practitioner will always balance his existence in this world.

ONE-ON-ONE with Jose M. Fraguas

Drinking from an Empty Cup

BY ANTONIO SOMERA

As evening falls, a warm orange-and-black glow, painted by sunlight and shadows, spreads over Sunset Boulevard in Malibu. Jose M. Fraguas is seated in the corner of a coffee shop, relaxing after a long day of writing. Clad in faded jeans and white tee-shirt, the creative writer and martial artist is remarkably still. Quiet though he is, his hands are never still. He drums the fingers on the table, and gestures with a mixture of cultural hands signs, from Italian to Japanese. He seems to delight in paradox. Everything he does is accomplished with a sense of economy, without deliberation or hesitation. It's a quality of contentment that goes beyond confidence and exceeds mere self-possession. "You are responsible for your own happiness," Fraguas says quietly. "You have to make yourself happy - but sometimes you have to go through real unhappiness to get there."

The Spain-born, Los Angeles-raised native is not keen on giving interviews. More often than not, he refuses. Fraguas fell in love with the martial arts when he was only nine years old and pursued his Karate ambitions by joining a school in his neighborhood - but things definitely weren't easy. "In the beginning, some training sessions were so intense that I couldn't fall to sleep and my body couldn't stand still in bed. I could get no rest at night," Fraguas recalls – philosophically, with a soft laugh. "I sure did learn how to drink tea from an empty cup."

His face still retains a glimpse of his young days in the streets of Madrid. His fingers compulsively running through his hair as if holding forth on the evils of the past as he says "I knew since I was a kid that the way was long and there were many difficulties ahead, but I believed, as Mencius said, that 'The way is lofty and beautiful. It leads to Heaven. It is far in the distance. But should we not try to bring it nearer by advancing a little, day by day?'"

While Fraguas – with more than 1,500 articles written and over 30 books published and translated into five different languages - still pursues martial arts and writing with as much youthful passion as ever, he now has a much more mature viewpoint of himself. "Everything in my life is based on a straight, logical approach. I'm committed to expressing myself as a human being. Some martial artist and writers doubt what they are doing and wonder if their success or recognition is just an illusion. But I know what I do is simply a natural expression of who I am, so I'm not afraid of looking into the mirror with strict eyes, empty my cup, and grow. I don't try to find in that mirror who I was once. I embrace who I am today and feel grateful for a great and challenging journey called life."

What's enviable about Fraguas isn't his life journey, but the way he has learned to come at it, uncomplicated by the self-lacerations that plague most creative individuals. He is ready to laugh [at himself too], able to relish the moment, even as he works for betters ones. "I have plenty of fight in me," he says, "I'm simply not wasting any of it fighting myself. I think I probably have a lots of drive. But I don't have any ambition. I never really had any. I don't have a hugely high opinion of ambition. I think of ambition as the need to prove something to others, and the need to be recognized. A need for regards outside of the works. Drive motivates you to do whatever it is you are doing as well as you can. That's an important distinction and always has been for me".

He has a reputation as a generous person and an unhealthy even sickening, work ethic [that makes him to get up everyday at 3am], a trait he shares with the most successful people I have met. All what he has accomplished in his life didn't come from luck or a cosmic fix. Every time I have spoken to him he's been in some state of intense emotional and existential transformation, I am not sure people really understand that level of daily commitment and what it takes to maintain it over a span of years. His "sickening" writing routine matches perfectly with his martial arts training, almost no days-off. "Once you are in shape you can get away with a few treats," he says. "But every day off, requires three days of work."

A perfectionist, Fraguas is aware that anyone who strives for absolute precision tends to have a very narrow focus. He also knows that when a person reaches their peak, it's not acceptable to go back and just be acceptable. "The difference for me as a writer is that I'm used to living in a constant state of anxiety that is driven by my desire to make very personal writing works and the need to make it commercial enough to please the public. You have to have the book there in your mind before you write it because if you don't, you are not a writer, you are a guesser. The same thing happens with martial arts. It's like walking on a tightrope – you need to have a good balance knowing where you are going and what you want. You need to conquer the heavens without burning in hell - you have to challenge them both. You have to give your best, regardless of what you're doing in life. I'm always strive to be better at whatever I do. It is not what do you, what is important, but how you do what you do, that really defines who you are."

"We have to differentiate between a challenge and a goal. Goals are single-minded pursuits and therefore limiting. Challenges can expand," he says. Fraguas makes it sound simple, and on one level it is. But is not so simple on a-day-to-day, real life level when we are all faced with personal choices and challenges. If you want to bring it back to simple – permanently – he advises first 'to bring yourself to a point of reckoning', just like he did. "Don't have this feeling that more is better. If you are doing a lot, people respect you more. It is like you are winning the game of life. That's wrong. Instead, learn a lot about yourself. Push yourself, challenge yourself, you should go to difficult places emotionally and you not always will be willing to do that. Our tendency in life is to narrow everything. Worldwide view, friendships, choices, feelings we have, our reactions to things become smaller and narrower. We lose our range."

Without seeming to do so, Fraguas through his articles, books and publications in Europe and USA has played a critical role throughout his career influencing people's mindsets in Martial Arts around the world. "I just like to write works that are positive in the sense that they deal with the dignity and essence of the true Martial Arts spirit," he says. "A writer [or martial artist] must never be satisfied with what he does. The writing piece or the martial arts technique never is as good as it can be. Always dream and shoot higher than you know you can do. Don't bother just to be better than your contemporaries or predecessors. Try to be better than yourself. I believe a genuine artist [of any kind] is a creature driven by demons. The only thing that can alter the good writer is death."

Back at his residence, Fraguas pulls up a collection of pictures of himself with some of the most respected Martial Arts masters of our time, music icons and movie celebrities. Japan, Hong Kong, Thailand, and several European countries, in traditional Japanese dojo, Thai training camps, historical "kwoons", the legendary "Mejiro Gym' and "Chakuriki" in Holland, etc. are the locations of these coveted collection of photos and training journey.

His more than 40 years of martial arts involves direct training under legendary masters, a resume that makes practitioners [who would give up their firstborn for 10 percent of this man's experiences] looking at him with healthy envy.

GOJU RYU LEGENDS

1. With Angel Lopez and Felipe Hita. Spanish National Team at 5th W.U.K.O. World Karate Championship. Madrid, Spain. (1980). 2, With Shigeru Sawabe Sensei (2005). 3. Practicing "Sepai" kata (1980). 4. With Fumio Demura Sensei (2007). 5. Practicing "Mawashi Geri" (1980). 6. With Y. Tsujikawa Sensei (1980). 7. With Ishimi Sensei and Sakumoto Sensei (1985). 8. Makiwara training: "sweat, blood [lots] and no tears." (1985).

1. With Y. Inoue Sensei (2010). 2. With Coach Antonio Oliva (2012). 3. With Kenzo Mabuni Sensei (2001). 4. With Teruo Hayashi Sensei (1980). 5. First generation of certified "Official Spanish National Karate Instructors" (1981). 6. With H. Nakahashi (1980). 7. With Kenei Mabuni Sensei (1980). 8. With Masahiro Okada Sensei (1978).

In the writing field, although he appreciates the many influences he received from a wide spectrum of individuals, he specially treasures his friendship and "cathartic experience" [as he likes to describe it], with Noble Prize Camilo José Cela, whom he met in Madrid, Spain during his youth.

"Camilo José Cela was a legitimate black belt in Judo and I wanted to do an interview with him because of my personal journey in writing and martial arts. He accepted and eventually I ended up having a friendship with him that I greatly treasured. He opened my mind to what a 'true' writer really is. He told me that a 'writer needs three things, experience, observation, and imagination — any two of which, at times any one of which — can supply the lack of the others. If he is interested in technique he should take up surgery or bricklaying. There is no mechanical way to get the writing done, no shortcut'. I was extremely lucky that I met him and that he shared his insight and wisdom with me. He passed away in 2002, but his many words of advise still echoing on my mind."

He still keeps some of the trophies and medals won during his competition days but they don't seem to be as much as relevant for him – the photos are a different sort of award, "I really don't show them to people. Some years ago, I have reached a point in life where I don't feel like letting others to know what I did in the past. One day I found out that it is no longer necessary for me to have a history to explain when I meet people. If you have no personal history to tell, no explanations are needed; nobody is disillusioned with your acts because nobody knows what you did or did not in the past. There is no label. No expectations to be met. And above all no one pins you down with their thoughts. This makes me completely free from the encumbering thoughts of other people. It is not bad to create, little by little, a fog around you and your life, so nobody knows completely who you are or what you do. I follow these four rules that were given to me by a very wise person: never ever talk about your weaknesses, personal finances, plans for your future and who you know."

He is a interesting bridge between tradition and progress, intellect and emotion, body and spirit. To all outward appearances Fraguas is a contradiction in terms. Yet with one foot planted firmly in yin and the other in yang, he is not divided by the light and the dark but rather is the line between the two.

"I believe that in order to become a man of accomplishment, one had to encompass what the Japanese call 'Bunbu Itchi' (the sword and the pen). Such parallel disciplines filled the life of the Japanese nobility, whilst this ago-old doctrine was expounded by Plato in his 'Timaeus', in which it was argued that the balancing of activities relating to mind and body were important in the pursuit of excellence. Only when these two parts are exercised equally could one rightly be called a fully developed personality. It is a regrettable feature of the martial arts in the West that much emphasis is placed on physical attributes, and so little on the mental development of practitioners," he says.

"On the other hand, philosophers do not, as a rule, have an easy relationship with their bodies. Descartes recognized that he had a body but insisted that it was not the same thing as himself. Plato sneered at the body's demands and shaped his philosophy from the desire to overcome them. Berkeley's body was a bundle of his own ideas, while Hume had great difficulties in establishing that his body existed at all - which is why he got so fat. Socrates is remembered by his body, but largely on account of its ugliness.

Nietzsche took exercise, fruitless attempting with his dumbbells to overcome the "blond beast" of his dreams. And Sartre took no more exercise than was required to get from his downtown apartment to the bar across the road. For some people both things don't match. As a martial artist, I like to train physically since that training reminds me that the body and the thinking of the self are one and the same."

A fervent admirer of Yukio Mishima - he owns all Mishima's works in their first edition - Fraguas founded in the prolific Japanese writer, a mirror image of his personal journey; the dichotomy of writing and Martial Arts impregnated with the samurai spirit of Bushido. "I was fascinated by this fact and eventually I became friends with people who knew him personally. For me, Mishima was about as famous as he was infamous. The enormous legacy left behind pretty much outshines his public suicide. When he was 30 years old, conscious of the inevitability of aging, and desiring bodily "perfection," he started a strict bodybuilding training that lasted for the rest of his life. His longing for a return to a spiritual Japan which respected the Bushido (way of the warrior) code inspired his training in Karate and Kendo. True Martial Arts, for him, allow one to experience the border between life and death. Regardless what anyone can think of him, no one can deny the symbolic significance of his life [and death] for Japan's post-war cultural identity, an identity that was rapidly changing in a country where Mishima seemed to embody the ultimate "lost samurai." Like the samurai of old, he succeeded in achieving the perfect death," he says.

"His philosophy was hard to understand for the Western world, even for a modern Japan. Mishima was seeking a faith, a religion, a God he could not find. Man cannot live by beauty alone: the esthetic and the romantic idea, when divorced from the whole context of existence, contains the seeds of extinction. They are death bearers, and his formula was one "in which Beauty, Ecstasy and Death were equivalent and together stood for his personal holy grail." The equation is suicidal. He was a man of a frightening talent."

It is clear that every one of us will some kind of leave a legacy behind when we die. The challenge is the same for all of us. So for Fraguas, the important question is what kind of legacy will I leave? Although he recognizes that does not spend much time thinking about his, he seems to have a clear idea about it. "I believe our main legacy as writers is to educate or even just re-echo those things that we believe are worthwhile - a subjective matter. Even if the idea is obvious or simple, we believe it deserves to be kept alive, and we do that using different ways current with the times; we broadcast our worldview with our family, friends, co-workers, and so on, " he says. "Ideally we live by our beliefs so as to lend them credence; the "unfollowing adherent" is just a meaningless mouthpiece - a preacher not following his own sermon. A legacy of values proven out by the bearer's own life would be a very good legacy for anyone. Life is motion, and the real goal of a writer should be to arrest that motion [which is life] and preserve knowledge by artificial means, and hold it fixed so that a hundred years later, when a stranger opens a book and reads it, it moves again since it is life. Since man is mortal, the only immortality possible for a writer is to leave something behind him that is immortal since it will always move. This is the writer's way of scribbling "I was here" on the wall of the final and irrevocable oblivion through which we all must someday pass."

A perpetual student of world cultures, a passionate reader of Eastern philosophers like D.T. Suzuki and Jiddu Khrishnamurti, and classic European thinkers such as Albert Camus, Soren Kierkegaard and Jean Paul Sartre, Fraguas prefers spending his free time reading and keeping in contact with the "real world," instead of pursuing the glamour of glittering ceremonies and social parties. "The other day," Fraguas says softly, "I was just walking barefoot around the block and the wind was blowing…" He stops momentarily, his gaze focusing inward, then continues. "…it was one of those perfects moments…like a perfect technique, like a perfect kata. Like Sisyphus, I think I have reached a point where I find contentment and meaning in pushing the rock uphill. What always mattered to me was to find a purpose, to see what it really was that I should be doing in this world; to find a truth which is truth for me, to find the idea for which I am willing to live and eventually…die."

Sometimes is hard to differentiate between Fraguas the man and Fraguas the martial artist. "The true greatness of martial arts lies in the depth and immensity of their underlying philosophies. They are the guiding aspect of our psychological unification and, most importantly, are the moral foundation of us as human beings. Martial arts, in the end, transcend the idea of winning and losing, and become a way of thinking and living. They become less about relating to the opponent's movement and more about

adapting and coping with the changing aspects of daily life. This is the real battle - to become the best you can be as a human being. Martial arts can aid the spiritual refining and polishing process and help to guide you toward the achievement of your goals, whatever they may be," he says. "Like Mishima said: 'A samurai is a total human being, whereas a man who is completely absorbed in his technical skill has degenerated into a 'function', one cog in a machine'. We need to strike that balance or we'll be defeated in life. It is either fighting or polishing your spirit. Following the first will take you to use your power to defeat others. In the second path, you struggle against yourself but the reward is much better. When you read in some places that martial arts are for peace, it means about 'polishing the spirit'. When the old Japanese swordmakers compared the value of their swords everything was boiled down to how the metal was tempered. Well, that's the real challenge of martial arts for me, instead of the blade there is only ourselves and our quality is tempered only by our spirit."

Certainly, if contentment can be attained through the gradual diminishing of worldly ambition, he seems well on his way to achieving peace of mind. This "polished spirit" is what Fraguas has been searching for, in one way or another, his entire life. It's where his stillness comes from today, and it reflects the peaceful state that readers and acquaintances can perceive while enjoying his works or simply by having a conversation with this unconventional "tea master."

Note: This article written by GM Antonio Somera was completed 4 months before his passing on October 21, 2013. It has never been published until now.

ANCIENT WARRIOR PRODUCTIONS & EMPIRE BOOKS

GOJU RYU KARATE
5 DVD SET

By Teruo Chinen

In this series, Sensei Teruo Chinen teaches the 12 Goju Ryu kata as well as special exercises and techniques seldom seen outside of Okinawa. In this classic and original "Ancient Warrior Productions" set comprised of 5 DVD, the legendary Karate master, Sensei Chinen unveils the secrets, principles and techniques of the Okinawa Goju Ryu style of Karate-do.

Volume 1 features Goju Ryu warm-ups, Sanchin kata, Nigiri Gami, Gekkisai Dai Ichi kata, Gekkisai Dai Ni kata and San Dan Gi. **(Approx. 60 min.)**

Volume 2 features Junbi Undo, Hojo Undo, Tensho kata, Saifa kata, Kigo Undo and Seienchin kata. **(Approx. 58 min.)**

Volume 3 features Hojo Undo and Junbi Undo, Shisochin kata, Kigu Undo-ishi sashi (stone hand weights), sanseiru kata and seipai kata. **(Approx. 58 min.)**

Volume 4 features Hojo Undo, Kururunfa kata, Kigo Undo-chi ishi (stone weights on a stick), Seisan kata and Kigu Undo-tan **(heavy log).** **(Approx. 55 min.)**

Volume 5 features kigu undo (makiwara), pinchurin kata and kakie (sticky hands). **(Approx. 58 min.)**

www.martialartsdigital.com

ANCIENT WARRIOR PRODUCTIONS & EMPIRE BOOKS

KARATE GOJU RYU MEIBUKAN

By Lex Opdam

This work reflects the system of education from the School of Dai Sensei Meitoku Yagi named the Meibukan. The Meibukan, in an educational sense, originated from the teachings of "the Empty Hand" that Chojun Miyagi adopted in his Goju-ryu Karate system and passed over to his student in turn, Meitoku Yagi. Sensei Yagi developed the system further and gave these teachings a personal interpretation. The reader will find many historical photographs of great Okinawan Goju-ryu karate masters who were the pioneers of this unique martial art. The syllabus in this book serves as a technical manual in which history, origins, practice, and techniques are arranged in an orderly way, allowing the identity of the style to emerge. This syllabus offers deep background that not only will serve beginning karatekas by giving them a rational framework to grasp this martial art, but also more experienced karatekas, who may reinforce or augment their existing understanding of the style's unique subtleties

#124 – 7 x 10 – 315 pages • ISBN: 978-1-933901-29-9

www.martialartsdigital.com

www.ingramcontent.com/pod-product-compliance
Lightning Source LLC
Chambersburg PA
CBHW081742100526
44592CB00015B/2272